CD START INSTRUCTIONS

1 Place the CD-ROM in your CD-ROM drive.

2 Launch your Web browser. *See below if you do not have a Web browser.

3 From your Web browser, select Open File from the File menu. Select the CD-ROM (usually drive D for PCs and the Desktop for Macs), then select the file called Welcome.htm.

* We have included the Microsoft Web browser Internet Explorer on this CD in case you do not have a browser or would like to upgrade or change your browser. Please review the CD-ROM appendix of this book for more information on this software as well as other software on this CD.

MINIMUM SYSTEM REQUIREMENTS

Designed to work on both Macintosh and Windows operating systems

Macintosh
Computer: 68030
Memory: 8 MB of RAM
Platform: System 7.0 or higher
Software: Web browser
Hardware: 2X CD-ROM Drive

Windows
Computer: 386 IBM PC-compatible
Memory: 8 MB of RAM
Platform: Windows 3.1, NT or 95
Software: Web browser
Hardware: 2X CD-ROM Drive

Out's
GAY &
LESBIAN
Guide to *the* Web

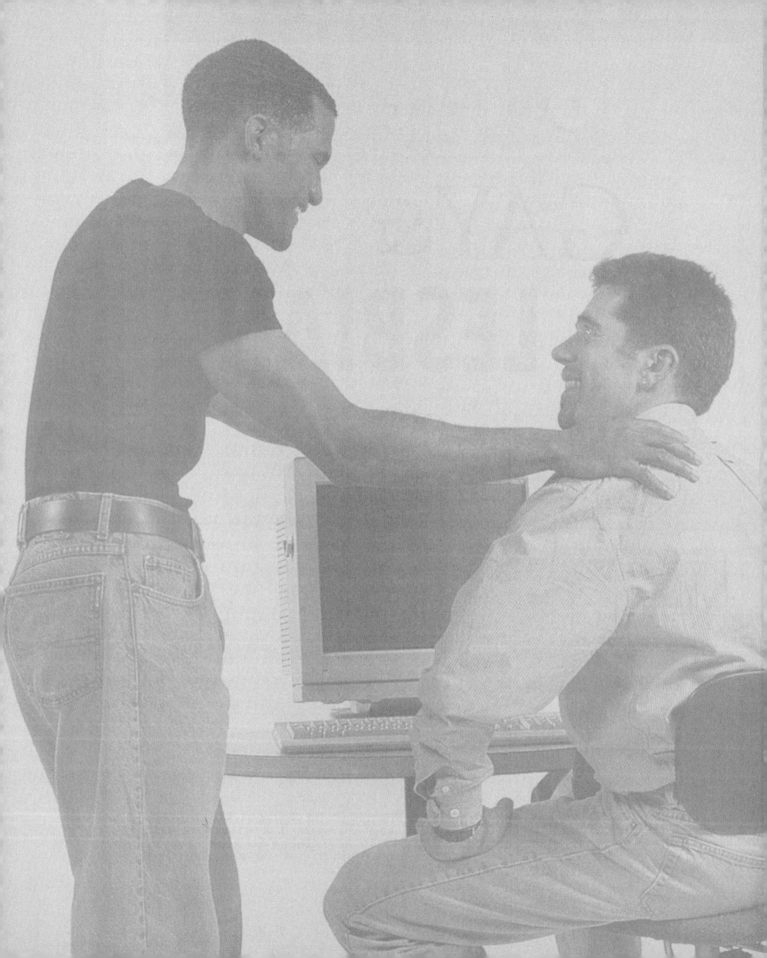

Out's

GAY&
LESBIAN

Guide to *the* Web

J. HARRISON FITCH

AND THE EDITORS OF

Out MAGAZINE

Lycos Press

An imprint of Macmillan Computer Publishing USA

Emeryville, California

Publishing Director	**Cheryl Applewood**
Acquisitions Editor	**Kenyon Brown**
Development Editor	**Katharine English**
Copy Editor	**Nicole Clausing**
Production Editor	**Madhu Prasher**
Proofreader	**Jeff Barash**
Cover Illustration, Design	**Bay Graphics**
Book Design and Layout	**Bruce Lundquist**

Lycos Press books are developed as a joint effort of Lycos and Que. They are published by Macmillan Computer Publishing USA, a Simon & Schuster Company.

Lycos ™ is a trademark of Carnegie Mellon University.

Lycos Press imprint books are produced on a Macintosh computer system with the following applications: FrameMaker®, Microsoft® Word, QuarkXPress®, Adobe Illustrator®, Adobe Photoshop®, Adobe Streamline™, MacLink®Plus, Aldus® FreeHand™, Collage Plus™.

Lycos Press, an imprint of
Macmillan Computer Publishing USA
5903 Christie Avenue
Emeryville, CA 94608
http://www.mcp.com/lycos

ISBN 0-7897-1059-5

Manufactured in the United States of America

10 9 8 7 6 5 4 3 2 1

Despite some knee-jerk backlash, it is plain to see that wired ain't tired yet. In a world where there are daily, real-life factors that keep us separated and isolated as gay men and lesbians, the Web has thrown out a newfangled and invaluable lifeline. Whether living quietly in lawned suburban enclaves or reclusively behind big-city desk jobs or out-loud-and-proud in one of our "ghettos," we all come along at different paces and in differing increments.

The complicated individuality of our lives and choices is something that we always try to keep top of mind at Out Publishing, the home of *Out* magazine, America's best-selling gay and lesbian magazine, and Out.com, our award-winning Web site. The premise behind our efforts has always been, in fact, that the more information our audience has, the stronger it will be to make determinations that suit its needs; facts are, ultimately, tools with which to do battle. And at Out.com we have seen firsthand the myriad exciting ways that the Web allows us to make new contacts, uncover vital information, and become part of an ever-widening net of gay communications.

But it's not just *if* we come out (one reality check: A survey of *Out* magazine readers from several years back had close to 60 percent of our subscribers asking to receive the magazine in a plain wrapper), but *how* we live our lives after we have done so. In a world of ever-multiplying options, the Web offers even newer ways to see ourselves and our choices. A kind of boost of rocket fuel, if you will, to an already powerful mission, the Web helps us navigate through new gay galaxies every day. Are you a gay couple looking for adoption advice, a lesbian in the military looking for legal counsel, or an armchair activist looking for an address to add to your burgeoning e-mail writing campaign? Look no further.

Now, quite delightfully, there are Web pages for nearly every stop along the way and in between—gay marriage activist home pages, massive HIV resources online, fan clubs for crushed out Keanu fans, you name it. And we think we've corralled quite a few in the pages of this tremendous guide. We've tried to keep it lively, up-to-date, chatty, and exhaustive. It's the first edition of, we hope, many, so dig in; there's more than you can imagine.

—Sarah Pettit, Editor in Chief/Vice President, Out Publishing

I wrote this book in Atlanta, so that's where I'll begin .... Thanks to all of my wireless friends who kept me engaged and amused in the real world when I was feeling like a robot. Special thanks to Jeffery Scott, whose wise words and twisted sense of humor are always an inspiration. Thanks to Jeff Roberts, who helped me with site surfing early on and who kept me abreast of Charro trivia and the worst of the Web. In San Francisco ... thank you thank you thank you to my development editor and dear friend Katharine English, my admiration for whom bleeds way off the page. Many thanks to my acquisitions editor Kenyon Brown—for all of the obvious reasons, in addition to the fact that he's such a friendly and professional guy. Same goes for the book's excellent copy editor, Nicole Clausing. In New York ... thanks to Dave, a gentleman and a scholar and a most excellent (site) surfer dude. Thanks to *Out* magazine editor Sarah Pettit and Out.com managing editor Christopher Barillas for doing such amazing things in print and on the Web. And at home ... thanks to Jeff Gibbs, my companion of many years, for friendship, advice, and support, without which I'd probably be at a loss for words. Finally, thanks to my dogs Micky and Moose, who often dragged me away from the Internet and made me go outside to play.

—JHF

In the brief time since the world has had point-and-click access to the multigraphic, multimedia World Wide Web, the number of people going online has exploded to 30 million at last count, all roaming about the tens of millions of places to visit in cyberspace.

As the Web makes its way into our everyday lives, the kinds of people logging on are changing. Today, there are as many Webmasters as novices, or newbies, and all are struggling to get the most from the vast wells of information scattered about the Web. Even well-prepared surfers stumble aimlessly through cyberspace using hit-or-miss methods in search of useful information, with few results, little substance, and a lot of frustration.

In 1994, the Lycos technology was created by a scientist at Carnegie Mellon University to help those on the Web regain control of the Web. The company's powerful technology is the bedrock underlying a family of guides that untangle the Web, offering a simple and intuitive interface for all types of Web surfers, from GenXers to seniors, from Net vets to newbies.

Lycos (http://www.lycos.com) is a premium navigation tool for cyberspace, providing not only searches but also unique editorial content and Web reviews that all draw on the company's extensive catalog of over 60 million (and growing) Web sites.

Lycos designed its home base on the premise that people want to experience the Web in three fundamentally different ways: They want to search for specific subjects or destinations, they want to browse interesting categories, or they want recommendations on sites that have been reviewed for the quality of their content and graphics. Traditionally, Internet companies have provided part of this solution, but none has offered a finding tool that accommodates all degrees and types of curiosity. Lycos has.

Lycos utilizes its CentiSpeed spider technology as the foundation for finding and cataloging the vast variety of content on the World Wide Web. CentiSpeed processes a search faster than earlier technologies, featuring Virtual Memory Control, User-Level Handling, and Algorithmic Word Compaction. This advanced technology allows the engine to execute more than 4,000 queries per second. CentiSpeed provides faster search results and unparalleled power to search the most comprehensive catalog of the World Wide Web. Lycos uses statistical word calculations and avoids full-word indexing, which helps provide the most relevant search results available on the Web.

In mid-1995, Lycos acquired Point Communications, widely recognized by Web veterans for its collection of critical reviews of the Web. Now an integrated part of the Lycos service, Point continues to provide thousands of in-depth site reviews and a thorough rating of the top Web sites throughout the world. The reviews are conducted by professional reviewers and editors who rate sites according to content, presentation, and overall experience on a scale of 1 to 50. Reviews are presented as comprehensive abstracts that truly provide the user with subjective critiques widely heralded for their accuracy and perceptiveness. In addition, Point's top five percent ratings for Web sites receive a special "Top 5% Badge" icon, the Web's equivalent to the famed consumer "Good Housekeeping Seal."

And for Web browsers who don't need a touring list of well-reviewed sites but who may not be destination-specific, Lycos offers its Sites by Subject. Organizing thousands of Web sites into subject categories, Lycos Sites by Subject gives the cybersurfer at-a-glance Web browsing, including sports, entertainment, social issues, and children's sites. A compilation of the most popular sites on the Internet by the Lycos standard—those with the greatest number of links from other sites—the directory provides Web travelers with a more organized approach to finding worthwhile places to visit on the Web.

Lycos was originally developed at Carnegie Mellon University by Dr. Michael "Fuzzy" Mauldin, who holds a Ph.D. in conceptual information retrieval. Now chief scientist at the company, Dr. Mauldin continues to expand the unique exploration and indexing technology. Utilizing this technology, Lycos strives to deliver a family of guides to the Internet that are unparalleled for their accuracy, relevance, and comprehensiveness. Lycos is one of the most frequently visited sites on the Web and is one of the leading sites for advertisers.

The Lycos database is constantly being refined by dozens of software robots, or agents, called "spiders." These spiders roam the Web endlessly, finding and downloading Web pages. Once a page is found, the spiders create abstracts which consist of the title, headings and subheading, 100 most weighty words, first 20 lines, size in bytes, and number of words. Heuristic (self-teaching) software looks at where the words appear in the document, their proximity to other words, frequency, and site popularity to determine relevance.

Lycos eliminates extraneous words like "the," "a," "and," "or," and "it" that add no value and slow down finding capabilities. The resulting abstracts are merged, older versions discarded, and a new, up-to-date database is distributed to all Lycos servers and licensees. This process is repeated continuously, resulting in a depth and comprehensiveness that makes Lycos a top information guide company.

Online providers or software makers can license Lycos—the spider, search engine, catalog, directory, and Point reviews—to make them available to users.

Lycos, Inc., an Internet exploration company, was founded specifically to find, index, and filter information on the Internet and World Wide Web. CMG Information Services, Inc. (NASDAQ: CMGI) is a majority shareholder in Lycos, Inc. through its strategic investment and development business unit, CMG@Ventures. CMGI is a leading provider of direct marketing services investing in and integrating advanced Internet, interactive media, and database management technologies.

HOW THIS BOOK IS ORGANIZED

Throughout this book, I have attempted to arrange the contents according to how gays and lesbians in particular may approach the issues covered—and based on the ways in which our issues are currently being addressed via the Web.

Why, you may ask, if a chapter is all about health, are HIV/AIDS resources primarily and most heavily emphasized? Because HIV/AIDS resources by and for gays and lesbians make up the majority of what is available in the way of Web sites addressing our collective health; at least for now.

I hope that you will find my often freeform construction logic to be an informative and fresh approach. It may be a little random at times. But then so is the Web.

This book comprises three parts: an introduction to the Web, a look at gay lifestyles in cyberspace, and, finally, a look at the Web's offerings in the way of gay business issues—both in the workplace and at home.

A nod to the throngs of gays and lesbians who get their first taste of the online world via America Online, Part 1 begins with a look at the world's most popular (and gay-friendly) online service. Without a doubt, AOL does a bang-up job treading the line between family service and throbbing gay Mecca, but is it—as many have suggested—the antiNet? .... The second chapter in this brief first part touches on what many consider to be the most invaluable resource available on the never-ending labyrinth of info we call the Web: a search engine. Using Chastity Bono and Tony Orlando as guinea pigs, Chapter 2 covers the ABCs of using a search engine to locate exactly what you're trying to find out there.

Part 2, "QueerCyberLifeStyles," deals with aspects of daily life as reflected on the Web. Art, for example—over the Web in its various forms—brings our diverse being colorfully and textually into focus.

Coverage in this section ranges from the online antics of the loud individuals who never fail to get a rise out of the Religious Right to a look at the surprisingly diverse spread of gay-oriented religion and spirituality sites that have found homes in the ether. Online reflections of pride from around the world round out the mix.

Part 3, "It's Your Business," begins with gay business groups and resources from around the world, and works through the virtual storefronts of establishments that proudly cater to gay and lesbian consumers. Along the way, you'll discover resources specifically for gays and lesbians as they conduct their personal business. You'll also get a hint of what worldwide business leaders are doing to ensure an equitable workplace for all employees.

In many instances, I've used sidebars to highlight certain issues or sites which seemed to warrant something extra. I have also borrowed content from the electronic pages of Out.com. You'll notice three conventions in particular.

- "Out-takes"—those bar and pie charts that decorate many of the pages—have been borrowed from GAI-Q surveys (it stands for "gratuitous anonymous intriguing questions") conducted by Out.com. The GAI-Q surveys offer statistical snapshots of life in the community, and they're included here because the surveys were conducted entirely by way of the Web.

- The unedited "Random Posts" which are scattered generously throughout the book may come off as nonsense at a glance. (Hey, folks, that's life on the bulletin boards!) In reality, these samplings from the many topical community forums of Out.com are intended to inject into the pages some random shots of personality from your queer peers in the virtual realm. A few of them even turn out to be a bit poetic.

- "Q&A," obviously, indicates the standard question-and-answer interview format. These interviews, however, have been conducted entirely over the Net. From the creator of KeanuNet to the Founder of the Deaf Queer Resource Center, you'll get the perspectives of a handful of the gay and lesbian trailblazers at work and at play on the Web.

I can't emphasize enough the fact that this collection of links—as jumbo-sized a package as it may be—is a mere sampling of what is out there waiting to be discovered. That leaves the majority of the work up to you. I only hope that what I have covered serves as a solid foundation for a lifetime of discovery, communication, action, and unity.

Part 1

WEBWARD HO!

Chapter 1

AMERICA ONLINE AND BEYOND

AMERICA ONLINE: IT'S COOL. IT SUCKS. IT'S WAY GAY.

In the wired age, few things remain the same for long. Just when you think you've got it, whatever it may be, it changes and you have to re-group, leap into action, and try to catch it again.

The variable "it" may be a modem. It may be a monitor. It may be a software version. It may be an entire operating system. It may be frustrating.

But there are a few constants that keep us grounded within the kinetic electronic culture.

There are the familiar line-dances of double-u's and colons and slashes and dots and coms that lead the way to the incomparable World Wide Web. There is the classic ice breaker, "Are you online?," which, these days, translates almost word for word to "What's your sign?." And there is the ongoing class struggle between the "Netizen" and the AOLer.

It's no secret that AOLers are the pariahs of the Net's social caste system; that the majority of Netizens, at least on the surface, consider America Online to be brain dead, juvenile, structured, chaperoned, and the antiNet in general. Show up somewhere on the Net with an AOL address—or, worse, admit you have one in public—and you'll immediately lose all credibility. Maybe even a date. Maybe even a job.

For lesbians and gays, the whole AOL issue eventually becomes a bit of a quagmire because it's a proven fact that all gays and lesbians started out on AOL, and that most of us still have memberships.

There are two good reasons for this. First, the world's most popular online service has the keywords we love to type: "gay," "lesbian," "entertainment weekly" (see Figure 1.1). Furthermore, AOL happens to do a bang-up job of treading the line between "family service" and throbbing gay Mecca.

Word travels fast through the gay pipeline, so it's no small wonder that gays and lesbians have been historically quick to jump on AOL's user- and gay-friendly bandwagon—often refusing to get off, even when it's high time to move on to a localized or more reasonably priced Internet service provider (ISP). A lot of times, we even insist on clinging to AOL's apron strings after we have enlisted another ISP.

We know better than to let go completely: At America Online, we have a genuine community; a gay phenomenon happening.

Since the DOS age, AOL has experienced a thriving presence in its Gay and Lesbian Community Forum (GLCF). Over the years, the GLCF area has mushroomed into a multiplex of more than 200 volunteers working around the clock—and the most used area on all of AOL. In fact, the GLCF claims to be the largest supplier anywhere of information and services to the gay community.

These days, AOL's gay community is, in its own words, "bursting at the seams." Like the rest of AOL,

the gay and lesbian section underwent a major re-tooling last fall. America Online got a brighter look and faster-loading graphics, licensed the theme song from "The Jetsons" and began marketing itself as some kind of Internet interpreter. Meanwhile, the GLCF checked in for a little makeover of its own, recruited some stellar talent, and began running around in new cha-cha heels calling itself "onQ!" The results, as usual, are impressive.

For seasoned gay Netizens and awkward newbies alike, the GLCF spread invariably delights. How do they keep it interesting? In the words of AOL Chairman and CEO Steve Case, "We remain committed to supporting the vibrant and diverse communities that populate our service."

A perusal of the current GLCF lineup (see Figure 1.2) makes it difficult to doubt the man. Here's a quick round-up of some AOL attractions of the caliber that make an increasingly passe membership worth keeping around.

The Transgender Community Forum
Keywords: GLCF TCF, Gender, TCF

Believe it or not, this one was founded on AOL way back in 1991. For its subject matter, the Transgender Community Forum strikes a surprisingly subdued pose; image

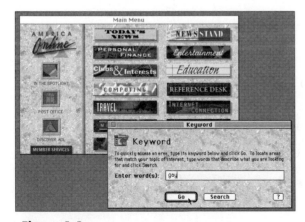

Figure 1.1
Gay keywords

Figure 1.2
The Transgender Community Forum

library notwithstanding. Download snaps with titles like "Halloween: Goth Girl" and "Mistress Kindra," as well as selections from someone's hammy Glamour Shots experience. Message boards dwell on specifics such as female-to-male youth transsexuals, and a quick search makes it ever so easy to locate news on an item like the alleged *San Francisco Chronicle* "Transphobia Attack." Details on *The RuPaul Show*? You know that's right, girlfriend. There's even a weekly support-group conference for transsexual post-operatives. And who can resist a peek into the "Tools & Utilities" folder here?

onQ Leather
Keywords: onQ Leather, Leather

Nay, the "onQ Dungeon." Absolutely no vanilla antics allowed, and no beating around the bush at AOL's home for members of the Leather Bondage/ Discipline/Domination/Submission/Sadism/Masochism community. Message boards exist for every imaginable segment and stretch of this increasingly popular subculture, from "Straight But Not Narrow" to "Flogging & Whipping." Elsewhere, one can do a quick-and-sleazy download of a generic "Master/Servant" contract, or bone up on "hankie code." And you thought this was a "family service."

The AIDS and HIV Resources Center
Keywords: HIV, AIDS

Perhaps the AIDS and HIV Resources Center demonstrates AOL in top form—as a networking ground for the marginalized, and as a pipeline to genuinely urgent information. Via the center's AIDS Daily Summary, the Centers for Disease Control and Prevention make available daily news summaries from a media sweep of more than 700 sources. The Positive Living Forum extends information and support to anyone affected by HIV, including caretakers and family members. And the Positive Living Room is staffed every night for topical discussions or casual chat pertaining to HIV and AIDS. Through the center's vast resources, personal (and oft overlooked) issues such as dating become as much a topic for discussion as late-breaking treatment news. Like no other aspect of AOL, this center becomes a way of life.

OutProud
Keyword: PlanetOut

Another of the finest offerings available to gAyOLers has actually been brought into the fold by PlanetOut. Inclusion of OutProud, the national coalition for gay, lesbian, bi and trans youth, is a bold step for AOL, and an excellent resource for the service's young gay audience. The section provides for youth-only chat and spreads the facts about HIV and violence to those who probably need them most. Progressive educators, too, will find much to celebrate here, including information on teaching positive values regarding homosexuality, and a "Lesbian, Gay, Bisexual and Transgender Bill of Educational Rights." Progress, progress, progress.

The Message Boards
Keyword: GLCF Boards

Whatever your case (gay, lesbian, bi, HIV+, transgender), a message board exists for you on AOL. The GLCF's "Heart to Heart" boards become a nifty electronic extension of the old gray "Same Seeking Same" personals. The "Just Friends" section means just that; bond virtually with other professionals, other 20- or 30-somethings, or other queers from your hometown. And wouldn't you know, the "Rainbow Classifieds" turns out to be your best bet for locating someone who specializes in "metaphysical learning," or, say, your very own British butler. Or maybe you're looking for a gay-owned electrolysis place; the latest copy of *Women's Wisdom*; men in the closet for research on a doctoral project; or just a damned good lesbian mechanic in Orlando.

Gay AOL Map
Keywords: GLCF News

Researchers and mainstream media junkies should start at the Gay Map, which lists alphabetically and by forum name every gay, lesbian, bisexual, and transgender folder available on the service. This means you find gay AOL folders outside of the GLCF, in places like the Adoption Forum, *The New York Times*, the Baby Boomers Forum, and Oprah. It's an excellent resource. (Too bad it's somewhat buried in the GLCF News and Politics section.)

Going AwOL

These services are but a fraction of what make AOL's GLCF worthy of your patronage. But if you, like so many, opt to limit your online experiences to those sponsored by America Online, you are missing the online pride parade in a big way. The World Wide Web may not be as organized and user-friendly as America Online, but it is infinitely more vast, more colorful, and more informative. If you're not getting out on the Web, perhaps it's time to go AwOL.

Is inability to surf the Web and traverse the Internet a reason to abandon AOL as an online service? Nope. Dyed-in-the-wool AOLers will be quick to note that, by way of AOL, one can easily get out on the Web. These days, it basically performs like any other access provider in that respect. Despite its bumpy arrival on the Web scene (with a browser set-up that can safely be described as really bad), AOL has, slowly but surely, made the steps to provide members with a quality browser (Microsoft Explorer), and a thoughtful variety of pricing options.

In December 1996, AOL began offering unlimited use of the service for $19.95, trumpeting "no more watching the clock or rushing offline to beat the charges." This was a major improvement over the former pricing plans, which charged between $1 and $3 per hour; and something that probably had to happen if AOL was to successfully compete with the myriad other online and Internet services.

Besides the unlimited plan, however, AOL rolled out even more options for discriminating users, starting with a "Light usage" plan which grants three hours of online time each month for $4.95. Not bad for those who are generally "over" AOL but who want to keep distantly in touch with the community there. For gay Webheads who want to fully experience the Internet *and* keep in close touch with the old AOL gang, perhaps the best option is the "Bring Your Own Access" plan. This one extends unlimited

GAI-Q Out Take

Out.com <http://www.out.com> regularly conducts a "Gratuitous Anonymous Intriguing Questions" (GAI-Q) survey, to learn more about the habits, passions, and opinions of the world-wide gay and lesbian community. All of the GAI-Q results are archived on the site, but you will also find excerpts from various surveys arranged topically throughout this book. (We'll call them GAI-Q Out-Takes.)

The figures below are taken from the June 1996 "Internet Survey" (see Figure 1.3). They reflect the respondents' overwhelming belief that the Net will grow in importance and will eventually compete with television. They also show that, as of last summer, three-fourths of the respondents had access to the Internet in their homes.

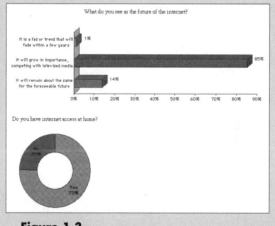

Figure 1.3
Out.com June 1996 Internet Survey

access, for $9.95 a month, to members who use alternative ISPs to connect to AOL.

The "Bring Your Own Access" plan is ideal because, as time passes, you're very likely to spend less and less time within the walls of AOL proper (essentially what you're paying for), and more and more time using the service to access the Web. Since AOL is designed with the lowest common denominator in

Get Online with a No-Frills ISP

The following list comprises a handful of Internet service providers being used by gay Netizens across the United States. (You'll notice that a few are even gay-owned and operated.)

The list includes both regional and national providers, but, with some 1,500 ISPs in the market, it is highly incomplete. If none of these works for you, check the listings under Internet access in your phone book. Or, better yet, scan your local gay and lesbian publication to see if any ISPs are advertising there.

AT&T Worldnet (International)
http://www.att.com/worldnet/
(800) WORLDNET

BackDoor Computer Products (San Francisco — gay service)
http://www.backdoor.com/
(415) 756-2906

BendNet (Central Oregon)
http://www.bendnet.com
(541) 385-3331

Best Internet Communications (San Francisco)
http://www.best.com
(415) 964-2378

CAIS Internet (Washington, D.C., and various East Coast cities)
http://www.cais.com
(703) 448-4470

Concentric Network (National)
http://home.concentric.net
(517) 895-0510

Creative.net (San Francisco)
http://www.creative.net/
(415) 495-0404

CRL Network Services (National)
http://www.crl.com/
(415) 837-5300

EarthLink (National)
http://www.earthlink.net
(800) 395-8425

Echo Communications (NYC)
http://www.echonyc.com
(212) 292-0900

Emerald OnRamp (New Orleans and Seattle—gay service)
http://www.eor.com
(504) 945-9955 (New Orleans)
(202) 324-6666 (Seattle)

Eskimo North (Seattle and various cities in Washington State)
http://www.eskimo.com
(206) 361-1161

Gay.Net (San Francisco—gay service)
http://www.gaynet.com
(800) 310-6626

HoloNet (National)
http://www.holonet.com
(800) NET-HOLO

IgLou (Kentucky, Ohio)
http://www.iglou.com
(800) 436-4456

InnerCity Communities Network (Dallas — gay service)
http://www.inrcity.com/
(214) 350-6995

Institute for Global Communications (National)
http:/www.igc.apc.org
(415) 561-6100

Intercall (New York and New Jersey)
http://www.intercall.com
(800) 758-7329

Internet Network Corp. (Florida)
http://www.innet.com
(813) 841-8603

Interport (NYC and other New York cities; Stamford, CT.)
http://www.interport.net
(212) 989-1128

ioNet (Arizona, Oklahoma)
http://www.ionet.net
(800) 360-5183

Kiva Networking (Indiana)
http://www.intersource.com
(800) 819-7018

Lobo AfterDark (Kansas City — gay service)
http://www.lobokc.com

MagicNet (Central Florida)
http://www.magicnet.net
(407) 657-2202

MCI (National)
http://www.mci.com
(800) 550-0927

MCSNet (Chicago and other Illinois cities)
http://www.mcs.com
(312) 803-MCS1

Mindspring Enterprises
http://www.mindspring.com
(800) 719-4332

NeoSoft (New Orleans and Houston)
http://www.neosoft.com
(800) NEOSOFT

Netcom (National)
http://www.netcom.com
(800) netcom1

Netlink Resource Group (Washington, D.C. — gay service)
http://www.netlinkrg.com/

New York City Net (gay service)
http://www.nycnet.com/
(800) 513-8065

Northern Lights (Maine)
http://www.nlbbs.com
(207) 773-4941

Panix (NYC)
http://www.panix.com
(212) 741-4400

PCNet (Connecticut)
http://www.lambda.org
(203) 316-4400

Pridenet (Boston—gay service)
www.pridenet.net

Primenet (semi-national)
http://www.primenet.com
(800) 4 NET FUN

Rainbow Net (Switzerland — gay service)
http://www.rainbow.ch/

Rt66.com (New Mexico)
http://www.rt66.com
(800) 586-Rt66

Shore.Net (Eastern Mass.)
http://www.shore.net
(617) 593-3110

Sirius Connections (San Francisco Bay Area)
http://www.sirius.com
(415) 865-5000

Siwash Communications Corporation (Vancouver)
http://www.siwash.bc.ca/

Slip.Net (National)
http://www.slip.net
(415) 281-3196

SprintLink (National)
http://www.sprintlink.net/
(800) 817-7755

Sprynet (National)
http://www.sprynet.com
(800) SPRYNET

SSNet (Delaware)
http://www.ssnet.com
(302) 378-1386

Suba Communications, Inc. (Chicago)
http://www.suba.com
(312) 929-8008

TDE Internet (Colorado—gay-owned and operated)
http://www.tde.com
(303) 455-4252

Teleport (Portland and other Oregon cities)
http://www.teleport.com
(503) 223-4245

Telerama (Pittsburgh and other Pennsylvania cities)
http://www.telerama.com
(412) 688-3200

Tezcat Communications (Chicago)
http://www.tezcat.com
(312) 850-0181

Thoughtport Authority (major U.S. cities)
http://www.thoughtport.com
(800) 477-6870

VoiceNet (Philadelphia and other Pennsylvania cities)
http://www.voicenet.com
(215) 674-9290

Westwind Consulting (Chicago — gay service)
http://www.westwind.net/
(773) 477-8191

Westworld Communications (Southern California)
http://www.westworld.com
(818) 718-4100

Whole Earth Networks (national)
http://www.wenet.net
(800) 2HOOKUP

Winternet (Minnesota)
http://www.winternet.com
(612) 333-1505

WorldWide Interconnect (Kansas City)
http://www.grapevine.com
(913) 492-4020

mind (a great thing if you happen to be a child or a newbie), it has its limitations as an Internet service provider. For what it is, AOL does an exceptional job of merging online service with the Internet and making it all make sense to the masses. But in the simplification process, it blocks off some shortcuts and clutters the road with traffic signs, so to speak. Once the ways of the Web become second nature to you, then, you'll most likely want to hook up with a no-frills ISP, and drop in on AOL only occasionally. Doing so with "your own access" is as easy as booting up a new application.

The market is loaded with no-frills ISPs—both regional and nationally based—that charge a flat monthly rate of $20, sometimes much less, for unlimited Internet access (see sidebar). Put your finger on one and set up an account today. Your new provider will rush all necessary Internet software your way and its technical support representatives will (one hopes) walk you through any "Netaches" you may encounter along the way. Within a week, you'll be navigating the Web like an old pro, seeing it in a different light, and enjoying a brand new identity that doesn't end with "aol.com."

AOL: The AntiNet?

Despite all its gay-friendly efforts and appearances, AOL has managed to send a fair number of its members reeling in search of other means of online service for purely ethical reasons. Notable among the problems are what some users have perceived to be dodgy billing practices, free-speech issues (like a situation in which some gay adult video titles were arbitrarily banned from mention), and a mean-old-aunt style of discipline directed at those who use frank language in chat rooms or on message-board postings. "Refer to the 'Terms of Service'"—a highly subjective and often confusing document—has become a kind of AOL mantra. "Guides," as the language police are called at AOL, lurk for the

protection of innocents and bashers alike. But let's face it: When you're engaged in chat about leather, or posting a message about being a transsexual teen, who wants to fret about some nameless, faceless guide's opinion of the language you may or may not be using? "Children may be online," the powers remind, and many will tire of shrouding their thoughts and language to appease.

The GLCF continues to sing the praises of its host, and points out that the issue of member discipline has actually been used on occasion to defend gay and lesbian AOL members from perpetrators of online homophobia. True, hate attacks at AOL are easily reported, and the memberships of violators are terminated immediately.

But AOL naysayers are a fortified and bilious little army, if not necessarily queer. A few of the individuals for whom AOL has left a bad taste in the mouth have taken it upon themselves to wage war with the big service by way of little sites on the Web. Their digital diatribes are heartfelt, if somewhat overwrought, but symbolically the outspoken "AOL Sucks" crowd provides for a good jumping-off point for a tour of "the pink side of the Web." What would surfing be like if it weren't for all of the marginalized thinkers to whom the Web cheaply and efficiently grants "publisher" status?

Well, it would probably be a little bit like America Online: massive, organized, relatively polite, packaged for the masses and, eventually, pretty boring.

Why America Online Sucks
http://www.aolsucks.org
The masters of this official org (see Figure 1.4) allow that AOL will become a key figure in the Internet's future, but ask, "What kind of leader will it be?" "AOL has a large staff devoted to cleansing the service of content and users the company deems undesirable," the site explains. "Its easy-to-use interface lacks the sophistication that Internet users expect. It makes chilling threats of litigation against those who criticize the service." Should such a company

lead the Internet into the future? Interesting observations abound and valid questions are raised. And perhaps the clincher is the internal AOL "Vulgarity Guideline," presented here in all its weirdness. From it, we learn (at least we *think* we learn) that "Dykes/Queers" is okay "if a member is referring to themselves. ... However, this word requires judgment." Elsewhere, "fags" is vulgar; "lambda" is okay; "whips & chains" is vulgar; "Nirvana kicks ass" is okay, though "Jenny is an ass" is not. Guess you had to be at the meeting.

AOL Sucks
http://www.en.com/users/tfinley/

An equally ferocious, though less organized AOL basher, this one suggests that the popular online service symbol-

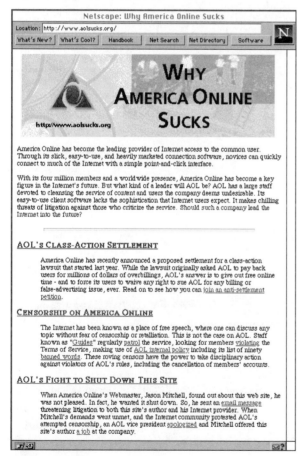

Figure 1.4
Not everyone is a fan of AOL

izes "the destruction of the Net" because of its "inability to educate users" and "a general attitude towards the Internet as a resource to be exploited." As if that weren't enough, a little hysteria is thrown in for balance. "America Online markets itself as a service safe for children to use, but nothing could be further from the truth," the Webmaster opines, adding, perhaps foolishly, that it is a "meeting ground for pedophiles and child-pornography rings."

Whether you agree with these opinions or not, it's probably impossible to be gay and not secretly dig the anarchic spirit and vitriol that these DIY publishers are able to spread freely around the globe. And if you think about it, the passion present at the "AOL Sucks" sites is probably not unlike that which must have driven Ron Buckmire to begin compiling his (now definitive) electronic Queer Resources Directory. Probably not unlike the energy that drove Tom Reilly to form his now legendary organization for queer mobilization through technology, Digital Queers.

THE PINK SIDE OF THE WEB

With AOL firmly behind us, the rest of this directory will focus specifically on the World Wide Web, and moreover, on helping you to see what's out there on the Web a lot more queerly. By general subject category, we'll examine the obscure and the blockbuster; the AbFab and the AbShab; the righteous and the riotous.

We begin with the big waves—the gay megasites and queer hyperlink collections—some of which you'll probably want to bookmark and visit regularly.

PlanetOut
http://www.planetout.com

Readjust your browsers ... hell, buy a bigger monitor—this thing is huge! The super-slick, multi-million-dollar PlanetOut (see Figure 1.5) launched simultaneously on the Web and at America Online last fall. Spearheaded by Digital Queers founder Tom Reilly, the queer megasite houses a variety of gay institutions. Among them: PopcornQ, an online home for gay and lesbian film fans and professionals; Ron Buckmire's gargantuan Queer

Resources Directory; radio-magazine "This Way Out" (broadcasts of which come via RealAudio); and an entertainment zine called "Shout," which keeps us abreast of everything late-breaking and queer on the box, on the shelf, in the player, on the screen, and in real life. PlanetOut hosts chat, with topical panel events on issues like "the joys and difficulties of being out in Holly-wood." Or Q&A sessions with the likes of Candace Gingrich and "Man of the Year" Dirk Shafer. It also boasts a substantial girl zone; from everyone's favorite lesbian comic strip, "Dykes to Watch Out For," to the online version of *Curve* magazine, featuring the interactive joys of the Curve Coffee Klatsch. Resource-wise, it's the Dog Star in the Web's queer constellation.

BRIEF HISTORY OF GAYOL: A CHARTER MEMBER CHATS ABOUT LIFE ONLINE NOW AND THEN

"benthere91@aol.com" is the archetypal gAyOLer. He joined the service way back in 1991, when membership was 300,000 and rising. These days, with membership hovering around 5 million, the thirty-something professional type is considered a charter member and enjoys special rates as a result. He signed up with "a real Internet-access provider" several years ago, though he doesn't see himself giving up AOL anytime soon. "Anonymity is great and probably still one of the most attractive things about gay life on AOL," he says.

Q: Why did you join?

A: At the time, AOL was the only service that really supported a graphical interface environment. CompuServe was text-based and Prodigy ... well, they were Prodigy. I wasn't aware of the gay aspects of AOL when I joined, so it definitely wasn't a gay thing.

Q: What did the original service look like?

A: It was NOT Microsoft Windows. They provided some subset of GeoWorks windowing that ran on DOS. It supported the mouse and multiple windows and some graphics—not much, but a major improvement over CompuServe and the other BBS text-only services.

Q: Describe the online gay scene back then?

A: I joined within a year of AOL's debut, and the Gay and Lesbian Community Forum had already been established. Seems like it consisted of four message boards and a resource library. ALL of the gay chat activity happened in the general chat area. There was no separation between the "AOL-sponsored chat rooms" and the "member chat rooms" like there is now.

When members were allowed to make up their own chat rooms, about half of them were gay. No kidding. So AOL, for appearances or whatever reason, made the member rooms two levels deep within the ser-vice. I guess this gave them an out. Plus, children can't get access to the member chat rooms. In reality, very little chat actually went on in those rooms. People basically went in and their sheer presence meant they were gay. Immediately upon entry, members would look up profiles of other people in the room and send private "instant messages" to the ones they liked. Then maybe they'd go off to a private room, or exchange phone numbers and get on the telephone.

Q: Did you ever hook up with anyone that way?

A: Not physically. I did get to know people by seeing the same ones online regularly. After a while, a phone number or two came my way. I NEVER gave mine out; paranoia of being outed at work. I called the guys who sent me their numbers. One liked me a lot and sent me free software from the computer store where he worked. It was good talking to other gay guys, and I really met some nice people.

Downside: Even with a 28.8 connection, the wait for information here is painfully slow. For its large and lethargic ways, though, PlanetOut is well worth your bookmark. It makes an impressive effort to create a "community" a la AOL's GLCF. Difference is, this community isn't afraid to turn you loose.

Out.com
http://www.out.com

Out magazine's electronic sisterfriend—and the number-one gay and lesbian Web site—delivers a generous sampling each month of the paper publication's authoritative look at gay culture, news and politics (see Figure 1.6). A pro like Michelangelo Signorile lends his distinctive point of

They all wanted to meet me in person, but I just knew they were 300 pounds and ugly! You know, everybody that owned a computer in 1991 and had AOL could not be as beautiful as they all said they were.

Q: What other kinds of impacts has AOL had on your life as a gay person?

A: Honestly, I would have to say that I credit AOL for provid-

boards and chat rooms I had my first extensive exposure to what I believe was a pretty good cross-section of the gay community. That added balance to my experiences with the bar crowd.

Q: How has the gay community on AOL evolved?

A: AOL has done two things, one positive and one negative. First, and most importantly, they have been very strong support-

much less controlled. But today it's much larger and there is a lot more information available as a result. There are essentially three kinds of gay AOLers: those looking for sex, phone or live; those who are very political; and those who are looking to learn about gay life, probably young and/or from rural areas where they are isolated. The anonymity is great and probably

> *"Honestly, I would have to say that I credit AOL for providing a forum for me to develop my self-acceptance of being gay."*

ing a forum for me to develop my self-acceptance of being gay. I knew I was, but my background had never let me be out and I hadn't met a whole lot of gay people ... especially in an environment where I could carry on a dialog without alcohol and the undercurrent of sex in the conversation. Not to say that never happened online, but I did meet a lot of people online that were more than willing to take their time to help answer my questions about being gay and help me understand that gay people weren't freaks like I had been taught growing up in South Carolina. Through message

ers of the gay community and have recognized the patronage of gay and lesbian customers by significantly growing the GLCF area. Second, and most unfortunately, they have buried the whole thing down deep in the bowels of AOL. I suspect—although I certainly hope this isn't the case—that is to satisfy some Christian coalition or something.

Q: Would you say that the gay scene on AOL is better or worse than it was back in the early days?

A: In some ways better and some ways worse. It was more "underground" back then, and

still one of the most attractive things about gay life on AOL.

Q: Does AOL suck?

A: Not at all, but you do outgrow it to a degree. In cyberspace, I would equate AOL to high school and the real Internet to college. After you first get online it's great, but then as you learn more, you realize there's a lot more out on the Internet. Most of the time, people know when they've outgrown it.

Figure 1.5
PlanetOut

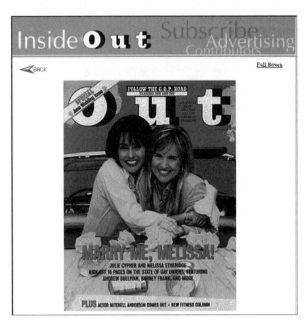

Figure 1.6
Out.com

view while the usual brood of frontline reporters and leisurely reviewers keeps us abreast of everything from Internet censorship to the latest Tori Amos opus. Unlike the print version, however, Out.com is able to deliver daily headline news (and gossip) as it maintains and grows the archives of past articles by subject ("Lesbian and Gay Youth," "State Laws and Initiatives," "International News"...). Interactive forums for specific groups such as teens, couples, and people of color can bring communities around the world into your living room. (The site's unique online dating service, MakeOut, might even reel in true love.) Tongue planted firmly in cheek, Out.com also serves up a few "gratuitous boy, girl" shots, updated regularly, "just to keep you interested." No doubt, jack in to Out.

Queer Resources Directory
http://www.qrd.org/qrd/
Ron Buckmire started the Queer Resources Directory (see Figure 1.7) as an electronic archive for Queer Nation in 1991. Since that organization's demise, the QRD has blossomed into an electronic library of epic proportions. The goal is "to contain every scrap of knowledge which has been used in or is part of the struggle for full equality" of sexual minorities—news clippings, political contacts, newsletters, essays, images; even "counterintelligence" documents from the Religious Right. Pore over anti-gay propaganda here, and do something about it with the "Fight the Right Action Kit." Like many of its

Web-based peers, the QRD has been "spiffed up" and included on the PlanetOut site. Around press time, Buckmire explained that PlanetOut would eventually be the exclusive host of the QRD, but that the transformation was nowhere near complete. Until then, he is maintaining his version at <http://www.qrd.org/qrd/>. Too bad it will soon be history; the no-frills original actually works better for serious research than the graphics-heavy version on PlanetOut. If you want something quickly, point your browser to the old QRD while it's still around.

InfoQueer
http://www.infoqueer.org/queer/qis/
Another excellent resource that has been smartly snatched up by PlanetOut, InfoQueer (see Figure 1.8) lists gay and lesbian Net resources by subject area—from "Arts & Culture" to "General Women's Sites"—and geographic area. As is the case with QRD, research here is more easily achieved in the rough than with the background images of trendy gays and lesbians that are constantly downloading over at PlanetOut. It's not nearly as extensive as the QRD; InfoQueer's most distinctive feature is its listing of the home pages of gay, lesbian, bi, and trans folks around the world.

Figure 1.7
Queer Resources Directory

Rainbow Links
http://www.cris.com/~rnbwlink/

A relatively new ad-based service, the goal is a "one-stop" world-wide link-a-thon for rainbow warriors. Rainbow Links (see Figure 1.9) will also design and maintain a Web page for you, and promises to donate ten percent of its profits to a U.S.-based gay organization. Directory-wise, subjects run the gamut from "Bears" to "Bars"; from "Professional" to "Pride." The service may be new, but the pages are streaming with information, broad and obscure. Great quick-reference for those with special interests.

Planet Q
http://www.planetq.com

Planet Q (see Figure 1.10) is a service from Active Window Productions, an Internet publishing, marketing, and consulting firm. It's nowhere near as content-heavy as its rival planet, but it does include some nifty features. Notably, the AIDS Virtual Library, which includes information on clinical trials, social services, statistical reports and more. The site's inclusion of an International Queer Events Calendar, organized geographically, is a novel concept. But it was almost completely devoid of information on a recent visit (unless "Party at Stella's House" in Denver is your idea of an event). An editorial staff provides a variety of voices via interviews ("Even Lesbian Avengers Get Confused"), Essays ("Homophobia in Latin

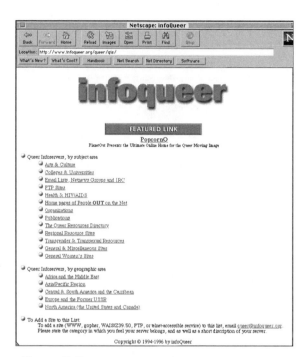

Figure 1.8
Infoqueer

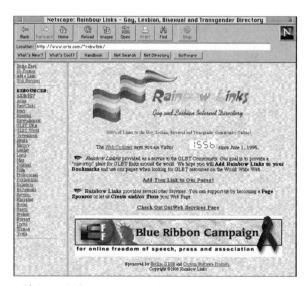

Figure 1.9
Rainbow Links

Figure 1.10
Planet Q

Figure 1.11
CyberQueer Lounge

America"), and Reviews ("My Evening with Annie [Sprinkle]"). Promised as coming: chat, bulletin boards, and CU-SeeMe broadcasts.

CyberQueer Lounge
http://www.cyberzine.org/

This members-only service describes itself as being "sort of like a phone book to the LGBT electrons ... designed to aid in your travels in this massive Internet cave." The CyberQueer Lounge (see Figure 1.11) wants to make your online experience better than TV, but it will cost you between $25 and $50 per year. What will a membership buy? Entrance to the "Backroom play area," for starters. (The play area includes erotica links along with public and private chat and messaging capabilities, wouldn't you know.) With lots of black backgrounds, animated flames, and the word "cum" regularly substituted for "come," the CyberQueer Lounge, at least on the surface, will not appeal to all. But let creator Tom Hicks 'splain: "It's a one-person band ... The Lounge is NOT connected with any giant like Microshaft (sic), or AOL or IBM." And because the Lounge has driven Hicks into "massive debt," he has been forced to limit access to certain areas to those willing to pay for it. Whether you decide to support the CyberQueer lounge or not, it offers

an undeniably well-organized directory for free. Subjects are both straightforward ("Homophobia") and whimsical ("The Happy Happy Joy Joy Channel," dedicated to "little tiny and big giant things that are important positive steps forward for LGBT people everywhere.") And don't forget to browse the "Satan's Little Helpers" section, in which Hicks provides pointers to various hate, fascism, and Rush Limbaugh sites.

Little Sites, Lots of Links

Best of the Internet for Gays and Lesbians
http://www.cyber-designs.com/pride/

Short on links, long on explanation, this site makes suggestions for "fun stuff" and "great links" as they apply to gays and lesbians. Free personal ads are also offered.

Brent Payton's Gay, Lesbian and Bisexual Links
http://www.fc.net/~zarathus/links.html

Monster link list, arranged alphabetically in categories like "Organizations," "AIDS information" and "Naughty Bits." Lots of personal pages, too.

Gay A to Z
http://www.centrum.is/~gusti/a-z/

Twenty-something Agust Smari Beaumont—"100 percent gay and love it!"—lists Web sites of gay interest, bit by bit, from his home in Iceland. His A to Z is a work in progress, but definitely getting bigger.

Gay/Bi Interests of all types
http://www.cris.com/~cmdrdata/gay-bi/

Eclectic collection of links, updated regularly. Pointers range from a "Gay Male Naturist Group" to a "Gay and Lesbian Star Trek" site. Top-heavy with sites of the "hot hot hot" variety, though no pay-to-use or commercial services are listed.

Gay & Lesbian Information
http://www.ping.be/~ping1678/gay/

Another link-a-thon, with gay Web pages by country or category, newsgroups, mailing lists, FTP, and gopher sites, etc. Respectable collection, though not updated often.

Gay and Lesbian Resources
http://www.3wnet.com/reference/gnl.html

Limited but straightforward page of popular resources and titles from the Reference Center of 3Wnet, an Internet presence provider.

Gay Resources
http://www.i2.i-2000.com/~ckossman/

A mother's info-laden Web shrine to her cute son, Wayne "How special must I be, that God gave Wayne to me," she writes). Right-on mom provides her own narrative for parents of gay people and for people who think they might be gay, in addition to links to some of the best queer resources on the Net (see Figure 1.12).

The Homosexual Agenda
http://www.tatertot.com/agenda/

Respectable browsing index of gay and lesbian Net resources with brief site descriptions. Points to gay-owned businesses, online services, and localized information. Updated regularly.

jimbo.Land
http://www.dnai.com/jimboland/

Jimbo's "faboo favs," arranged by subject. Includes multiple listings for such categories as "activism," "humor," "sci-fi & fantasy," "Wicca," and more. Searchable database.

Kerry's Miscellaneous Queer Links Page
http://www.geocities.com/WestHollywood/2555/gaylinks.html

Rundown of one Kerry Shatzer's queer favorites on the Web, accompanied by spirited mini-reviews. Includes links for travel, shopping, activism, and entertainment.

Figure 1.12
Some moms take the news better than others....

```
Random  Posting

Subject: New on the Net
I have just acquired my email and my
fingers are ever so bored! Oh gosh Im
so naive at what all this can do. Any
tips from Cyberqueens would be welcome
Thu Sep 19 2:29:03 EDT 1996 - ()
```

LesBiGay Information Center
http://soho.ios.com/~ski4ever/

Personal selections for "choice" LesBiGay-related sites, a site of the week and more.

LesBiGay & Queer Resources @igc
http://www.fair.org/lbg/lbg.resources.html

Great big list of resources, by subject, from the good folks at the Institute for Global Communication. Subjects include "Domestic Partner and Family Issues," "Media Resources," "College Groups," and "International Gay/ Lesbian Rights Groups."

Q Planet
http://www.geocities.com/WestHollywood/ 1271/

Another aspiring planet—the most indie so far—this one collects hot links (with a "hot men" bias). Includes gossipy and wishful commentary along the way. Nice amateur effort.

Queer Information
http://www.cs.cmu.edu/afs/cs.cmu.edu/user/ scotts/bulgarians/mainpage.html

This hellacious URL compiles topical articles "snarfed" off of the Net. Sections are devoted to gay history, domestic partnership, and scientific evidence for a genetic basis of sexual orientation, among other things. Links are accompanied by concise commentary.

Queer Related Links & Referrals
http://macav.chautauqua.com/Queer.html

The "huge full list" available here is a monster. (We're warned it can take up to three minutes to download if you're using a slow connection.) If you are using a slow connection, you might want to shoot for the site's "small old list."

The Rainbow Room
http://www.crl.com/~heath/rainbow/ rainbow.html

No dancing and dining at this Rainbow Room, just queer links galore—from statistics and research to the "Creme de la Femme" of the Web. Quotables and queer headlines, too.

Sappho Central
http://ourworld.compuserve.com/homepages/ sappho/

Sappho Central is an Athens (Georgia) woman's guided tour of the Web, particularly (but not limited to) lesbian and women-oriented sites. She also specializes in "odd, bizarre, weird, unusual, twisted, screwy, strange, quirky, daft, or just-plain-not-quite-right" stuff.

Skippy's Queer World
http://www.geocities.com/WestHollywood/ 3430/index.html

With a name like Skippy's Queer World, it has to be good. Queer media, queer activism, queer places to go and spend money; yep, Skippy has covered all the bases. Don't miss his "Kweer Kennel," now boarding guys' home pages from all over cyberspace.

Steph & Lil's Queer Links
http://www.teleport.com/~rocky/queer.shtml

Steph & Lil's page is mostly a girl zone, with links to fun stuff like "Lesbian Barbie," "FaT GiRL," "Dyke Street," and more serious items like the "Lesbian Herstory Project" and "Sapphic Ink: A Lesbian Literary Journal." Shopping, too.

GAI-Q Out Take

The graph below (Figure 1.13), from the June 1996 "Internet Survey," shows how gays and lesbians think the Internet has affected their ability to gain information about and participate in the gay community at large. Close to 90 percent said they get more information as a result of the Net; nearly 75 percent said they get information faster; and 45 percent said they communicate more with other gays and lesbians because of it.

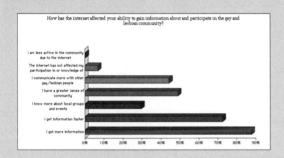

Figure 1.13
June 1996 Internet Survey

Yahoo! (Society and Culture: Lesbians, Gays and Bisexuals)

http://www.yahoo.com/society_and_culture/
sex/gay__lesbian__and_bisexual_resources/
index.html

The URL's a killer to type in, but if you make it to the Yahoo! Net directory for Lesbians, Gays and Bisexuals, you're in for thorough, updated coverage. From "African-American" to "Youth" subcategories, the links tend to number in the hundreds.

Chapter 2

SEARCH IN STYLE

Net vets know it well, and even the most naive nonliners have heard it whispered in the dark: the Web is a wild and woolly frontier; a never-ending labyrinth of information; a page-turner that will never reach a conclusion. Depending on your personality type, the concept is either infinitely appealing, or instantly off-putting. But don't lend the naysayers too much credibility. In time, they'll all be wired and surfing and loving it.

After one has truly experienced the Web, the conclusion is bound to be that its structure, or lack thereof, is a big part of what makes it so much fun. Random surfing can account for hours of play and education, often a combination of the two. It's the randomness of it all that enables the direct links and seamless transitions between a chain of entities such as Out.com and the Human Rights Campaign and Cyber-Queer Lounge and Adult Children of Heterosexuals and Holy Titclamps and FaT GiRL and the Andrea Dworkin Online Library and on and on and on. As it is with the tube, when you're over something you pick a new subject and you change channels. Unlike the tube, however, you don't exhaust the options at channel 59. In fact, it's safe to say that you'll never exhaust your options on the Web.

But sometimes when you get online, you really mean business. And if you have no idea what you're doing, where you're going and what you're looking for, it won't take long for that sense of randomness to translate to tedium.

FINDERS, SEEKERS

Many services exist to assist you in making sense of too much information, to help you effectively use the Web for subject research—or even for a quick spelling check. Most likely, you'll find a "search engine" to be the essential Web helper. A search engine is an automated "machine" (with a Web interface) which magically turns subject queries to hyperlinks, allowing users to locate lists of, and link out to, Internet-based resources and documents on any given subject. You should get to know one intimately, and keep it close by.

Web-based search engines are as common as corner stores in big-city neighborhoods. Most of the major engines are advertiser-driven (free to you), and each incorporates its own unique blend of options for tracking down and sorting through the information floating around out there. Some smaller engines are audience-specific (see sidebar); others attempt the daunting task of covering all aspects of life on the planet—and beyond. For examples in this book, I'll focus almost exclusively on using the all-purpose Lycos search. But as you become more of an experienced Netizen, you'll probably want to experiment with a variety of different engines. Choose one you like the best; or use them all, as I often do.

Lycos can be as direct and user-friendly as they come (see Figure 2.1). Each time you use Lycos for a keyword search, the engine sifts through more than 60 million documents contained in what is commonly known as the "catalog of the Internet." With Lycos, conducting such a search is as easy as typing **http://www.lycos.com** into your Web browser of choice. Bookmark it for easy access. Or, if searching becomes a big part of your life online, configure your browser to make Lycos your automatic home page.

Once you have arrived at the Lycos home page, simply enter the word or group of words that best identifies the subject in which you're interested.

Figure 2.1

The Lycos search engine sifts through more than 60 million Internet documents each time you enter a search term.

Keep in mind that most engines—Lycos included—will ignore prepositions, articles, and conjunctions ("the," "a," "an," and "and"), so it's best not to use them as keywords.

For a trial run, let's suppose we're attempting to gather the most general collection of Web information available on Sonny-and-Cher-progeny-turned-lesbian-activist Chastity Bono. On the Lycos home page, simply type the words "Chastity Bono" in the search box and click "Go Get It." Within a matter of seconds, the engine will generate thousands of hyperlinked documents, ranked in order of relevance based on the keywords you entered (see Figure 2.2).

Ten results are displayed on each page by default. On the first page of the search for Chastity, we find results ranging from an "Outlines" article titled

"Chastity Bono: Out, Proud and in Chicago," to a Chastity quotable tucked away in the CyberQueer Lounge ("My father's Republican. I'm a Democrat. We keep things on a very friendly and loving plane, so we don't really talk to each other about politics").

Sound and Vision

One of the more novel Lycos features is the fact that it enables users to search specifically for pictures and sound files of or "about" specified subjects. (That way, you can look at a picture of Chastity and listen to a sound file of her parents singing together.) With just one added step, it's as easy as a simple keyword search.

To the left of the box in which you type keyword terms on Lycos, you'll notice a pull-down menu. By default, the menu is set to "search the Web" (Figure

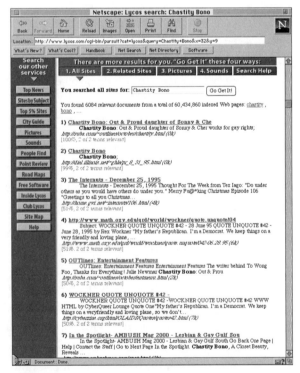

Figure 2.2

A simple Lycos keyword search for "Chastity Bono" turned up 6084 documents. The first results page includes the 10 most relevant links.

2.3a). By pulling down the menu, however, you can customize a search so that results only turn up sound files or images of a desired subject. Select "pictures" from the pull-down menu to display GIF, JPEG, and MOV files dealing with the topic in question (Figure 2.3b). Or select "sounds" to display WAV, SND, RA, and AU files (Figure 2.3c).

DON'T GET STONEWALLED BY A SEARCH ENGINE: CUSTOMIZE YOUR QUERY

When you're using Lycos, what may seem to be the simplest of tasks—finding information on Stonewall, for example—can turn up some pretty mindboggling results; often thousands of them at once. By approaching the quest from the search box on the Lycos home page (by entering the keyword "Stonewall"), your first page of results may range from the

Figure 2.3

By using a pull-down menu, the Lycos engine enables users to search the entire Web (a), or search specifically for pictures (b) or sounds (c) related to a subject.

Stonewall Inn at 53 Christopher Street; to the town of Stonewall, just 24 kilometers northwest of Winnipeg; to the top gas producers for Stonewall County. Likewise, a search for a picture of Chastity Bono may turn up undesirables like "Bono leaning back," "Bono looking dapper" or "Young Virgin Autosodomized by Her Own Chastity."

Feeling a bit stonewalled? It happens, and developers of good search engines realize it.

The simple Lycos keyword search does just fine in most instances. But every once in a while, you will need to get more specific, and these times require a different way of asking for the information to ensure that what you want is what's appearing at the top of your results list.

More advanced searches don't have to be difficult, either. At Lycos, they're actually quite easy once you understand the features and the lingo.

Boolean Rhapsody

You've probably at least heard of the Boolean search, which refers to retrieval of information containing specific combinations of words. If you want to get real geeky about it, a Boolean search involves a logical combinatorial system treating variables—such as propositions and computer logic elements—through the operators AND, OR, NOT, IF, THEN, and EXCEPT. (It's named after mathematician and logician George Boole, of Boolean algebra fame.)

The Lycos engine doesn't support a full Boolean search like some of the other major search engines do (Alta Vista, **http://www.altavista.digital.com**, for example). Rather, it incorporates a variety of its commands into pull-down menus that enable you to easily "customize your search." That way, you don't need to be a bang-up Boolean to perform adequately refined searches—say, to locate all documents containing Tony Orlando without Dawn (hypothetical, of course).

These Days, We Even Have Gay Search Engines ...

While the Lycos database includes items from every stretch of the imagination, at least one such search tool exists solely for use by the gay, lesbian, bisexual, and transgendered community. For sure, more help is on the way.

Rainbow Query
http://www.rainbowquery.com

Rainbow Query (see Figure 2.4) boasts "the power of the major search sites, but with content that matters to the gay, lesbian, bisexual, and transgendered community." This excellent free service, which claims to be the "largest, most complete 'gay-only' index on the Internet," offers full text search capabilities and category-specific searches. Or, if you're up for some browsing, surf by category—200 of them, from "Alumni Groups" to "Youth 'Zines." It's a service of GL Web (http://www.glweb.com), a gay online resource and business community.

Figure 2.4
Rainbow Query

Boolean "AND" searches are automatically available when you perform a search using the box on the home page. Simply enter whatever words you want in the search box ("Tony Orlando"), and click the "Go Get It" button (or hit return on your keyboard).

Notice that, despite the fact that we didn't type in the keyword "Dawn," there she is, alongside Tony, number one again, after all these years (see Figure 2.5). Lycos cannot assure that Dawn won't show up when you do a search for Tony Orlando, but by customizing your search somewhat, you can attempt to reduce the chances.

Symbolica

(-)

Begin the term with a hyphen in front of Dawn ("Tony Orlando -Dawn"). This will lower the relevance score (and therefore the ranking on the list) for Tony Orlando sites containing the word "Dawn." Dawn may be coming to the party, but by inserting a hyphen before her name, you eliminate her from your A-list.

(.)

Use a period at the end of a term to limit it to no expansions. "Out." will bring up only results with the keyword "out" and ignore expansions like "outback," "outhouse" and "outré."

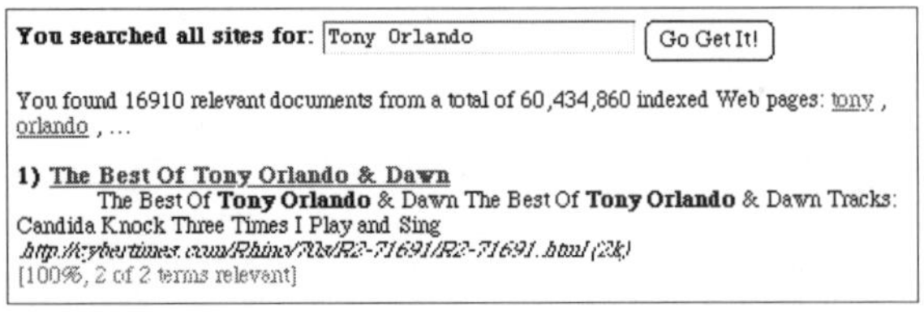

You searched all sites for: Tony Orlando   Go Get It!

You found 16910 relevant documents from a total of 60,434,860 indexed Web pages: tony , orlando , ...

1) The Best Of Tony Orlando & Dawn
The Best Of **Tony Orlando** & Dawn The Best Of **Tony Orlando** & Dawn Tracks: Candida Knock Three Times I Play and Sing
http://cybertimes.com/Rhino/R0s/R2-71691/R2-71691.html (2k)
[100%, 2 of 2 terms relevant]

Figure 2.5
A simple keyword search for "Tony Orlando" turns up 16,910 relevant documents.

($)

Place the dollar symbol after a term to make the search engine expand it. The search term "homo$" will bring up results like "The Uselessness of Homonymophone Debates," "Homophobia," and "Homosexualite et Sida." This is a great feature for those who have a clue, but don't quite know what they're looking for. (Great, too, for etymology freaks who have far too much time on their hands.)

Customize Your Search with Pull-down Menus

If your search requires even more fine-tuning, the customized search form **http://www.lycos.com/customsearch.html**—hyperlinked adjacent to the search box on the Lycos home page—should be your next destination (see Figure 2.6).

By customizing a search this way, you can:

• Make your search more narrow

• Make your search wider

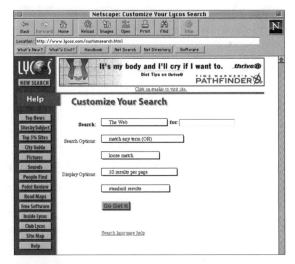

Figure 2.6
For specialized queries, Lycos offers a page enabling users to "customize" searches by using pull-down menus.

- Have the search match ALL words in your query, rather than the default ANY words
- Search for a number of terms different from the number you entered (for example, search for several possible spellings of a word AND some other word)

The search form offers two ways to control your search (search options) and two ways to control the display (display options) of your search results.

For search options, you can "match all terms" (like the Boolean "AND"), or you can "match any term" (like the Boolean "OR"). You can also match from two to seven terms via this menu. Your other selection of search options includes choices for "loose," "fair," "good," "close," and "strong" matches.

By default, Lycos finds all documents matching "any" word you type in your query (except for words like "a" and "the," which are generally not meaningful in a search). If you type "Patrick Stewart" as your query, Lycos will find all documents containing either "Patrick" OR "Stewart." This is the "match any term (OR)" search option—what you use, by default, if you type a query into the search box on the Lycos home page.

Sometimes you want to find only documents which match ALL the words in your query. This is the "match all terms (AND)" option.

And you're probably wondering why you would need to "match 2 terms," let alone "match 7 terms." These options simply give you more flexibility. Suppose you want to find references to Candace and Newt Gingrich, but you're not sure whether Candace is spelled "Candice" or "Candace." You would enter the query "Candace Candice Newt Gingrich"; to get the best results, you would use the "match 3 terms" search option. This will match at least three terms in each document. Since it's highly unlikely that Candace will be spelled two different ways in

the same document, the results returned will have references to one of the two spellings of Candace AND Newt AND Gingrich. (So, you'll locate the relevant documents AND learn how to spell Candace's name correctly.)

Another search option allows you to adjust the selectivity of the Lycos search engine to "loose," "fair," "good," "close," and "strong" matches. When you select a "loose match," you will get more results, but many of them will tend to be less relevant to your query. Selecting "loose match" allows you to cast the widest net in a search. On the other hand, if you want your search to turn up only the most relevant documents, set the search option to "strict match."

For display options, you can choose to receive 10, 20, 30, or 40 results on a single display page. Your other set of options for display includes "summary results," "standard results," and "detailed results."

Lycos supplies all of the results, or "hits," that match your query; even if there are hundreds or thousands them. Of course, the hits aren't displayed all at once. Ten hits are displayed on each results page by default, with a "next 10 hits" link located at the bottom of each results page in a series. If you'd like to see more than 10 hits at a time, however, you can vary the number of hits displayed—up to 20, 30, or 40 per page—by way of the display options menu.

Options also allow you to control the amount of information displayed about each result. Lycos offers three levels of result detail: standard (default), detailed (all information displayed), and summary (the minimum amount of information displayed).

The standard setting displays the most relevant and frequently used information about a site—typically an outline and an abstract.

The detailed setting might provide such additional information as site ranking (regarding your query), number of links to outside resources, and words matched on the page.

The summary results option displays only the hyperlinked site title and its relevance. This is useful if you need to browse quickly through a large number of sites.

STILL STONEWALLED

Got all that down and still feeling a bit out of the loop? As it is in the real world, in the virtual realm you should never be afraid to ask for help. The Net has its fair share of Mother Teresa types lurking about. The Lycos Help page (**http://www.lycos.com/help.html**, see Figure 2.7) brings it all together by flouting the everyday FAQ sheet (frequently asked questions) and opting instead for a YAQ, or "your answered questions." Search tips and details on other Lycos features are right around the corner. Take up any burning questions which remain unanswered at this point with "Webmaster Triage" (webmaster@lycos.com). But don't rule out the possibility that a site dealing with Tony Orlando without Dawn simply doesn't exist.

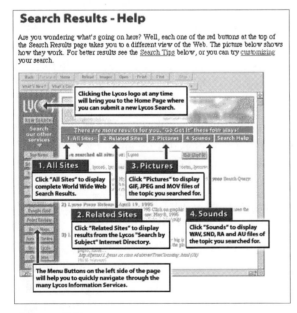

Figure 2.7
Help is usually just a click or two away.

SWITCH HITTERS

Rest assured, there is search life beyond Lycos. New search and directory services seem to pop up every day. Users often switch back and forth between a few popular services, depending on whatever their immediate needs may be. The following three—Search.com, Yahoo!, and HotBot—are but a few of the other popular, free Web-based search options available.

Search.com (**http://www.search.com**), one of many fine services from c|net (**http://www.cnet.com**), brings together the best of the Net's search engines; large and small, subject-specific, and general. It recruits such disparate forces as AltaVista and the Anagram Generator, and—despite its utterly mindnumbing array of options—is easy (even fun) to use. Browsing Search.com's subject-specific searches is also one of the best ways to get hip to the Web's top content providers.

The multi-purpose Yahoo! service (**http://www.yahoo.com**) is most notable for its gargantuan Net directory (which is hierarchical to an almost nauseating degree). Because of its massive size, Yahoo! always weighs in with the Net's no-nonsense search engines. For keyword searches, you'll fare better elsewhere, as Yahoo! results pages tend to be convoluted at best (though Yahoo! will automatically deliver AltaVista search results along with its own). If you have time for newsstandesque browsing by subject, however, Yahoo! is the real gem. Its whimsical design and freestyle approach to cataloging are truly the essence of the Web.

Offered in conjunction with HotWired, *Wired* magazine's electronic baby bro, HotBot (**http://www.hotbot.com**) wins the search engine so-hip-it-hurts award, hands down. It's powered by Inktomi Corporation (exploiter of breakthrough UC-Berkeley supercomputing technologies) and claims to be the first Internet search tool with the horsepower to handle the entire Web, promising "the largest, freshest, most flexible Web search database on the planet."

It's a cool cat, fer sure. Besides the *Wired* neon colors, though, you probably won't notice much of a difference between HotBot and the rest.

AT LAST: A SEARCH TOOL FIT FOR A DIVA

To say that Wynn Wagner III is a mover and a shaker on the Net is somewhat of an understatement. His Net ventures (and there have been many) seem to have picked up shortly after he was "fired from some of the better radio stations in Dallas during the 1970s." These days, the Chief Systems Architect for Computer Language Research in Carrollton, Texas is also the guy behind DivaNet. Contrary to the way things sound, DivaNet is not the long overdue Web hub of Jessye Norman. Rather, it's the base page for Wagner's commercial Web server, which houses the Gay Dallas Page and the Dallas Gay/Lesbian Alliance, among other sites.

Besides the great name, DivaNet's most invaluable offering to the non-Dallas set is its excellent Quick-Search Page. As Wagner succinctly puts it, "I keep a collection of search engines on one Web page. Using my Quick-Search page, you can find almost anything on the Internet."

DivaNet Search Page
http://www.divanet.com/search/

This diva isn't content with the services of one search engine. She wants them all! "I found that I spent as much time sifting through search engine forms as I did actually searching for things," Webmaster Wagner explains, "so I created a collection of shortcuts to the searching tools I find most useful." His DivaNet Search Page (Figure 2.8) enables visitors to do simple keyword searches (and some customized searches) on the Web by way of all the major engines, including AltaVista, Excite, HotBot, and Lycos. But there's more: It also allows you to search Usenet for a newsgroup, AT&T for an 800 number,

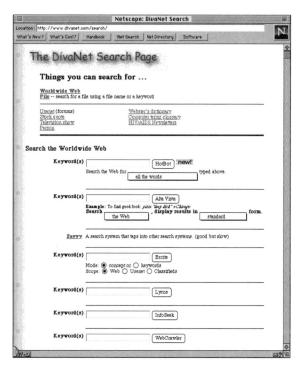

Figure 2.8
Gay Netizen Wynn Wagner III developed an all-in-one search page for his DivaNet guests.

PAWWS for a stock quote, and TV One for a television show. "It's intended to be handy, not pretty," Wagner notes. (But don't tell the diva.)

YOU GO GET IT, GIRL

Okay. Now you're armed with the essentials, and hundreds of pages brimming with the best of the gay and lesbian Web await you. Surf the link-a-thons listed in the previous chapter 'til your heart's content. Find a queer megasite that fits your personality, jack in and make it your virtual digs. Customize your search for obscurity. Whatever you do, don't just get online. Get informed. Get active. Let these pages, and the Web sites they explore, be your guide. You'll find that the good times just come with the territory.

Part 2

QUEERCYBERLIFESTYLES

Chapter 3

THE WEB'S BIG GAY HE(ART)

The arts are a reflection of who we are, where we've been, and where we're going. In lieu of traditionally documented histories, we often find ourselves turning to things like Sappho's romantic poetry and Michelangelo's lusty paintings and sculpture as reminders that, yes, we've been here a long time, and that over the years we have created and accomplished many great things. We look at art inspired in the age of AIDS to remember what we've lost, or maybe to develop a stronger sense of compassion. We listen to the harsh sounds of a new style of queer music, and we are reminded that our culture is always in transformation.

Like no other medium, the Web enables us to bring our very diverse being colorfully and textually before us, whisking us within a matter of minutes from old times to the newest times. That, and everywhere in between.

This section, then, is really an exploration of us. The Web puts us on display in all of our ways, shapes, and forms. For an instant, we may be just like everyone else. And then without notice, we might be like nothing you've ever seen before.

POETS, ARTISTS, MADMEN, AND MADWOMEN

In a Different Light
http://www.uampfa.berkeley.edu/exhibits/idl/
dlhome.html

We're no strangers to this phrase, and we're no strangers to the forces at work behind this 1995 exhibition from the University of California at Berkeley. Thankfully, the now closed exhibition exploring "the resonance of gay and lesbian experience in 20th century American art," lives on in cyberspace. On display: works from Man Ray, Diane Arbus, Nancy Grossman, and Deborah Kass facing issues such as unrequited love ("Other"), imitation ("Drag"), and emptiness ("Void"). Also on-site: links to topical organizations and resources like a pro-sex, safer sex guide for teens, and a gay marriage rite.

Lesbian Images in Art
http://www.sappho.com/lart/index.shtml

The images on these pages were chosen because they have "a lesbian appeal to them, depicting emotional or romantic interaction between women." An offering of the Web's Isle of Lesbos, the site features more than 65 works from 40 artists. Browsing by era, the images date back to the early 1500s. It's a tour through the art history of sapphic relations, from Peter Paul Rubens's "Juniper and Callisto" to Gustav Klimt's "Girl Friends."

ArtAIDS
http://www.illumin.co.uk/artaids/pages/
home/

The creators of the ArtAIDS project (Figure 3.1) envisioned an alternative to the "Day Without Art" that many organizations around the world hold in memory of those who have died of AIDS. Rather, they wanted a day—every day—with art. An awareness raising project for CRUSAID, a leading U.K. AIDS fundraising charity, ArtAIDS uses the Web as a virtual quilting loom, allowing artists from around the world to contribute their images as individualized patches. It uses biological concepts of

Figure 3.1
ArtAIDS

"transmission," "modification," and "replication"—commonly used to describe the passage of the virus—as a model of association and change. Having been viewed by more than 500,000 people, it also acts as a resource for education, fundraising, and health awareness. The gallery, which contains some 170 images, takes visitors on a guided tour. Sit back and watch images pass across the screen. Click on items that catch your eye, and even download them to your desktop.

Angel Web
http://www.a-r-k.com/angelweb/

"A site based around open-minded creativity"? There's *got* to be a story at Angel Web (Figure 3.2). Sure enough; Story Waters, to be exact. Waters, a creative and very open-minded twentysomething gay male from Kent, England, started the Angel Web in 1995. (Subsequently, he has moved into his own Web site design business, promoted heavily here.) If Mr. Story looks anything at all like the underwear model-cum-angel who graces his site, you'll want to hightail it to Kent and make an appointment with him in person. What he has set up here is a virtual museum in which his work is displayed (4th floor) along with the work of anyone else who's interested (levels two and three). On level two, the Aphrodite Gallery is a fine place to start for poetry and prose concerning love (from "Friday Night: "Oh bloody hell ... Ironing is a bleedin' mystery to me, so the shirt always emerges with two long, burnt creases.") Love deluxe indeed, Aphrodite! The Hestia Gallery fares better with some homoerotic photography, and upstairs in the Dionysius Gallery, things really begin to heat up with "work relating to love and sexuality." At long last, on the 4th, we meet Story himself. He provides frank information for young gay men coming to terms with their sexuality ("The main thing I suppose I don't want you to be doing is going to cottages for your first sexual experience") and dazzles with sizzling photos of—you guessed it! "It may worry you to know," he confesses, "I'm a cross between ... Catherine, Louie,. and Edward." FYI, that's Catherine, the ice-pick-wielding bisexual from *Basic Instinct*, Louie, the gloomy one from *Interview with a Vampire*, and Edward, a.k.a. Mr. Scissorhands. You must visit the site to learn the rest of the story.

Now, if you're really up for something different, try Story's companion zine, A-R-K (http:www.a-r-k.com), a serious read with a "strong philosophical underpinning." Translation: you probably won't get a lot of it. But it sure is neat to look at. Click around a little and you'll find some interesting items, like a "fictitious interview with George Michael" (Figure 3.3). Startlingly dull (perhaps that's the point), the conversation covers the mysterious singer's songs and character. This is novel, and no doubt George Michael fans will scramble to A-R-K to see what it is he would say if he were a talented gay Webmaster.

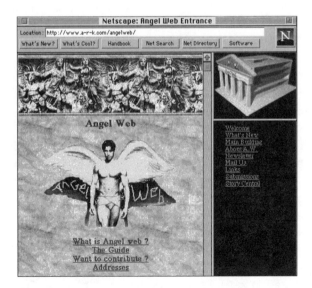

Figure 3.2
Angel Web

Figure 3.3
A-R-K

Alternative Creations
http://www.alternative-creations.com/

Alternative Creations is a lesbian-owned and operated business for production and promotion of art for and by women. The goal is to design and distribute products that are "not only fun but are also needed in our society." Items are offered in a variety of categories, including jewelry, sculpture, cards, and videos. Pick up a matted and framed print of the hot Melissa Etheridge PETA poster, or check out the hip review column by *Claire of the Moon* author/director Nicole Conn.

Free Spirit Rainbow Art
http://www.gcrc.ufl.edu/~cchurch/fsra.html

For those who thought original uses for the rainbow flag had been exhausted. Check out Ocala, FL-based Charlie Church's hand-sculpted figurines, incense holders, and magnets in the flying colors.

Mirror Images
http://www.acmeweb.com/mi/index.html

Colorado Springs-based Sandra Marin founded this Internet gallery to "promote womyn artists and feminine culture." Her own pen 'n pencil show, "Impressions of a Graceful and Elegant Culture," is on display (and for sale), and she invites other artists to join her online.

For Lesbians: The Art and Poetry of Women
http://www.goodnet.com/~stacey/staceys_other.html

"Now this is what I call art and poetry," exclaims Art and Poetry of Women Webmistress Stacey, who announces to visitors that she'll be leading them through "not an exploitation of the female body, but total and complete artistry." Without further ado, Stacey points her guests in all kinds of directions. **Edward L. LaBane's Fine Art Nudes** page (**http://www.rt66.com/swest/labane/indexilj.html**) showcases the still photographer's work with the female form. Stopping off at the official Patrick Nagel site, **@Nagel** (**http://www.PatrickNagel.com/Nagelgirl/index.html**), we get to preview or purchase digital images that were immortalized in the eighties by Spencer Gifts stores and that Duran Duran album. Getting a little more serious, the **Women Artists Archive** (**http://www.sonoma.edu/library/special/WAA/**) shines through by giving exhibit space to colorful works like Betty LaDuke's "Africa" series and more grisly encounters like Eleanor Dickinson's "Crucifixion" images. Next stop, **The World's Women Online!** (**http://wwol.inre.asu.edu/artists.html**); hundreds of 'em. In alphabetical directory style, the service out of Tempe, AZ, lists women artists along with an example of their work and a statement as to what they're all about. One can even contact artists via this service. "For something a little more spicy," Stacey leads the way to "a different kind of art form," pin-ups from the past. **Picture Palace's Pinup Calendar** (**http://www.ids.net/picpal/pinup.html**) leads to the most famous pinup of all time (Betty Page) and definitely the most frightening (Russ Meyer). Good show, Stacey!

Artists, Briefly...

Michelangelo Buonarroti's "David" is the ultimate showstopper when it comes to homoeroticism. No surprise that the artist's work and story are alive and well in cyberspace. Check out **Michelangelo** (**http://quistory.clever.net/qih/michelan.htm**) for an excerpt from the book *Queers in History* and a glimpse at David. And swing by Cappella Sistina (**http://www.christusrex.org/www1/sistine/0-Tour.html**) and check out Michelangelo's ceiling treatment and his "Last Judgment" painting over the altar.

Another master of the homoerotic, **David Hockney**, can be found in on the Web. The WebMuseum, Paris offers a bio (**http://sigma.samsung.net/louvre/paint/auth/hockney/**) and an exploration of his 1967 work, "A Bigger Splash." The David Hockney Reference Page (**http://www.artincontext.com/listings/pages/artist/8/2i3qorj8/menu.htm**) is best for those seeking galleries and dealers and information on exhibitions.

And thanks to the Web, one doesn't have to go to Pittsburgh to visit the ultimate shrine to the most enigmatic of gay enigmas, Andy Warhol. The **Andy Warhol Museum** (**http://www.clpgh.org/warhol/**) presents itself as "the essential to the understanding of the most influential American artist of the second half of the 20th century ... a primary resource for anyone who wishes to gain insights into contemporary art and popular culture." The site whisks visitors on a virtual museum tour with some of the finest "museum tour" narrative you'll find in cyberspace.

Sneak a peek at some of the feminist lesbian art of Austin, Texas-based artist **Amalia Litras** at her impressive online gallery (**http://ns1.world-net.net/users/cypher/**).

The work of American painter **Lari Pittman** explores themes from gender and sexuality to the cycle of life. The University of Southern California at Santa Barbara hosts an online installation, Lari Pittman Drawings (**http://humanitas.ucsb.edu/depts/museum/uam_past_exh/pittman/pittman_exh.html**).

Last time we checked, Cincinnati-based queer photographer **Alan Bratton** and "dancegrll" **Erin Watson** were rotating the Breath and Movement (**http://www.geocities.com/SoHo/3287/**) space to display their works, consisting of highly sensual lesbian imagery.

BOOK-MARKINGS

Attempts have been made, but let's face it: The Web just can't compete with the paper page when it comes to a good, long read. (Imagine curling up in bed with your PowerBook.) As any number of amateur poets will tell you, though, the Web can be a dream outlet for seeing one's work in print for the first time. Book retailers are also making good use of the medium. For the wired consumer, tracking down that outdated anthology of lesbian fiction is probably just a few keystrokes and clicks away these days.

Poetry

The Web has published many an otherwise unpublished poet. Poetry is almost a given on personal home pages these days (you can surf around and dig up some of it if you really must). For easy access, lesbian poetry wins the gold star of organization hands down. Where? The Isle of Lesbos, of course.

Lesbian Poetry
http://www.sappho.com/poetry/

Direct from the Isle of Lesbos comes an exhaustive collection of works by poets who, over the ages, have written about romantic love between women (Figure 3.4). Poet, nonfiction writer, and photographer Alexandria North (**http://www.persephone.com/alix/**) did the research on her own, finding much of this work "has been ignored and suppressed, despite the historical interest and literary value contained within." Works here run the gamut from Sappho to Gertrude Stein to Elsa Gidlow. North even throws in some lesbian poetry by men, for good measure. "The work of several of these men (such as Pierre Louys and Paul Verlaine) inspired the writings of the female poets on the list (such as Renée Vivien and Michael Field)," she reminds.

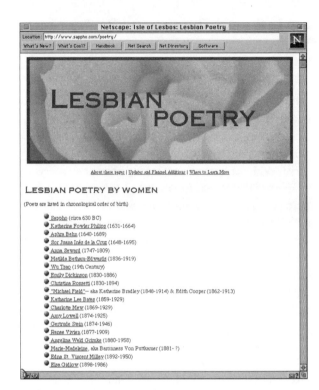

Figure 3.4
Lesbian Poetry

Sapphic Ink
http://www.lesbian.org/sapphic-ink/

An online lesbian literary journal, Sapphic Ink delights each month with short fiction ("Electra Woman and Dyna Girl"), book reviews (Emma Donoghue's "Hood") and yes—be still, beating hearts—lots of poetry. The publication's layout is no-nonsense, and a snap to navigate. Submission information is included for those who want to let the Sapphic ink flow.

Wit's End Literary Cyberzine
http://www.skylink.net/~corwalch/index.html

Also for aspiring artists, poets, and creative types in general, the inspired Wit's End Literary Cyberzine offers a queer-friendly online environment for electronic publication glory.

Figure 3.5
A Different Light Bookstore

Gay Asian Literature

http://www.geocities.com/WestHollywood/
3821/

The site's Webmaster originally wanted to point visitors
to a variety of resources available to the gay Asian community. For now, the site settles for a listing of books.
The impressive listings, to be exact. Browse titles in the
fiction, non-fiction, and anthologies categories.

Bookstores: Browsing the Shelves from Home

A Different Light Bookstore

http://www.adlbooks.com/

With branches in New York, San Francisco, and West
Hollywood, A Different Light (Figure 3.5) is a touchstone
for many. Its online bookstore is no exception. Localized
information about signings and events is available for
each of the branches. The "ADL Review" catalog is also
on hand, along with its companion, online ordering capability. Across the way, the "Cafe" section hosts an open
chat forum on queer literature, art, culture, and society.
It's Java-based, natch.

Lambda Rising Bookstore
America Online
Keywords: lambda rising, gaybooks

For those of you with access to America Online, the
Lambda Rising Bookstore offers one of the finest shopping experiences you're likely to find there. (It claims to
be the world's leading source for gay, lesbian, bisexual,
and transgender literature.) Pick up the latest titles—
even many that are out of print—along with CDs and
cassettes, videos, and various gay-themed gifts. The
store hosts a chat room ("The Rainbow Cafe"), and
holds "virtual signings" in its "Stonewall Salon." A major
Web presence was forthcoming at press time, so keep
an eye open for it.

Crossroads Market & Bookstore
http://www.crossmarket.com/welcome/

Browse through bestsellers and new releases in gay and
lesbian literature. "Great flicks" in the video section, too.
Place an order online.

Affinity Books

http://ns.cent.com/affinity/

Affinity may be located in beautiful downtown St. Petersburg, FL, but with this site, it becomes your local gay and lesbian bookstore, no matter how remote you are.

Afterwords Bookstore

http://www.afterwords.com/

Rainbow-tinged bookstore and espresso bar. You can't taste the espresso here, but you can buy books, videos, music, and gifts online.

Ex Libris

http://www.clo.com/~exlibris/

Toronto-based online bookshop specializes in new and used gay and lesbian literature. Special services include a discount for prepaid orders, and a "loan programme" by which you can make a deposit and pay a rental fee and take a book on loan.

Girlfriends Coffeehouse and Bookstore

http://www.bonzo.com/girlfriends/

The girls of Tucson await, with women's books, prints and music, metaphysical gifts, and "mouth watering treats to eat." Run, don't walk.

Glad Day Bokshop

http://www.tiac.net/users/gladday/

Boston's Glad Day Bookshop claims to be the second-oldest gay bookstore in North America. More details at its Web site.

Hungry Head Books

http://www.teleport.com/~bwilga/

Everybody's got a hungry head, and this Eugene, OR-based bookstore knows how to feed the craving. Whether its with *Hallucinogenic and Poisonous Mushrooms: A Field Guide* or *Stallions & Other Studs*.

The Sacred and the Profane, Booksellers

http://www.cruzio.com/~profane/index.html

... and lots of things in between. Browse the store's catalog with categories like "African Diaspora," "free love," "hippies," and "world art & literature."

Sisterspirit Bookstore

http://www.elf.net/sisterspirit/

Located in San Jose, CA, Sisterspirit is a non-profit, all-volunteer org, designed to promote women's community and unity. The Web space features news, book reviews, and a reference section.

Gay-Mart Entertainment Stop Books Library

http://www.gaymart.com/2catalog/
shopes.html

The Gay-Mart Entertainment Stop Books Library peddles its wares in chatty, gossipy fashion. Take the bait on "find out the true gay story from your favorite gay personality when you sample this selection of autobiographical picks!" and you'll end up staring at product numbers for the Greg Louganis and Bob Paris & Rod Jackson books. When finished browsing for books, you can always visit one of Gay-Mart's other action aisles. Alas, Jacqueline Smith and her shopping cart are nowhere to be found.

Little Sister's Book & Art Emporium

http://www.lsisters.com/default.htm

Little Sister has been serving the community for nearly 20 years with gay and lesbian books, music, video, magazines, cards, and adult toys. The site features product and ordering information, along with a special section on censorship.

Sapphisticate

http://www.sapphisticate.com/

The Sapphisticate ("for the dykescriminating reader") was created to provide access to lesbian literary work by those who "choose not to visit gay/lesbian bookstores or conduct credit card transactions with gay/lesbian identified sites." Billing goes through Amazon.com books (hello!), which "carries practically every book in print, and therefore specializes in nothing."

Thunder Road Book Club
http://ourworld.compuserve.com/homepages/
Thunder_Road_Book_Club/

Bruce Springsteen has absolutely nothing to do with this Thunder Road, which deals in discounted mail-order lesbian books and videos. Catalogs and shipping available in the U.S. only.

OH, THE DRAMA!

What would gay life be without a little drama? Most of us experience more than our fair share on a daily basis. Community theaters often play a bit-part in the process. The Web makes it cheap and easy for typically underfunded gay and lesbian troupes to get the word out to patrons. Same goes for Broadway. Is it dead? Well, with the recent wave of gay fantasias and queer knee-slappers/toe-tappers taking the Great White Way by storm, it's probably safe to say that, for us at least, it's just beginning to happen.

Theatre Central
http://www.theatre-central.com/

The "hub of theatre (sic) on the Internet" is as good a place to start as any. Whether you're a butch thespian or fey theater-goer, you'll find the dramatic goods to light your fire here. Theatre Central (Figure 3.6) boasts the largest compendium of theater links on the Net, a "call board" with jobs and auditions, and a searchable database for contact info on wired theater pros.

Playbill On-Line
http://piano.symgrp.com/playbill/

Diva talk with Bernadette? *Miss Saigon* chat? *Tango is Forever*? Gawd, this place is too good to be true! Chuck your shabby paper copy of *Playbill* underneath the theater seat and get online for everything that's everything, anyone who's anyone, in New York theater and beyond. (Yep, you'll even find the sordid details of all those bus-and-truckload blockbuster tours that are coming soon to a city near you.) Need to make sure you get in to see

David Copperfield on your next trip to the big apple? Order the tickets online here.

The Show Must Go Online!

Norma, *Medea*, *Victor/Victoria*! If they're fabulous, they've all found a fanatical fan base on the Web. Here's a rundown of some notable shrines to block-buster productions. (Just for kicks, the *Cats!* page has been omitted.)

Aspects of Love Home Page
http://ernie.bgsu.edu/~joshw/aspects/

Bring in 'Da Noise, Bring in 'Da Funk
http://www.publictheater.org/cgi-bin/
noifunk.cgi

Chess
http://students.cs.byu.edu/~mason/chess.html

Forever Plaid
http://www.softaid.net/webmap/plaid/

Figure 3.6
Theatre Central

Subject: Nathan Lane
Can anybody honestly and positively
tell me if Nathan Lane is gay or not?
Has he said anything about his
sexuality at all?
Fri Jun 14 21:36:14 EDT 1996 - ()

Hair: the American Tribal Love-Rock Musical
http://www-leland.Stanford.edu/~toots/Hair/hair.html

Hello Dolly
http://www.geocities.com/Broadway/1250/
See Figure 3.7.

The Les Miserables Home Page
http://www.ot.com/lesmis/lesmis.html

Medea, the Musical
http://www.webcom.com/shownet/medea/

Miss Saigon Page
http://www.clark.net/pub/rsjdfg/

Nunsense
http://obryan.com/Nunsense/Home.htm
See Figure 3.8.

The Phantom of the Opera Home Page
http://phantom.skywalk.com/

Plan 9 from Outer Space, the Musical!
http://ourworld.compuserve.com/homepages/mjd/plan9.htm

Rent Home Page
http://www.shadow.net/~dbsccp/rent.html

Starlight Express
http://www.iscs.nus.sg/~anghuiho/starlight.html

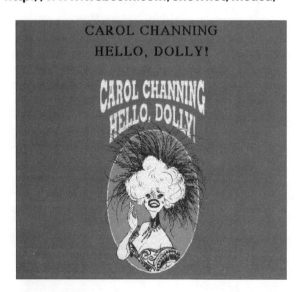

Figure 3.7
Hello Dolly

Figure 3.8
Nunsense

Sunset Boulevard National Tour Home
http://www.sunset-tour.com/

Victor/Victoria Home Page
http://www.hqe.com/victor/victoria/
index~1.htm

Pope Joan Workshop Web
http://orlok.vs.mcs.net/popejoan.html

This "love story based on the rise and fall of the only fe-male Pope" uses ecclesiastical accents and a bubbly pop score to explore modern and age-old themes. But *Pope Joan* (Figure 3.9) is much more than a gender-blender stage production; it's also a one-of-a-kind online theatrical workshop. Through stage diaries and background informa-tion the producer conveys behind-the-scenes realism as to what it takes to get a new musical produced on a Chicago stage. Roll up your sleeves and jack in to *Pope Joan*.

Theater Rhinoceros
http://www.vidaviz.com/adpages/rhino/
rhino.html

The rhinoceros is mild and peace-loving unless pro-voked, and that's something with which this San Fran-cisco-based non-profit theater org can identify. Theater Rhinoceros is devoted to the development and produc-tion of theatrical work by gay and lesbian artists, and/or those addressing gay and lesbian issues. Get details on the upcoming season, and on the organization in general, at this home page.

Execution of Justice
http://www.randy.com/executionofjustice/

Playwright Emily Mann brings the trial of Dan White (the guy who shot and killed Harvey Milk) to the San Diego stage in an award-winning production. The Web site to promote the play is none too shabby itself. (It's even sticking around after the play has completed its run.) Along with ticket information and actor bios, visitors can also use this as a link resource for everything imaginable about Mr. Milk.

Figure 3.9
Pope Joan Workshop Web

One in Ten Theatre Company
http://www.azstarnet.com/~jdbanks/
1in10.htm

The Tucson, AZ-based gay theater company posts its current schedule and information, and that's about it.

Wings Theatre Gay Plays Series
http://www.brainlink.com/~cjeffer/gay.html

New York City's Wings Theatre provides information here on its current and upcoming productions. The the-ater specializes in new plays and musicals by American playwrights geared for a gay audience.

Catalog of Lesbian Plays by Carolyn Gage
http://www.monitor.net/~carolyn/

The title says most of it. Carolyn Gage provides synopses of her lesbian-themed plays here (with price lists and or-dering info), as well as a special "Take Stage" section in which she gives instruction on how to direct and pro-duce a lesbian play.

And for the rest of you playwrights ....

The Dramatic Exchange
http://www.dramex.org/

A Web site "dedicated to archiving and distributing scripts," the Dramatic Exchange gives new meaning to the word "playground." The free service provides a place for playwrights to "publish" and distribute their plays, and a place for producers to scout out ones they may want to produce. One can spend hours reading bizarre and moving plays here. A recent plot goes like this: "Man meets hippie (in a dress), man learns to hate hippie, man tries to kill hippie in the surrealest possible way." Wahoo, the full script is available!

THE SOUND (AND THE LOOK) OF MUSIC

Making the transition from gay theater to gay music is easily accomplished by way of the Big O. Believe it or not, the global opera community is loud and boisterous on the Web. Buffs will find an unimaginable array of professional organizations, companies, and fan shrines to choose from. Here are some of the operatic highlights. And you may want to start right here.

Opera for Dummies
http://www.dn.net/schultz/opera.html

"Welcome to another wonderful world of sex, alcohol, and profound carnage," writes Webmaster John Schultz, tenor. "Welcome to the wonderful world of opera." Schultz urges his visitors to tear themselves away from the TV just long enough to read his fun-page report. He provides a list of the most common female characters in opera ("the whore ... the heroine ... the heroine/ho ....") and the most common male characters ("suave, debonair, selfish, womanizing pig").

OperaGlass
http://rick.stanford.edu/opera/main.html

OperaWeb
http://www.opera.it/English/OperaWeb.html

Both the tragically gray OperaGlass and the splish-splashy OperaWeb have set up plump information services for lovers of the art form online. Visitors to these sites are treated to details, details, details, including performance histories, synopses, libretti, discographies, and pictures. OperaWeb is by far the busiest and most stylish of the two (it's Italian, wouldn't you know), and its features are far more playful. Sections include an "Opera Sing-Along," an interactive quiz, and "The Crazy Opera." For the fast facts, OperaGlass works just fine.

Parterre Box: the Queer Opera Zine
http://www.anaserve.com/~parterre/

Remember when opera was queer and dangerous and exciting? Well, Parterre Box (Figure 3.10), the queer opera zine, is all about making it that way again. Take it from Wayne Koestenbaum, author of *The Queen's Throat:* "Parterre Box is fabulous!" The zine's Web presence is mainly for promoting the paper version of PB, but author James Jorden serves up plenty of goodies from back issues. Get the latest gossip about repertoire, casting, and backstage drama. Read "totally biased" performance and recordings reviews.

Figure 3.10
Parterre Box: the Queer Opera Zine

Maria Callas

http://borg.ncl.ac.uk/miscellaneous/scott/callas.html

Debuts, fan clubs, a bibliography, and discography are among the offerings at this lovingly produced fan page for Callas, who, the creators believe, is "one of the greatest and most versatile operatic singers in recent history."

Opera America

http://www.operaam.org/

The professional organization Opera America services its field by providing informational, technical, and administrative resources to the greater opera community. Find out about its advocacy and awareness programs here, or peruse the listings of schedules and the various databases.

The Opera Schedule Server

http://www.fsz.bme.hu/opera/main.html

As Webmaster Tamás Máray explains, "there is a constant demand for information about the schedules of different opera companies, and this server will try to satisfy that demand." Search the massive, no-frills database by date, city, artist, title, or composer. The server also links directly to various companies and opera resources. Got a burning opera URL of your own? Plug it in right here.

Beyond the Big O

The Derivative Duo Opera

http://www.nwlink.com/~rainier/duo.html

They wreak havoc on the classical music scene, though not with heavy does of rap or discordant homocore. Rather, the Seattle-based Derivative Duo (Figure 3.11) creates opera parodies (à la Weird Al) to illuminate pressing social issues of our day—things like gays in the military, P.M.S., and cat psychology. Hear this if you must, on the site, in RealAudio.

Gay Discography

http://www3.dk-online.dk/users/Christ_H/discography.html#S

Hans Christophersen has painstakingly arranged "these fragments of a manuscript" he made while producing

Figure 3.11
The Derivative Duo Opera

radio shows for Danish gay radio. The work has never been finished, but the notes on musicians and their gay-themed material are arranged in A to Z format for easy access. It's a little messy, but it often makes for a fascinating read.

Sweet Music: Sisters on Stage

http://www.qworld.org/DykesWorld/sweetmusic.html

This lesbian link-a-thon is dedicated to "women in the music biz who are more or less out as being women-loving women." Many are less out than more, but it's still an excellent place to start for women's music on the Web. Artists range from Toni Braxton ("soulful sister with a thrilling voice!") to "pink punk dyke bands" like 7 Year Bitch.

SHE SHRINES

We love our out, proud, and popular artists. And so many of the straight ones are gay friendly these days that it actually would take less effort to compile a list of those we can't stand. Here's a by-no-means-exhaustive rundown of some she-shrines and boy-noise supersites of interest. Boys and girls are welcome on either side, of course. And you'll have to fast-forward to the CattyCorner section in Chapter 4 for RuPaul's House of Love.

Tracy Chapman Internet Fan Club
http://www.rrze.uni-erlangen.de/~sz1526/tracy.html

Ani DiFranco
http://www.columbia.edu/~marg/ani/

disappear fear
http://www.fish.com/music/disappear_fear/

Melissa Etheridge Information Network
http://fanasylum.com/melissa/
See Figure 3.12.

Fem2Fem
http://fem2fem.landqmedia.com

Melissa Ferrick
http://www.best.com/~kluce/www.htm

Ferron
http://ferronweb.com/html/Ferron.html
See Figure 3.13.

Figure 3.12
Melissa Etheridge Information Network

The Drown Soda Hole Pages
http://www.clysmic.com/hole/

Janis Ian Home Page
http://songs.com/noma/jian/index.html

Lifeblood: a Collection of Indigo Girls Information
http://www.hidwater.com/lifeblood/

Random Posting

```
Subject: relations
Hello I'm Barbara a lesbian who's girl
just turned 18.I love to listen to
music by Janis Joplin, Melanie safka,
Neill Youngh. My hobbies are listening
to people like melanie, donovan and
others, drawing cartoons.one of them is
coming out soon in an underground-
cartoonsshop. How do I look. Well, I do
have long dark/blond hair I'm not fat,
I wear glasses. I would like to e-mail
with a girl wholooks like Janis Joplin
or Melanie safka And who knows one of
them (atleast)
Mon Jul 22 12:55:17 EDT 1996 - ()
anonymous
```

Figure 3.13
Ferron

Obvious Gossip: Official k.d. lang Fan Club
http://www.infohouse.com/obviousgossip/

Cris Williamson and Tret Fure
http://www.hypernet.com/cris&tret.html

BOY NOISE

GutterNet: The Marc Almond Page
http://www.why.net/home/torero/marcpage.html

Boy George Home Page
http://www-personal.umich.edu/~geena/
boygeorge.html
See Figure 3.14.

Erasure Home
http://www.erasure.com/

The Flirtations
http://www.provincetown.com/village/stars/flirt/
flirtations.html

Imperial Teen
http://www.inquo.net/~dana/imperialteen/

Elton John—Captain Fantastic
http://www.ccnet.com/~reg/elton.htm

**Understanding Liberace: Grooving with the
Fey Heckler**
http://www.birdhouse.org/words/scot/liberace/
liberace.html

Cemetry Gates—Morrissey and the Smiths
http://www.public.iastate.edu/~moz/
See Figure 3.15.

Pet Shop Boys—Dedicated
http://home.interlynx.net/~rwerner/psb/

Figure 3.14
Boy George Home Page

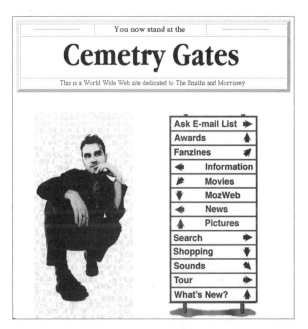

Figure 3.15
Cemetry Gates—Morrissey and the Smiths

Pink Punk

If you thought gay and lesbian music had to incorporate a wailing diva, a pounding electronic bassline, or a woman embracing an acoustic guitar, it's time to enter the current decade. Introducing ... homocore and punk feminism!

Homocore Chicago

http://www.tezcat.com/~homocore/

Joanna Brown and Mark Freitas created Homocore Chicago as a space where queer punks could hang out and listen to live queercore music and feminist punk together (as opposed to hanging out and listening to hi-NRG tunes with either men or women). There aren't too many queer punk shows anymore, their informational site laments, but Homocore Chicago continues to keep visitors abreast of what is going on by way of the Web.

The Official Pansy Division Page

http://www.woodworks.com/pansydiv/

They're innovative, in your face, punkish, openly queer, and they want to rock your world with their "humorous gay-themed lyrics." Might as well let them in. The official Pansy Division site (Figure 3.16) shares lots of the humorous lyrics, and some up-close-and-personal info on each of the three band members. As if that's not enough, we're even treated to an underwear modeling spread the band did for "a popular fashion designer."

Figure 3.16
The Official Pansy Division Page

Queer Music Explosion

http://www.io.com/~larrybob/musicexp3.html

What started out as a paper explosion is now in flames on the Web. The Queer Music Explosion index is jamming with concise reviews of some queer bands that even those who get out fairly often may not have heard of. Bandit Queen? Vaginal Davis? Womyn of Destruction? What ever happened to the Indigo Girls?

Candy-Ass Records

http://m3.monsterbit.com/candyass/

Outpunk Records

http://www.jett.com/outpunk/outpunk.html

They're queer underground music labels and they're responsible for a lot of this new pink noise. Outpunk doubles as a fanzine; Candy-Ass is "lesbionic." Rock on, dudes.

QUEER FILM, HOMO VIDEO

PopcornQ

http://www.planetout.com/kiosk/popcornq/

Livin' large on PlanetOut, Popcorn Q (Figure 3.17) is the definitive online resource for queer film buffs and professionals alike. The colorful site is based on the book *The Ultimate Guide to Lesbian & Gay Film and Video* and has landed on the Web thanks to Jenni Olson, former codirector of the San Francisco International Lesbian & Gay Film Festival. The site's fan section is the place to turn if you want to find out about a current Fassbinder Retrospective or what Sandra Bernhard is up to these days. Elsewhere, services for industry pros include production updates and extensive professional listings. Fun extras accent the site, like an ongoing poll of the all-time faves of queer celebrities and media professionals (Bruce La Bruce's number one is Jerry Lewis's *The Ladies Man*). Beyond that, you still have the "Film Fest Directory" and "Links Galore!" Appropriately, this movie site is graphics intensive. So get thee to a big pipe and a big monitor and you'll really be in show business.

Figure 3.17
PopcornQ

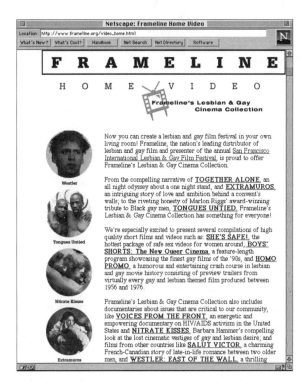

Figure 3.18
Frameline

Frameline Online
http://www.frameline.org/

Frameline Distribution
http://www.frameline.org/distrib_home.html

San Francisco International Gay & Lesbian Film Festival
http://www.frameline.org/festival.html

Strand Releasing
http://www.strandrel.com/

Frameline is a nonprofit organization dedicated to the exhibition, distribution, promotion, and funding of gay and lesbian film and video. It's responsible for the annual San Francisco International Lesbian & Gay Film Festival and for Frameline Distribution, the U.S.'s only distributor solely dedicated to gay and lesbian film and video. The Frameline home video showcase (Figure 3.18) contains information on acclaimed titles like Marlon Riggs's *Tongues Untied* and Barbara Hammer's *Nitrate Kisses*. And you can order titles by way of Strand Releasing, which also maintains a catalog online.

Hollywood Supports
http://www.hsupports.org/hsupports/

Not everyone in Hollywood is in the closet, as is proven by this entertainment industry workplace education and support project. Launched in the fall of 1991 by "leading entertainment industry figures," Hollywood Supports works to stamp out discrimination based on HIV status

for spearheading the annual "Day of Compassion," on which television programming highlights compassion and support for people affected by HIV and AIDS. Get details on Hollywood Supports and the various workshops it offers here.

Internet Movie Database Search
http://us.imdb.com/cache/list/genres=gayll
lesbianllbisexualllaidslltransvestitism

Call up this URL within the monster Internet Movie Database and you'll arrive at a ready-matched listing of hundreds of films (with titles linked to more information) that mention in descriptions any or all of the words gay, lesbian, bisexual, AIDS, or transvestism. Basically, that means *Ace Ventura: Pet Detective* to *Zorro, the Gay Blade*, so you may be better off narrowing things down with your own search.

Subject: Gay Videos Collection!
I have to get rid of my videos. They are
a lot and good ones. Send me mail, then
I'll respond soon. Price? Not expensive
at all. Almost 50% off from original
prices. Collection from HIS, Vivid,
HotShot, etc.etc.etc.! Need to be
responded soon.
Mon Sep 2 15:51:27 EDT 1996 - ()

The GLBO-Centered Film List
http://www.io.com/~topman4u/glbohead.html

Greg Havican of Austin, Texas, maintains this excellent listing of gay, lesbian, and bisexual oriented films. The list is broken down by film type ("Gay Centered U.S. Films," for example) and brief summaries are provided. He also includes a list of film distributors and their addresses. It's all in text (no hyperlinks), but it's still a fine source of information.

Homosexuality in Film
http://www.movienet.com/movienet/sonycl/
celluloid/misc/history.html

Think of "Homosexuality in Film" as a quick hypertext version of *The Celluloid Closet*. With a flowing narrative, the article picks up with a primitive image of two men dancing together (made in Thomas Edison's studio) and leaves off in modern times, exploring films like *Philadelphia* and *Fried Green Tomatoes*. Hyperlinks out to curiosities like Marlene Dietrich and Mariel Hemmingway make for an excellent non-linear read and history lesson.

Tinseltown's Queer Web Site
http://www.gaywired.com/ttownqueer/

Nicholas Snow is "Tinseltown's Queer" (Figure 3.19) (You knew there was one somewhere around there, didn't you?). His mission is to dismantle Hollywood's closet, and he considers himself both "a queen's version

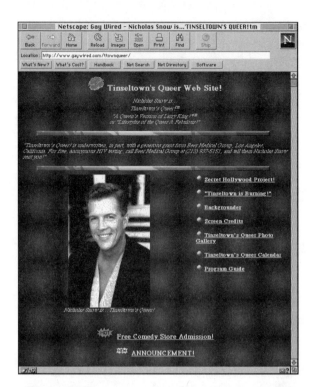

Figure 3.19
Tinseltown's Queer Web Site

of Larry King" and a sort of "Lifestyles of the Queer & Fabulous." He even has his own theme song. Visit Snow's Web home for details on his "Secret Hollywood Project" and "Tinseltown's Queer Calendar." Just don't be surprised if you find the calendar empty.

Beyond Tinseltown

National Library of Australia's Gay and Lesbian Films Checklist
http://www.nla.gov.au/2/film/gay.html

Australia's national library gives just what the title promises, a quick checklist for directors and films of gay interest. The "Memorably Marginal or Obligatorily Oblique" section gets dishy, with items like "*All About Eve*: Hints remain that Eve was originally written as a lesbian."

Queer Asian/Pacific Related Films
http://www.tufts.edu/~stai/QAPA/films.html

This labor of love comprehensively lists films of gay Asian/Pacific interest, or films by queer A/P directors. It also throws in a few articles, like one on AIDS on the Asian/Pacific screen.

Pick Flicks

The Birdcage
http://www.mgmua.com/thebirdcage/

Come as you are to the official promo site for the mainstream drag success story (Figure 3.20). Set up like a clickable tabloid—"The South Beach Inquisitor"—the site is an imaginative hoot. It also allows visitors to download some choice QuickTime movie clips. Let's hope it stays online long after *The Birdcage* has run its course in the video stores.

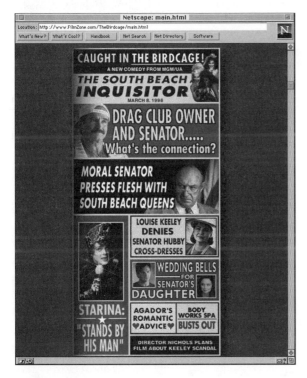

Figure 3.20
The Birdcage

The Celluloid Closet
http://home.earthlink.net/~tellingpix/

Telling Pictures, coproducer of the acclaimed documentary about gay and lesbian images in film history, presents an overview, a history of the film, and some fabulous stills.

The Incredibly True Adventure of 2 Girls in Love
http://www.flf.com/twogirls/index.htm

Check out the official movie poster, read a transcript of an interview with the film's writer/director, and hear the sounds of *Two Girls in Love*. Dreamy.

The Kung-Fu Dyke
http://www-unix.oit.umass.edu/~yvicious/kfd/index.html

It's definitely not lining the walls at your neighborhood Blockbuster, but if you'd like to purchase a copy of Yid Vicious's kicker picture ("filmed in the spring of 1996 in Northampton, MA"), you'll find all the information you need at the Web site, along with some tantalizing stills of the fierce Kung-Fu dyke in action.

Man of the Year
http://www.newfilm.com/

Why is Dirk Shafer directing in his underwear? "Does he have to be gay?" What's a "docu-dramedy," anyway? For answers to these and other questions, hit the Web site for the "comedy movie based on a true story of the centerfold who revealed everything ... but the truth" (Figure 3.21).

To Wong Foo
http://www.digiplanet.com/universal_pictures/to_wong_foo/

This promotional effort from Universal Pictures was apparently so fabulous that it had to be archived. We're greeted by lots of pink and Miss Vida Boheme (the Patrick Swayze one), who invites us on a road trip, starting in New York City at a drag queen contest. "Chicken, can you imagine—three drag queens go on the road and find danger, adventure, and fun fun fun," says Miss Vida. (Chicken?) Whatever you do, don't forget to stop at the rest area, where you can download the choice soundbite, "I got more leg than a bucket of chicken."

Figure 3.21
Man of the Year

And on the Tube...

On the Air, from the *Washington Blade*
http://www.washblade.com/
ONTHEAIR.HTM#top

D.C.'s excellent gay weekly provides notes on queer television scheduling and a day-by-day look at what's of interest to gays and lesbians in TV-land.

Planet Out's Shout Guide
http://www.Planetout.com/kiosk/shout/96/02/
box_oct.html

Shout, the arts and entertainment zine on PlanetOut, provides an instant, ready-made schedule of queer-themed programming for the month.

Gay/Lesbian/Bisexual Television Characters
http://home.cc.umanitoba.ca/~wyatt/tv-characters.html

David Wyatt of Manitoba, Canada, has compiled this mindblowing list of television programs that have included gay characters—either regularly or semi-regularly—as part of their casts. His index looks at characters by decade of debut, or by alphabetical listing of program titles. One thing is obvious: This guy watches too much television.

Dyke TV
http://www.dyketv.org/

It's television "to incite, subvert, provoke, and organize." It's "Dyke TV" (Figure 3.22), a half-hour bi-weekly program of news, politics, and culture, produced by lesbians, for lesbians. The New York City-based program debuted in 1993 and now airs in more than 60 cities across the U.S. Pull up the organization's Web page for a brief her-story, a program and network schedule, and to learn how to get involved. There's even some stylish "Dyke TV" gear up for grabs in the merchandise area.

In the Life
http://www.inthelifetv.org/

"In the Life" is a national television newsmagazine reporting on gay and lesbian issues and culture. It is broadcast on nearly 100 public TV stations. Get press clips and air dates, and check out what's coming up in the season.

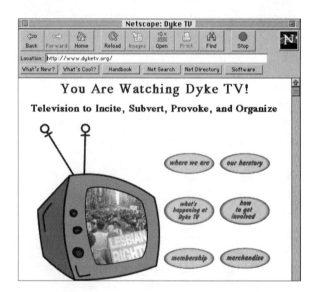

Figure 3.22
Dyke TV

LambdaCom Corporation
http://www.tde.com/~lambdacom/

LambdaCom is a nonprofit Denver-based organization that produces cable and public television programming for the gay and lesbian community. Get details here on "The Lambda Report," a weekly news report, and "The MCC Connection," spiritual programming for the gay and lesbian community.

Outlook Video
http://www.OutlookVideo.org/

"Outlook Video" is a monthly gay and lesbian news and entertainment program for cable television. It is broadcast throughout the San Francisco Bay Area, Sacramento, Nashville, and Dallas. Get program and episode highlights here, or find out what's going to be taped at the next shoot.

The Gay & Lesbian Star Trek/Sci-Fi Home Page
http://ccnet4.ccnet.com/gaytrek/

"Star Trek" clubs and organizations around the world (and there are gazillions) refer to themselves as ships. The gay and lesbian "Star Trek" club (Figure 3.23) follows suit, unleashing "the USS Harvey Milk." The site is a place where gay and lesbian Trekkies can exchange commentary, reviews, and stories that relate to "Star Trek" and the inclusion of gay and lesbian characters. Like most "Star Trek" sites on the Web, this one is loaded to an almost exhausting extreme. It's enchanted, it's political, it's techie. Check it out.

Smithers
http://www.snpp.com/family/
smithers.sexuality.html

And for those of you who prefer the simplicity of "The Simpsons" but are going bonkers trying to figure out whether or not Smithers is gay, point your browser accordingly.

Figure 3.23
The Gay & Lesbian Star Trek/Sci-Fi Home Page

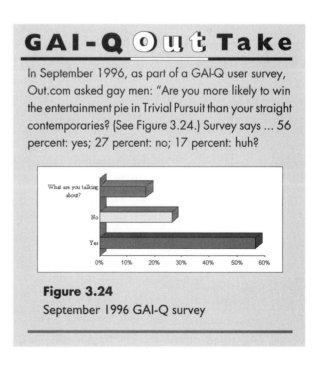

GAI-Q Out Take

In September 1996, as part of a GAI-Q user survey, Out.com asked gay men: "Are you more likely to win the entertainment pie in Trivial Pursuit than your straight contemporaries? (See Figure 3.24.) Survey says ... 56 percent: yes; 27 percent: no; 17 percent: huh?

Figure 3.24
September 1996 GAI-Q survey

Chapter 4

CATTY CORNERS OF THE WEB

Reporter: *Do you suppose that gay content on the Web could be fabulous or only pedantic and earnest?*

Trudy: *Me voilá.*

Who's this Trudy?, you might be wondering; and what the hell makes Trudy such fabulous content? With apologies to RuPaul, Data Lounge's so-called Trudy is nothing less than the busiest and the wittiest queen in cyberspace; a queen for whom clacking noises emanate from a keyboard, and not from heels clipping across a stage. In a legendary interview with the elusive Trudy, excerpted above, the "reporter" poses a valid question: While we're busy using the Net to build communities and push through action items, do gays and lesbians forsake laughs and fabulousness for all things pedantic, earnest, and utterly dull?

Absolutely not. Trudy's living (okay, virtual) proof of that, but the good times don't stop there. Who's your favorite icon? Chances are, he, she, or it is the object of a fabulous fan shrine—perhaps even a pedantic fan shrine—floating around out there in the ether. If there's a better way to exhibit nutty infatuation than construction of a shrine for all the world to see, it's not coming to mind.

Finally, where would all of our catty correspondents find jobs if it weren't for the world's second-favorite pastime of digging up hot scoop? A handful of gay and lesbian correspondents have elevated talking trash to an art form.

As we all know, when you're hungry for dish, you must have it now. And as you will discover in this section, with Internet access and a few strategically placed bookmarks, you'll never go hungry again.

THE VIRTUAL PERSONALITY

Data Lounge
Trudy in Cyburbia
http://www.datalounge.com

If it's twisted content you seek, Trudy is the madcap creator to follow. You'll find her letting it all hang out in her own cyburbian hell at Mediapolis's Data Lounge. It is by way of the flowery Data Lounge that Mediapolis presents its portfolio of gay-oriented Web creations all in one place. The collection—including Out.com, POZ, Q San Francisco, and GLAAD—is fierce. But it's the giddy prose of Trudy, "Big ol' Fussbudget and basically everybody's lovable boss," who secures the Lounge's bookmarkability ad infinitum.

Trudy is basically turned loose, with at least one very talented graphic designer, to do things like host Miss World Wide Web Pageants, take snapshots at NYC Pride, and create instant drag names for guests (see Figure 4.1). One must pull up a chair and interact with these little projects to truly appreciate them, and the same can be said about the vicious nonlinear reads available in our heroine's public diaries, "Trudy in Cyburbia." Trudy also stamps her seal of approval ("Trudy Approved") on a smattering of site royalty across the Web. And she has given at least one interview to date—with a "young lady reporter of infinite potential, dressed in a smart tailored pinstripe suit" and blindfolded.

SassyFemme
http://www.txdirect.net/~sassyfem/
mainpage.html

SassyFemme (Figure 4.2) doesn't have a force like Mediapolis behind her, and she apparently doesn't have anything to promote besides her incredibly true adventures

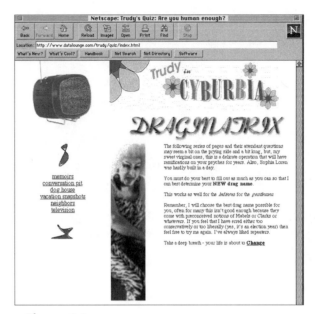

Figure 4.1
Trudy in Cyburbia

as a lesbian. If you must know, she's feminine with a bit of sass—and a slightly warped sense of humor. We like all that, and if this description is sounding like a personal ad for which you'd enthusiastically lick a stamp, do drop in on SassyFemme. Check out her writing, aka her "musings from the heart," on things like her commitment ceremony and life with her partner's daughter. Delve into the deviance of her pets via their "arrest reports" ("the Phantom Plate Licker"). And don't miss her "Life of a SassyFemme" diary, subtitled "I see you snooping into my life!" We've got an excerpt.

After getting back from the carnival yesterday I was sitting in the office when I heard this loud bang on the dining room window. I turned around just in time to see a bird fly away after hitting the window. Fran and I jumped up and ran to the window, but didn't see any sign of the bird.

Ouch! Is that the truth, or is it SassyFemme's warped sense of humor at work? "All Things Barbie" are also of primary interest in these parts. You know, that "so-called perfect blonde who'd really fall on her face from overendowment if she were a human." Like a good dream, SassyFemme brings Barbie back into perspective. "Was she your constant companion? ... Did she have a secret

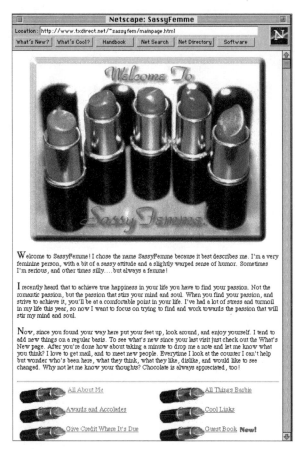

Figure 4.2
SassyFemme

spot for doing nasty things with Ken? Was she pushed aside in favor of GI Joe?"

GIMME SLEAZE

You know you want it. Do a search on Lycos for the word and it's a sure thing that the name Adam Curry will pop up. (At least within the first two pages of results.) You remember Adam: the long- and purty-haired video-jockey who used to work for MTV when it still pretty much played music videos. But who cares about that. What's the dude got to do with sleaze?

The Vibe: Sleaze
http://metaverse.com/vibe/sleaze/

As grand poobah over at The Vibe (Figure 4.3), a kind of GenX, MTVesque 'zine for the Web, Curry gets the honor of shoveling buckets of sleaze every weekday. In his words, "Each opinionated report brings you your up-to-the-minute dose of doctor-recommended 'sleaze' from the sordid worlds of music and entertainment." Well, let's just say that Curry isn't losing any friends over the nuggets you'll find here. This is mild Curry: "Soul singer Stevie Wonder had President Bill Clinton tapping his feet and clapping his hands ...." And this is extra-spicy: "Marlon Brando ... was recently spotted putting away six pizzas and three plates of pasta in a Los Angeles restaurant." Curry's editor is named Jill "The Diva" Stempel, but we know she's not a queen. This dish is far too polite.

On to the next big glossy online pop thing, E! fares much better and, frankly, sets off the gaydar every damn time a page comes up. As you know if you've seen the television version of "E!", the gossip here is some of the best.

E! Online—Gossip
http://www.eonline.com/Gossip/

Unlike Adam Curry, sleazemonger Ted Casablanca doesn't seem to be afraid of losing, or at least infuriating, a few friends in the industry. The catty pen behind E!'s

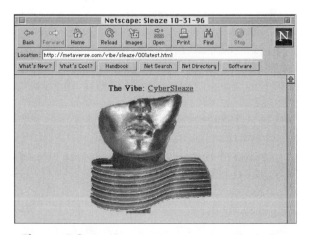

Figure 4.3
The Vibe: Sleaze

"Awful Truth" column (Figure 4.4) let his courage be known and put his reputation on the line during the pre-*Evita* season last year, for example, by a) referring to the flick as "you know, Madonna's latest effort at a movie career" and b) daring to suggest that a notable lack of buzz after the first screening was "ominous." Sacrilege! But there's much much more beyond "The Awful Truth," because gossip is pretty much all E! does. *Print Soup* (like *Talk Soup*, on Prozac) tells you which current magazines you should buy and why. Gossipeuse Samantha Fein plods through the relatively subdued "E! Files," which covers more the car crash/gangsta tragedy/heart attack beats. And that still leaves hours—okay several minutes—of fun with "The Diary of Madonna's Baby" (Figure 4.5) and, wow, "The Best of the Gossip Show." For real, E!'s better online than it is on the tube.

Premeire Magazine—Back Lot— Celebrity Bytes
http://www.premieremag.com/backlot/ celebytes/

While making the rounds of the substantially underwritten and professionally written dishrags online, might as well stop off for a rest break at *Premiere* magazine's passé online digs. The magazine has become incredibly, dare we say it, colorless and puffy in recent months, but one can sidestep the front door and head straight to the "Back Lot" for the "Celebrity Bytes" archive. The Anne Bancrofts, the Drew Barrymores, the Tom Cruises ... they're all hanging out here, just waiting to be examined in all their complexities. The rest of the site, um, bytes.

Pathfinder
http://www.pathfinder.com/welcome

Forget that Time Warner's hyperactive Web conglomerate is where you'll find CNN & Time news, *Money* magazine, and alarmingly serious coverage of what's happening with O.J. Simpson. Cut to what Pathfinder does best—rabid coverage of celebrities. Start with the welcome page. At best, it's a guilty pleasure; at worst it's a convoluted jumble of blocks, icons, and color. For the most satisfying results, zero in on key words like "entertainment" and "people," and then click on them ....

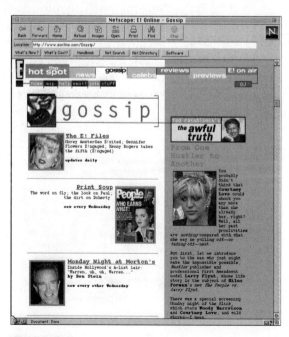

Figure 4.4
E! Online—Gossip

Figure 4.5
Madonna's baby diary

Entertainment Weekly Online
http://pathfinder.com/ew/

Entertainment Weekly (Figure 4.6) has been highly inclusive of gay- and lesbian-themed content from the get-go (k.d. lang graced the magazine's first cover). With its weekly format and daddy's bottomless pockets, it flat-out covers everything, so all-inclusiveness would be expected. This one, however, goes the extra mile and is perhaps the only mainstream publication that regularly runs with gay cover stories. Like the paper version, EW Online offers a good, quick read, albeit without some of the goodies you would normally find on the newsstand. Never fear, Jim Mullen's witty "Hot Sheet," an EW institution, is here in all its glory, along with something you can't find on the newsstand: archives.

People Online
http://pathfinder.com/people/

You know you're close to rock bottom when you flip through a copy of *People*. But, then, you know you always peek when you're stuck in line at the supermarket. The good folks at Pathfinder spare you the embarrassment of being caught red-handed by piping the schlock right into your office. From the home page (Figure 4.7), go directly to the "Peephole" for polite celebrity gossip as gathered from tabloids and other "sources."

Random Posting

```
Fri Nov 1 10:29:38 EST 1996 - ()
anonymous
Subject: Gina Gershon
Does anyone have any info on this
GORGEOUS woman? One can only dream that
she is a sister....I love her! I dream
of her! I need her!!! Help me.
```

Hot Hollywood Gossip
http://member.aol.com/editorman/gossip.html

You have to subscribe to get this over-the-top tabloid dirt once a week. It's free, and worth every penny. A sample of what you'll be reading: "Sharon Stone once slammed a boyfriend's private parts into a door."

Mr. Showbiz
http://web3.starwave.com/showbiz/

For more of the same, check out the Mr. Showbiz home page for hyperlinked headlines. This is a service of the Starwave folks (creators of Nascar Online and NBA.com, for what it's worth). Mr. S also features reviews, interviews, and industry charts.

It's safe to say the gossip industry is teeming with people like us, and perhaps their shrouded style is what

Figure 4.6
Entertainment Weekly Online

Figure 4.7
People Online

makes all of the "mainstream" gossip so much fun to follow. But the Web offers plenty of opportunities for the straight gay-dope, as well.

Out.com—Culture—Today's Gossip
http://www.out.com/out-cgi-bin/ page?p=CULTURE&f=content&x=1

Get your daily dose here from the sources at Out (Figure 4.8). Need to spill something yourself? Out's very own mistress of mischief, Linda Simpson, hosts the celebrity gossip forum here. Shades of the "Celebrity Chat" folder at gAyOL.

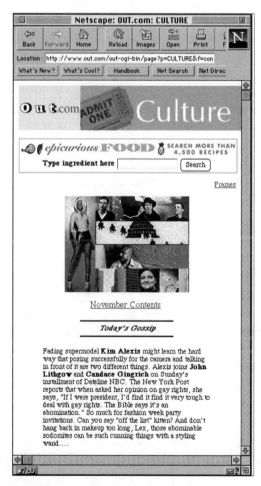

Figure 4.8
Out.com—Culture—Today's Gossip

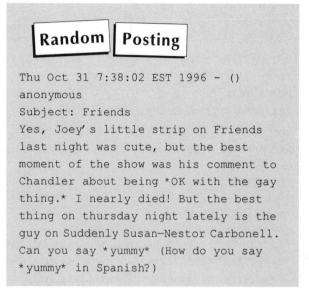

Thu Oct 31 7:38:02 EST 1996 - ()
anonymous
Subject: Friends
Yes, Joey's little strip on Friends last night was cute, but the best moment of the show was his comment to Chandler about being *OK with the gay thing.* I nearly died! But the best thing on thursday night lately is the guy on Suddenly Susan—Nestor Carbonell. Can you say *yummy* (How do you say *yummy* in Spanish?)

PlanetOut: NewsPlanet
http://www.planetout.com/kiosk/newsplanet/

As the name would imply, PlanetOut's NewsPlanet is infinitely more newsy and substantiated than the run-of-the-mill fluff you'll comb off of the entertainment sites each day. But the Planet always manages to mix in some frivolous fun with the hard news, so it should be a definite stop-off, even if you're just digging in the dirt.

HX
http://www.hx.com/hx/cat-index.html

The très trendoid guide for queer New York nightclubbers will tell you what to see, where to be seen, and pretty much everything in between. The gossip gets top billing here, and it comes in two flavors: dyke and homo.

WEBWEENIE DU JOUR

Gay Daze

http://www.gaydaze.com/sstory/index.html

It may be Los Angeles, and it may be the story of a doctor, a dancer, a lover, a loser, a father, and a natural woman, but rest assured: "Gay Daze is not just another melodrama." Rather, it's "a gay and lesbian saga of colossal proportions." (See Figure 4.9). Think of it as a combination of daytime soaps, "American pop fiction" and interactive entertainment. (Or just think of it as "The Spot" with gay characters.) Meet Andrew (he'll eat anything if there's *sake*); Eric ("unable to hide from himself"); Frances (hates beef, loves sea bass); Greg ("personal trainer by trade, artist in spirit); Hugo ("everybody's

Every Picture Tells a Story

Sometimes pictures are all you need. Thank Doug Stickney for creating stellar online galleries and one hell of a meditation on silver-screen sirens. Liz, Lauren, Rita, Greta, and more await at the following URLs.

Doug Stickney's Silver Screen Siren Website

http://users.deltanet.com/users/dstickne/index.html

Ingrid Bergman Image Gallery

http://users.deltanet.com/users/dstickne/bergman.htm

Greta Garbo Image Gallery

http://users.deltanet.com/users/dstickne/garbo.htm

Rita Hayworth Image Gallery

http://users.deltanet.com/users/dstickne/rita.htm

Veronica Lake Image Gallery

http://users.deltanet.com/users/dstickne/veronica.htm

Hedy Lamarr Image Galley

http://users.deltanet.com/users/dstickne/hedy.htm

Lizabeth Scott Image Gallery

http://users.deltanet.com/users/dstickne/lizimage.htm

Elizabeth Taylor Image Gallery

http://users.deltanet.com/users/dstickne/ltimage.htm

Gene Tierney Image Gallery

http://users.deltanet.com/users/dstickne/tierney.htm

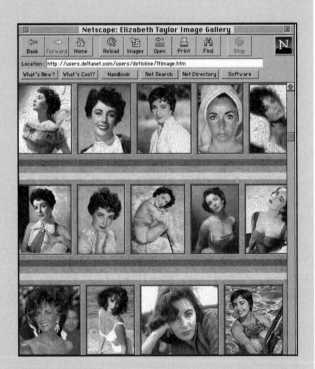

Elizabeth Taylor Image Gallery

Figure 4.9
Gay Daze

daddy"); and Miguel (if he wasn't a dancer, he'd be a con man). Hooked yet? Get up close and personal with the dubious lot in this long-overdue online alternative to "Melrose Place." But wait, there's more. The on-site "Fairy Tales and Dyke Dramas" archive is brimming with short stories from "you, out there."

WE LOVE YOU

The Paula Abdul Web
http://www.pabdul.com/

No kidding. It's artist approved and "created by fans with contributions from many wonderful people."

Drew Is Love
http://www-personal.umd.umich.edu/
~melindab/Drew/drew.html

"Since so many have asked, Why I love Drew: Once upon a time I had a friend who was in a band. This girl played guitar. She looked very much like beloved Drew. I became slightly infatuated with this girl. I first really became interested in Drew when I saw her on the cover of Interview magazine, no not the one with her in a pool, but an earlier one, she is wearing something pink. She looked so stunning (if anyone has this magazine please, please, tell me). But now my interest continues on, hence this page you are admiring!"

Julia Child Uncensored
http://shoga.wwa.com/~sluggo/julia/

Ed Special, of Ann Arbor, Mich., gives "everyone's favorite grandmother figure" (and everyone's favorite curdled voice) the opportunity to speak out from cyberspace. Choice audio file: "When you get it, you want to smell it."

The Montgomery Clift Homepage
http://members.aol.com/stallen/clift.htm

This would be Steve Allen's first attempt at a home page (Figure 4.10), and he can't think of more worthy subject matter. Good point.

The Completely Un-official Ellen DeGeneres Home Page
http://www.hamline.edu/~drhagel/
EllenHome.html

When she's not strumming her guitar, Webmaster Deb may be found adding quotables or pictures to this "completely Ellen-friendly" zone for the world's favorite Lebanese comedian.

Catherine Deneuve
http://www.generation.net/~vincy/
cdeneuve.htm

"The goddess of cinema" didn't like the idea of having a lesbian magazine named after her. Wonder how she feels about this Web site.

Figure 4.10
The Montgomery Clift Homepage

The Jodie Foster Gallery
http://www.tcp.com/~mary/foster.html

Webmaster Mary Cardenas admits that, in a dim way, she's beginning to understand fan obsession. With an intro like "Ms. Foster, we truly respect and admire your intellect, education, achievements, and trapezius development," you probably never would have guessed that.

The Nicole Kidman Worship Page
http://www-personal.umich.edu/~rkmead/
kidman.html

The lovely and talented Australian actress is painted here as an inspiration to redheads everywhere. Miscellaneous facts point to her "sheer coolness."

Steve and Mark's Madonna Page
http://www.buffnet.net/~steve772/
maddy.html

Steve and Mark are just two ordinary college students that happen to be burning up for Madonna. They share their passion, their photos, their Madonna poll results (Figure 4.11), soundbites, and videos with fans around the world via this exemplary shrine. Enjoy their efforts, but heed their request: "We do not have contact with her, nor do we know her e-mail address, so stop asking."

Time in New England:
The Barry Manilow Fan Club Web Site
http://www.cris.com/~Shaked/

Music and passion are always the fashion at the Barry Manilow Fan Club site (Figure 4.12), and "New England" may just be the hottest spot north of Havana if you're a Man' fan. Find the lyrics to "Mandy," photos galore, possible pen-pals, and learn when he'll be appearing on "Regis and Kathy Lee."

The Unofficial Bette Midler Web Site
http://www.nwrain.net/~jstewart/
bettehome.htm

Experience the divine ... online (Figure 4.13).

Liza Online
http://www.oberlin.edu/~dfortune/
lizapage.html

Start spreading the news. Two photo galleries, a sound room, and lots of Liza links.

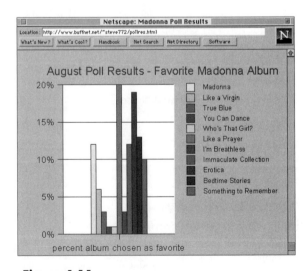

Figure 4.11
Steve and Mark's Madonna Page

Figure 4.12

Time in New England: The Barry Manilow Fan Club Web Site

Figure 4.13

The Unofficial Bette Midler Web Site

Lovejoy's Marilyn Monroe Image Gallery
http://studentweb.tulane.edu/~llovejo/marilyn/

Webmaster Lee Lovejoy writes, "she possessed an ability to command attention greater than any other's and can still, after so many years, captivate me." And with that, a graceful collection of images from fans across the Net is on display.

We Hate Your F*cking Guts, Marilyn
http://www.africanet.com.br/~nailbomb/mm/

From the other Marilyn camp: "Marilyn was the one who taught a whole generation how to hate women." Click on thumbnails of her if you'd like to see larger versions. "And if you want to fill yourself with misogyny, you may also right-click on the images to save them." Sca-ry.

Rosie O'Donnell, Queen of all Things
http://www.mindspring.com/~moomoo/rosie.html

Yo! Sound clips and episode guides for Ro's show and links to info about her life in general. Just in case you don't know enough already.

Random Posting

```
Thu Oct 31 20:30:44 EST 1996 - ()
anonymous
Subject: RuPaul
Has anyone heard RuPaul's new album?
I'm just curious if it is any good
before I buy it.
```

ERIC PERKINS'S EXCELLENT ADVENTURE: THE MAN, THE FAN, BEHIND KEANUNET

For Eric Perkins, Keanu Reeves is more than the star of "Feeling Minnesota" and the bass player for Dogstar; he's a way of life. Virtually. The gay Manhattan-based 46-year-old writer and graphic designer began his Web hub for all things Keanu in 1995. Since then, he's amassed awards, personal satisfaction, and the thrill of speaking with and meeting like-minded people from all over the world. More importantly, his collection of Keanu memorabilia has grown by leaps and bounds. Perkins took a time-out from the Keanu-watch to answer a few questions about KeanuNet and Keanu in general.

Q: Why KeanuNet? Why not DeppWeb or DandoNet?

A: DeppWeb? Dando-Net? Well, it had to be KeanuNet, because I've been a longtime fan of Keanu Reeves. About a year and a half ago, I got the opportunity to have my own Web site, and was thinking about what I should do. I didn't want one of those personal pages that tells all about myself. They're mostly boring, in my opinion. I was aware of other celebrity sites, and looked around for something about Keanu. There wasn't very much, and what was there was sparse. I decided that if I was going to do a site, it would have to be as complete as possible.

Drawing from my Keanu collection of stills and magazine articles, I put up the first KeanuNet on July 1, 1995. It took a month of 50 hour weeks to get it up, so to speak. It's constantly evolving.

Q: How much time out of your week does KeanuNet occupy these days?

A: Well, I no longer spend 50 hours a week on it, that's for sure. I would say about an hour or so a day, unless I'm doing a project or major updates, then it can be much more. When Keanu is working, as he is right

Keanu.net

now, on *Devil's Advocate*, I spend more time digging around for facts. Fortunately, his publicity people and the studios are very cooperative.

Q: Have you ever met him?

A: Yes, just recently. I ran into him on the street in New York. He was very polite, and we chatted briefly, as we were both off to the theater and it was nearing curtain time. Hopefully, I will get a chance to meet him again.

Q: Is he a Mac user, or a PC guy?

A: To the best of my knowledge, Keanu doesn't own a computer, and is not online. However, I'm told that he has been shown the Internet by some friends. He is well aware of my site and the others that have recently sprung up about him.

Q: Do you know whether or not he digs KeanuNet?

A: I'm told by his management that he finds the Web sites amusing.

Q: You're pretty protective of the facts about Keanu. That is, you don't like to print malicious gossip. Seems like everyone else on the Net does. Why do you hold back?

A: First of all, I don't want to offend the man. Secondly, Keanu is often the butt of stupid rumors and I refuse to give credence to such things until proven true. And it's not only on the Net that stupid rumors fly. It's just a way of gaining readership. KeanuNet has a dedicated following. I don't need to sling dirt to attract viewers.

Q: How many hits do you get on an average week?

A: Between 7 and 10,000 generally. More when a film is opening.

Q: In general, what kind of people visit your site? Young girls? Guys in their twenties and thirties?

A: I don't keep statistics, but judging from my mail, there is a very wide range of people who visit. I would guess that the biggest viewership is actually women in their thirties and forties, although I get people of all ages.

Q: So I see in the News section of your site that Keanu has been offered a role as a gay man. Do you think he'll take it?

A: Keanu is never scared off by any subject matter, which is proven by his choice of films that he has acted in. So whether the character is gay or not, will not be much of a consideration. His decision will be based on the other elements. It must be a good script—which is the main reason he turned down *Speed II*; the script wasn't very good—and the character has to be interesting. Additionally, he has to be interested in the director and supporting cast. Keanu is at the stage now where he can pick and choose, without worry-ing about it. I have not heard how good this script is, but apparently many top actors are pursuing the role, so they must smell a hit!

Q: What do you think of his choices of roles lately? *Chain Reaction* and *Feeling Minnesota* ....

A: *Chain Reaction* was a script that Keanu found interesting, and it had a top director and costar attached as well. Strong elements. Also, he needed to make a picture at Fox, and he does try to make some films that will be commercial. It certainly looked at the beginning that the film would do very big box office. Personally, I thought the film was a lot better than the critics did, but expectations were that it would be another *Fugitive*, and that obviously didn't happen.

A: *Feeling Minnesota* was a very interesting quirky film, the kind of thing that Keanu enjoys doing. I thought Keanu was very good in it, the best acting he has done since *River's Edge*. For those that insist that Keanu cannot act, and there are many, they should take a look at some of his earlier films.

Q: What's your opinion of Dogstar?

A: I haven't formed an opinion about Dogstar yet. I did attend one of their concerts, and I have to admit that I'm not a fan of that type of music. The volume was so high that I really couldn't hear the music! Mostly, it's Keanu and friends having a good time. Although they are serious about it, for Keanu and Rob Mailhouse (also an actor) it's a second-ary occupation. For Bret Domrose (the lead singer and writer of most of the material), however, it's his only occupation.

Q: A lot of people have been saying that Keanu has put on too

> ## "For those who are Keanu fans, and are regular visitors to KeanuNet, his weight fluctuation was no hindrance to their loyalty."

much weight lately. Has that had an effect on the traffic on your site?

A: Another rumor, actually. Keanu was never fat. Keanu's weight does fluctuate ... he loves to eat! But he wanted a slightly rounder appearance for his role in *Chain Reaction* as a graduate student. He thought the character would not be eating properly, and certainly wouldn't be hanging out in the gym. Unfortunately, after filming was completed he broke his ankle and couldn't get back to the gym to take the weight off. When I met him recently, he had lost the weight and was back to his usual good looks. For those who are Keanu fans, and are regular visitors to KeanuNet, his weight fluctuation was no hindrance to their loyalty.

Q: What's the future of Keanu-Net look like?

A: Bigger and better. I'm always adding to it, and it goes through constant redesigns. It's sort of my beta site for the other sites I design, none of which are fan related.

KeanuNet
http://www.aok.com/
keanunet/knet.html

RuPaul's House of Love

http://www.glasswing.com/~rupaul/

She's conquered music, books, screen, and television, and at Travis Prebble's Web creation, RuPaul is crowned "Queen of Cyberspace." Come on in to the House of Love (Figure 4.14), where the positive love energy will knock you out of your chair! Inside, you can find the latest dish (in a recent MSNBC poll, viewers selected RuPaul as the ideal mate for Dennis Rodman); accessorize (with the 1997 RuPaul calendar); and write to Ru (the girlfriend even responds to some of the letters personally).

The Tracey Ullman "Go Home" Page

http://www.inforamp.net/~amitch/index.html

She's played more characters than anyone else in history, and this is a towering shrine to all of 'em. A brief hypertext history of Ullman, song samples, and the Tracey Ullman Database, if you have a few days.

Figure 4.14
RuPaul's House of Love

WHEELS ON FIRE

The gay one-liners file would be severely lacking if it weren't for Patsy and Edina, who have carelessly left us in a holding pattern and a loop of "Absolutely Fabulous" reruns as we anticipate their next move. Will it be a movie? Another guest appearance on "Rosanne"? Meantime, their spirits have been preserved in the ether, both by those who stand to make a profit from reruns, and those who don't. Lights, models, guest list ....

The Absolutely Fabulous Home Page

http://comcentral.com/abfab/abfab.shtml

And the reruns keep coming! Comedy Central hosts this shabby bash (Figure 4.15), a not-so-subtle reminder that you're definitely better off turning on the telly for an AbFab fix than turning up online. At least to this address. The BBC has requested that Comedy Central remove a variety of the site's mulitmedia clips "to comply with British entertainment unions' policies"—how utterly unAbFab of them. Still, the site holds a few charming features for hopeless hangers on. It's hard to resist a GIF of Pats clutching her Stoli and lighting up as a helicopter looms overhead—or just a picture of Pats clutching her Stoli and lighting up, for that matter. Beyond the images, you'll find episode synopses and air schedules. Oh, and you can go shopping at the Comedy Central mall for AbFab briefs and leotards. It's nothing like Harvey Nicks'; Pats and Edina wouldn't be caught dead near the place.

The Global Absolutely Fabulous Pages

http://online.anu.edu.au/nceph/Tor/welcome.html

Leave it to AbFab-fan-deluxe Victoria Smith, aka Tor, to kick Comedy Central's ass in the sweetiedarling department. Tor recalls the days when she used to sit up Friday nights on her own to watch "AbFab" before it attained its cult status. She's collected the best of the fabulous,

Figure 4.15
The Absolutely Fabulous Home Page

and shares it all right here. (She has since become obsessed with Gillian Anderson of "X-Files," but that's another story.) Tor's illustrated FAQ covers the essentials, like "What is Bubble's accent?," "What's Lacroix?," and "Is Saffy a virgin?" And judging from her sound and vision gallery, the BBC hasn't caught up with her yet. Here's to Tor: Cheers, sweetie. Thanks a lot.

AND SAFFY, TOO!

The Unofficial Julia Sawalha Homepage
http://www.geocities.com/Hollywood/3465/mmain.html

Home of the Julia Sawalha Appreciation Society answers the burning questions—like who the hell is she?—and helps visitors "watch out for those Julia appearances that you usually miss!" These fans mean business. The on-site picture gallery is private, and invitation only. We're assured that it contains more than 150 pictures and "should be well worth looking out for." Funny, funny.

GAI-Q Out Take

In an April 1996 GAI-Q survey (Figure 4.16), Out.com asked viewers how much influence a designer label has on a clothing purchase. Results are illustrated below. (We'll assume that at least 17 percent of the respondents relate intimately to "Absolutely Fabulous.")

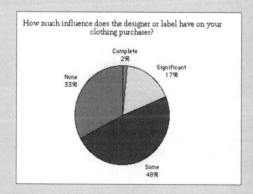

Figure 4.16
April 1996 GAI-Q survey

Chapter 5

HOMOS@HOME

This section is dedicated to anyone who enjoys throwing a dinner party, doing yardwork, raising a family, and, moreover, anyone who is destined to meet their mate while waiting in a line at Home Depot ....

HOME ARTS

HomeArts
http://www.homearts.com/

Good Housekeeping
http://homearts.com/gh/toc/00ghhpc1.htm

Country Living
http://homearts.com/cl/toc/00clhpc1.htm

Popular Mechanics
http://homearts.com/pm/toc/00pmhpc1.htm

Okay. The "five tips for turning up the heat in your bedroom" (excerpted on the HomeArts site from *Redbook*'s "How to Be a Sex Goddess in your own Home") are not launched directly at gays and lesbians. Nor are the tips from Ellen Welty on the site's breathless Kiss.Net. But pointers like "Give him a head massage" can be read under at least as many shades of light as "She Monopolized My Dinner Party." In other words, we can relate.

Hearst Corporation publications are meant to appeal to the masses. So if you're an all-around homebody, might as well drop a bag of chamomile, pull up a stool, and jack in to HomeArts (Figure 5.1), Hearst's friendly empire online.

HomeArts houses all of Heart's popular favorites: *Good Housekeeping*, *Country Living*, *Popular Mechanics*, and more.

At the click of a country mouse, *Country Living* will keep you abreast of the latest news in sandwich glass, clock dials, and vintage bookmarks. And don't hesitate to "Ask Helaine," a pro appraiser, about the value of your rugs, sewing tables, and other homey collectibles.

While we're talking advice, you may be surprised to discover inky stalwarts Heloise and Dr. Joyce Brothers wired and constantly queued just across the hall at *Good Housekeeping*. Heloise beams through the monitor with all of her conventional wisdom as it applies to missing puzzle pieces and bra repair. And Dr. Brothers? Well, looking spiffy as ever in her pink blazer, she tells it like it is, answering all the questions she receives that are fit to print. ("Fighting as Foreplay," anyone?) Perhaps HomeArts's most stellar feature is *Popular Mechanics* (Figure 5.2), which goes so far as to offer online home improvement "clinics." Here, you'll get step-by-step instruction on domestic practices such as installing wainscoting, replacing a dryer belt, and taping drywall. All in a day's work at HomeArts.

Figure 5.1
HomeArts

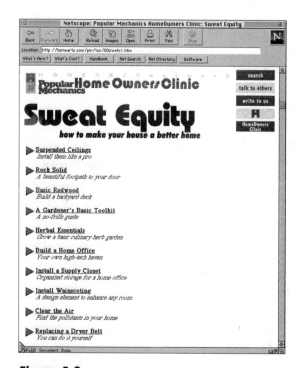

Figure 5.2
Popular Mechanics

CraftNet Village

http://www.craftnet.org/

The diverse crafts and computers scenes collide in this village, a virtual community and marketplace where citizens are armed with soldering irons and glue-guns. Browse articles of interest on the site's magazine rack, or send off for free catalogs for days.

CraftWeb

http://www.craftweb.com

CraftWeb claims to be the premiere online community for professional craft artists. It fosters an environment where pros and artisans meet, swap tips, and promote fine craftwork around the world. Peruse the online crafts gallery, or track down an obscure book title for instructions on whatever it is that you're trying to do with all those sequins and pussy willows.

Collector's Corner

Whether it's kitsch or coins you collect, the Web probably hosts an online community for people just like you. Some online societies of interest follow.

The Action Figure Web Page

http://www.aloha.com/~randym/action_figures/

News and views on classic and ultra-modern action figures. Blast Cape Batman, Deluxe Martial Arts Robin, *et al.*

Action Girl's Guide to Female Figures

http://members.aol.com/sarahdyer/index.htm

Collector's guide from the producer of Action Girl Comics. Don't miss the site's dynamite Master (er, Mistress) List of femme action figures; from Annie models to glamorous American Gladiators.

The American Numismatic Association

http://www.money.org/

If, unlike most of us, you actually save your coins, this is the nonprofit, educational org for you. Warning: chartered by Congress!

Random Posting

```
Subject: Aquariums
Does anyone know where I can purchase
some "Gay themed" aquarium decorations?
I'm thinking something pink-triangl-y
or better yet a waterproof David for my
certainly queer fish to swim around.
Anyone?
Sat Sep 7 21:32:51 EDT 1996 - ()
103165.3514@compuserve.com
```

Antiques and Collectibles

http://willow.internet-connections.net/web/antiques/

Offers information, pictures, and examples of antiques ranging from china to jewelry; from swords to wall hangings.

AquaLink

http://www.aqualink.com/

An oceanography student spearheaded compilation of this deep sea of information pertaining to fish tanks and the aquarium scene in general.

Autograph Online

http://www.io.org/~akennedy/

Features autographs—both authentic and questionable—of people like Lily Tomlin and Bette Midler, along with resources of interest for those who collect John Hancocks.

Birding on the Web

http://www.birder.com/

Serial Mom surely turned a few people on to this practice. New bird songs, bird alerts, and scientific discoveries appear almost daily here. Birding software, to boot.

Brit-Iron

http://ezinfo.ucs.indiana.edu/~cstringe/brit.html

Brit-Iron provides a friendly forum for riders, restorers, and admirers of the classic machines. And who can resist a name like Brit-Iron?

Burlingame Museum of Pez Memorabilia
http://www.spectrumnet.com/pez/

PEZ exhibit! PEZ information! PEZ for sale!

Cyber/Darts Home
http://www.infohwy.com/darts/

Everything imaginable in the world of darts, from the basics to a complete tournament calendar. If you're on a team, be sure to add it to the list.

The International Paperweight Society
http://www.armory.com/~larry/ips.html

Dedicated to furthering awareness of the art of the glass paperweight.

G.I. Joe—Action Soldier
http://www.netaxis.com/~petebuilt/gijoe/

The Webmaster writes: *GI Joe is the only toy I can recall that stimulated the imagination ... GI Joe let the imagination run wild and a new adventure was created every afternoon.* For sure, many men can relate to this.

Harley Owners Group
http://www.magicnet.net/mni/hog.html

The group has given up on the "good folks in Milwaukee" for authorization, but continues to blaze down the Info-SuperHighway with information about local HOG chapters, activities, and memberships.

Joseph Luft's Philatelic Resources on the Web
http://www.execpc.com/~joeluft/
resource.html

You can't lick this fine assortment of links into the wild world of stamp collecting.

The Movie Poster Page
http://www.musicman.com/mp/posters.html

From *Adventures of Baron Munchausen* to *Vengeance of Bruce Lee*, everything's on display, and on sale.

The Online Knitting Magazine
http://www.fearless.net/knit/

Handknitters and spinners unite and take over the Web. Includes patterns, a directory of knitting suppliers around the world, and a calendar of upcoming events for knitters.

The Plastic Princess Page
http://deepthought.armory.com/~zenugirl/
barbie.html

Believe it or not, the Plastic Princess Page is not just for kicks. It's a zine "for adult fashion-doll collectors," offering "information from collectors for collectors." Ordinary gawkers can meet the usual assortment of Barbies and Kens, in addition to "Billy, the world's first out and proud gay doll" (see Figure 5.3). Find out how to order "Sailor Billy" and "Muscle Boy Billy," too.

Figure 5.3
Gay Billy

The Puppetry Home Page
http://www-leland.stanford.edu/~rosesage/ puppetry/puppetry.html

Puppetry history, types, and associations around the world, Lambchop.

Eat. Drink. Virtually.

StarChefs
http://starchefs.com/TOC.html

Top-shelf chefs and cookbook authors are the toast at the overstuffed StarChefs site (Figure 5.4). Interviews with an impressive variety of chefs, along with some of their favorite recipes, are the main entrees. The "Rumbles & Murmers" page pours the culinary gossip, and several newsgroup-type forums enable users to post opinions on such back-burner issues as "Fusion cooking: Do you like it? Do you eat it?" and "What are your five favorite pantry items?"

Epicurious Food
http://www.epicurious.com/a_home/a00_ home/home.html

From the folks at Condé Nast, Epicurious Food (Figure 5.5) is served up fresh "for people who eat," which only leaves out a few unfortunate supermodels. Like most of the Epicurious offerings, the site's brilliant recipe file is set up as a searchable database. (Run a search for the word "dates," for example, and you'll unearth a list ranging from Fruitcake Brownies to Bacon-Wrapped Stuffed Dates. Mmmmm.) The Epicurious Dictionary is another user-friendly winner. It boasts conversion charts for temperature and the metric system (to and from it) and contains an expert's book of definitions, from "abbacchio" to "zwieback." Likewise, in the Epicurious Drinking guide, you'll find recipes for hundreds of libations and definitions for all of the drinking lingo known to mankind. Into wine? The site's interactive sommelier will help you assemble a personal list based on your preferred type, price range, and region. One could spend days playing around at Epicurious. But your stomach is bound to growl eventually, reminding you that it's time for a good meal and a bottle of wine. Not necessarily in that order.

Figure 5.4
StarChefs

Bon Appétit
http://www.epicurious.com/b_ba/b00_home/ ba.html

Gourmet
http://www.epicurious.com/g_gourmet/g00_ home/gourmet.html

Epicurious also integrates the online versions of Condé Nast's essential *Bon Appétit* (Figure 5.6) and *Gourmet* magazines. If you're bored with the thick glossy stack on your coffee table, drop in for an interactive cooking class with *Bon Appétit*. Or, for those who don't subscribe, pick up free highlights from the issue that's currently on the newsstand. Gourmet's tastiest treat is an interactive city guide for the best in dining out around the world.

Food Network's CyberKitchen
http://www.foodtv.com/

The big, well-resourced but relatively insignificant CyberKitchen features instant access to recipes from all of the Food Network cooking shows you may or may not have heard about. Other treats include Q&A with "CyberChef," and cooking news that is updated daily.

Figure 5.5
Epicurious site

Figure 5.6
Bon Appétit

Veggies Unite!
http://www.envirolink.org/orgs/vegweb/
The Veggies Unite! site (Figure 5.7) set up shop in 1994 with a few recipes and a search engine. Today, it has mushroomed into a site of more than 2,000 recipes and 17,000 members, and it receives some 60,000 hits a day. The VU mission is to enhance public awareness of the benefits of a vegetarian diet and lifestyle. And what a lifestyle it is; this site is proof. Veggies Unite! is stuffed with features like VegWeb chat, a weekly meal planner, and a composting guide. Bulletin board forums are on hand for topics like animal rights, health, and veganism. Purchase of a $15 per year (U.S.) membership is requested, but not mandatory.

Vegetarian Pages
http://www.veg.org/veg/
Intended to be a definitive guide to what's out there on the Net for vegetarians, these pages are loaded with

news, organization contacts, and updates on major vegetarian events around the world. Stargazers will get a kick out of the site's long list of famous vegetarians.

How to Become a Fruitarian
http://www.islandnet.com/~arton/fruit.html
Hey, no wisecracks. A fruitarian is a person who eats lots of fruit, with some nuts and grains thrown in for good measure. "We have never been 'censussed', but to the present writer's certain knowledge, there are at least two of us. We are healthy, light in body and spirit." If you're still interested, the site offers an entire book on the subject. Download it for free.

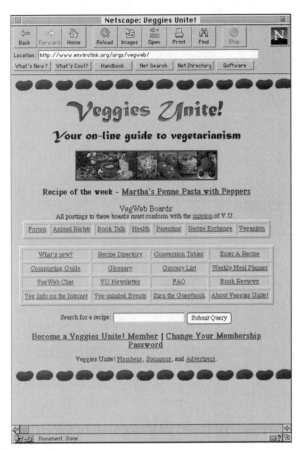

Figure 5.7
Veggies Unite!

Vegan Bikers Home Page
http://www.nildram.co.uk/veganmc/

Get your motor running ... pack your tofu weenies ... head out on the highway ....

Home Page of Blu
http://www.geocities.com/WestHollywood/3985/ccc.html

Blu is a married bisexual woman who can talk cooking and crafts 'til she's blue in the face. If you can relate, might as well check out her personal page, where she shares a handful of her favorite food- and craft-related links.

Recipes, Recipes, Recipes!
http://www.txdirect.net/~sassyfem/recipes.html

SassyFemme offers a page of good down-home lesbian cooking. She offers recipes for appetizers (a cheese dip that goes great with Bugles), main dishes ("Messy Chicken"), and some awfully yummy-sounding desserts (like "Whoopie Pies").

Farm Direct Marketplace
http://www.farmdirect.com/main-2.0.html

It's the Net's "first marketplace run by real farmers," but don't let that scare you away; these farmers are as Net-savvy as they come. And they're aiming to please with fresh produce and specialty items—ordered online and delivered right to your doorstep. Whether it's North Carolina Fuji apples, Cape Cod cranberries, or simply "The Right Potato" you seek, this is the market for those who don't have time to go to market.

Miss (Good) Thing

At one point, the Web was teeming with sites dealing with Martha Stewart, the "doyenne of domesticity." Mostly they were kooky parodies that now seem to have vanished into thin air. Did the jokes rot on the vine, or did Martha get crafty with the toothpicks and thumbscrews? She's rumored to be whipping up something extra special for the Web as we speak. Until then, her cult following will have to settle for two Web titles; one that is an earnest tribute (yawn) and another that may have you reaching for your American Express and the nearest craft knife.

The Web Guide to Martha Stewart
http://www.du.edu/~szerobni/

Kerry Ogata paved the way for this "really great thing," now maintained by real-live Martha freaks Leslie and Shari. In lieu of an official Martha site (although one is supposedly in the works), this one keeps fans abreast of Martha's recent media appearances and her latest recipes. It also provides links to other Martha fans. There were eight on the Web at the last count.

The Lair of the Anti-Martha
http://www.cris.com/~akiyama/martha.html

Lea Hernandez does her own cooking and child-rearing and has a maxed-out AmEx card to cut up. Oh, and only one modest-sized wreath (Figure 5.8).

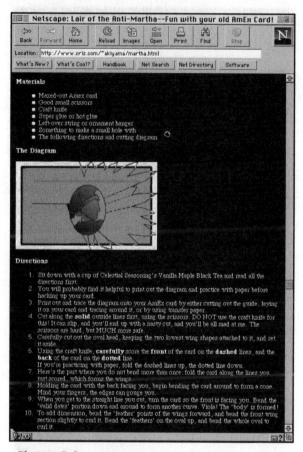

Figure 5.8
The Lair of the Anti-Martha

POINT-AND-CLICK PARENTING

Two, four, six, eight,
Not all moms and dads are straight!
We are proud, We are Gay,
We are in your PTA!

It's a chant that gets louder and louder as more gay parents come out of the closet and as already-out individuals assume their rightful positions in the maternal and paternal arenas. Tolerance on the issue of gay parenting can vary drastically from community to community and, once again, the Net scores as a sure-fire means of global support and networking. From a directory of gay dads around the world to a documentary on the first summer camp for children of gay and lesbian parents, the many facets of gay parenting have found homes on the Web. Many of these sites contain a considerable overlap of information. But with each personal creation comes a new Webmaster, and a personalized spin on the issues.

GAI-Q Out Take

Results of an Out.com GAI-Q survey from March 1996 suggest that nearly half of the respondents consider themselves to be potential parents (Figure 5.9).

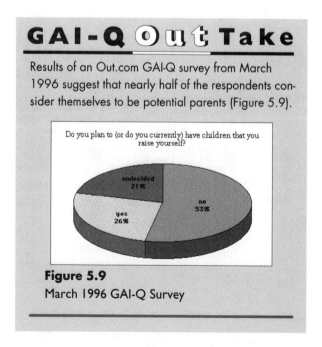

Figure 5.9
March 1996 GAI-Q Survey

Family Q
http://www.athens.net/~familyq/

Enter the Web's premier resource for gay and lesbian families. Family Q (Figure 5.10) seeks to provide lesbians and gays with information regarding family building and maintenance. From the many options and methods for starting a family (alternative insemination, fostering, and so on) to legal information for gay families; from books and articles for adults to a list of fun links for your kids, Family Q serves up the information in a concise and easy-to-use fashion.

Gay and Lesbian Parents Coalition International
http://abacus.oxy.edu/QRD/www/orgs/glpci/home.htm

The family values at Gay and Lesbian Parents Coalition International include "love and nurturing; integrity and responsibility; acceptance, respect and inclusion." The advocacy, education, and support group serves gay people in child-nurturing roles and their families in all their diversity (emphasis on "all"). The bank of GLPCI offerings includes an adoption resource packet, and a "Straight Spouse Support Network." The org has member chapters all over the world.

The LesBiGay Parenting Home Page
http://www.albany.net/~gelco/

"Ms. and Mrs. LieghAnne Farber," of New York state, maintain this site for lesbian, gay, and bisexual parents in the face of "hate and disinformation being fostered by the radical religious right." Their creation includes pages on "Myths and Facts about Lesbians and Gay Men," "Sexual Orientation and the Law," "Starting a Family," and, of course, "Fighting the Radical Right."

Out At Home
http://www.OutAtHome.org/

With Out At Home (Figure 5.11), Ben Felix has created a colorful online dedication to gay and lesbian families with children. The site contains current news, a bibliography of titles for both adults and children, and a nice selection of links to other sources. Perhaps the best aspect of this site, however, is the way it puts faces to parents and kids from around the world in an on-site Family Album.

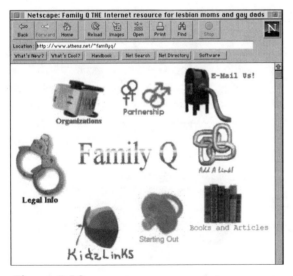

Figure 5.10
Family Q

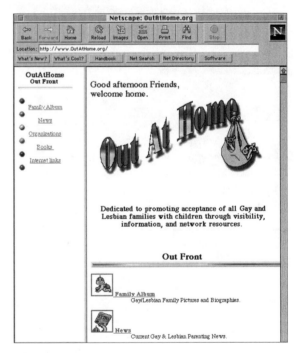

Figure 5.11
Out At Home

ParentsPlace
http://www.parentsplace.com/

Gay and Lesbian Parents Message Board
http://www.parentsplace.com:8000/dialog/get/samesex.html

The straight-but-not-narrow ParentsPlace site (a monster for all-around parenting resources) extends this message board to gay and lesbian parents. Postings range from "We are pregnant now—it is exciting and scary—I would love to speak to other parents in similar situations" to "Love is what makes a family." The message board can be a strong medium for sharing the challenges and joys of raising children.

Lesbian Parenting
http://moon.jrn.columbia.edu/NMW/twomoms/index.html

Robin Eisner and Paula Murphy, both students at the Columbia University Graduate School of Journalism, present this provocative look at "Two Women and a Baby." Their newsy site on lesbian parenting (Figure 5.12) includes a four-part fact-based story, along with in-depth looks at the legal aspects and the insemination process. It's a refreshingly creative approach to the subject.

The Lesbian Mom's Web Page
http://www.lesbian.org/moms/

"If you need a doctor, get one, if you need legal advice, see a lawyer, if you are looking for the wisdom and life experiences of other lesbian moms...read on," suggests the Lesbian Mom's Web Page. Pretty much tells it like it is.

Lesbian Mothers Support Society
http://www.lesbian.org/lesbian-moms/

The Calgary, Alberta-based Lesbian Mothers Support Society is a nonprofit org which sets up social functions and children's activities to enable lesbian families to share experiences and build support networks. Of course, this aspect of the group will only benefit those who happen to live near Calgary, but the LMSS Web site does an excellent job of compiling links to articles and organizations of interest to lesbian parents from all around.

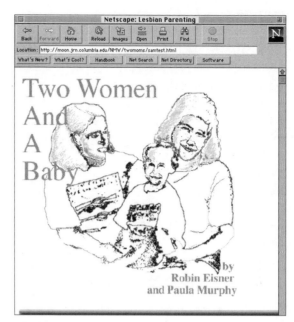

Figure 5.12
Lesbian Parenting

Gay Fathers
http://members.gnn.com/euromixer/featurenov.htm

Thomas Fronczak, CSW and Vicki Jo Campanaro-Cummings, MS Ed. wrote this academic article, based on their experiences counseling gay and bisexual fathers and their spouses. (Fronczak works with the fathers; Campanaro-Cummings works with their spouses.) Fronczak relays the experiences of several of his clients ("out of the fear of being unacceptable I have lived someone else's dream and forgotten who I am and what my dreams are"), while Campanaro-Cummings focuses on what she has identified as the eight "stages of grieving and healing" that occur with women married to gay men. The article is a brief, though informative, read. And thanks to hypertext, it links readers up with a well-rounded batch of other Net resources on the subject.

Subject: HELP NEEDED IN SOUTHERN WISCONSIN!

I am a 32 year old married mom who has been hiding behind a straight lifestyle for toooo long I am looking for female friend to talk with possible more in the future. I need to know everything I can. I have no experince with women and have no idea where to start any help would be appreciated thanx all

Thu Aug 22 23:24:35 EDT 1996 - ()

ballen@midplains.net

A Coming Out Guide for Gaydads
http://userwww.service.emory.edu/~librpj/gaydads.html

Gay-pop-who's-out Richard Jasper publishes this resource guide for gay fathers (Figure 5.13) and uses his personal story as the glue. Even men who are not fathers will find it easy to relate to Jasper's frank telling of courtship/marriage and eventually coming out to his wife. (Jasper is a reporter by trade, so his information is very well organized.) His site's FAQ answers questions that he asked himself over and over again when first coming out, while another page gives step-by-step instruction on coming out to children. Perhaps the most impressive aspect of the site, however, is its directory of gay fathers across the world, complete with bios, personal home-page links, and e-mail addresses. "Considering that putting together an online community was vitally important in my own coming out process, it seemed to me that the next logical step was this directory to help pave the way for other gaydads in doing the same thing," Jasper explains.

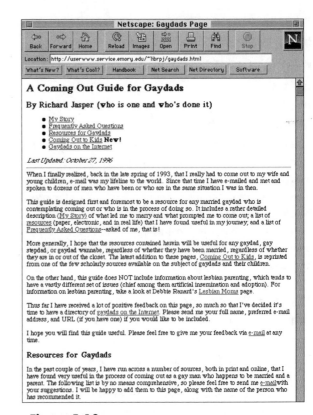

Figure 5.13
A Coming Out Guide for Gaydads

Gay Fathers Coalition of Baltimore
http://members.aol.com/MDLambda/gfcbalt/index.htm

Gay Fathers Coalition of Washington, D.C.
http://members.aol.com/MDLambda/gfcdc/index.htm

The various city chapters of the Gay Fathers Coalition (an affiliate of the Gay and Lesbian Parents Coalition International) provide services to gay fathers, their partners, and their friends. Much of the GFC activity is localized, so residents of the Baltimore and D.C. areas should check with their respective city sites for details of special events.

Alternative Family Project
http://afp.OutAtHome.org/

San Francisco-based Alternative Family Project offers affordable family counseling, support, and advocacy services for families with gay, lesbian, and transgender members. The program is staffed by interns, affiliated with San Francisco State University, and bases fees on family income and dependents.

Camp Lavender Hill
http://www-leland.stanford.edu/~trigon/clh/

Award-winning documentarian Michael Magnaye focuses on the children of gay, lesbian, and bisexual parents for his current project, "Camp Lavender Hill." The setting is the first summer camp for children of gay parents, and Magnaye strives for "a balance between the light-heartedness of the camp and the seriousness of issues campers face in less idyllic settings." The project's home page (Figure 5.14) provides some background and images, and asks for assistance ranging from fundraising to distribution.

COLAGE: Children Of Lesbians And Gays Everywhere
http://www.colage.org/

They may be based in San Francisco, but the community on which this site is based is open to children of gays and lesbians everywhere. The org says it is as diverse as any group of children who come from different areas of the country—different ethnic backgrounds and different economic levels. Their common bond is that of having a gay parent in a homophobic society. The site offers fun facts, membership information, and plenty of networking opportunities. By joining the COLAGE Internet Club, children are placed on their very own mailing list.

Rainbow Flag Health Services
http://www-leland.stanford.edu/~blandon/rainbow.html

This known-donor sperm bank expressly serves the gay and lesbian community of the San Francisco Bay Area. (It is the only sperm bank that accepts gay and bisexual donors.) The service is limited to providing services only to residents of Northern California. Philosophy, goals, and the service's unique mission can be explored on-site.

Figure 5.14
Camp Lavender Hill

GAI-Q Out Take

The results of an August 1996 Out.com GAI-Q survey (Figure 5.15) show that 75 percent of the respondents place a good deal of importance on the right to adopt children.

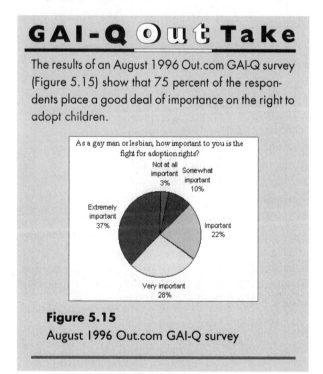

Figure 5.15
August 1996 Out.com GAI-Q survey

Chapter 6

WWW.HEALTH

Glancing at the composition of this health chapter—perhaps predictably top-heavy with resources dealing with HIV/AIDS—it's obvious that the collective gay and lesbian community has channeled its heart and soul (and bandwidth) into fighting and living with the epidemic. But while creative and useful HIV/AIDS resources abound on the Web, relatively few exist for dealing with the general wellness needs of the gay and lesbian population.

That said, you may have to dig a little deeper for gay and lesbian wellness information, but it is increasingly beginning to spring up. We learn that the Human Rights Campaign has made lesbian health an action item. And that the Washington, D.C.-based National Lesbian and Gay Health Association is hard at work specifically on physical and mental health-related issues as they impact our lives.

The Web also shows us that minds and bodies are getting stronger by way of gay sporting organizations around the world; be it through membership in a gay bowling league in New Jersey, or through participation in a queer karate club in Paris. Here's to our health.

HIV/AIDS

The good news is, government bureaucracies have used the Net to streamline resources within the complex, surging, and vital stream of HIV/AIDS information. Elsewhere, active Webheads have used their imaginations to come up with personalized HIV/AIDS resources above and beyond what one might expect. The range of what's out there—from humble homemade creations, to volunteer-driven libraries, to full-blown educational multimedia experiences—is astonishing. Community orgs are online in full force; activist groups have adopted HTML as a new kind of bullhorn; individuals have used Web space to construct touching memorials to those lost. The services are novel, some allowing viewers to search databases of available clinical trials, or to explore the details of studies that are currently seeking volunteers. Finally, there are entities like OUTline <http://www.out.org>, a volunteer-run San Francisco organization which arms PWAs with computers, software, and Internet access—access to empowerment through technology, and access to the hope and promise of this very powerful medium. In that respect, there is only good news to be found in this section.

Spreading the Word

AIDS Resource List
http://www.teleport.com/~celinec/aids.shtml
College student and Web consultant Celine Chamberlin compiles and updates regularly this thoughtful, narrative directory to what's out there and what's new in AIDS resources on the Net.

AIDS Treatment News Archive from Immunet
http://www.immunet.org/atn

AIDS Treatment News Internet Directory
http://www.aidsnews.org
John James's eight-page, bimonthly "AIDS Treatment News" (Figure 6.1) is commonly recognized as the best AIDS treatment newsletter available. Previously distributed on the Net via newsgroup, ATN's hundreds of back issues and latest editions now have a searchable home on the Web thanks to Immunet, a nonprofit org dedicated to "harnessing the power of the Internet in the battle against AIDS." Elsewhere, the ATN experts deliver a no-frills Internet Directory with pointers to experts, spiritual guidance, treatment advocates, and more.

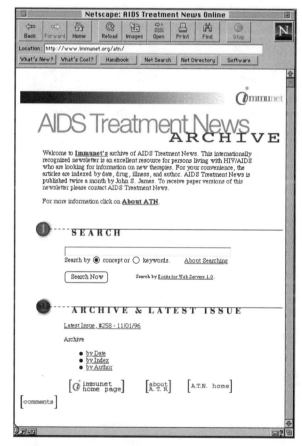

Figure 6.1
AIDS Treatment News Internet Directory

AIDS Virtual Library
http://planetq.com/aidsvl/index.html

Planet Q hosts the volunteer-driven AIDS Virtual Library, which deals with the social, political, and medical aspects of HIV and AIDS. Link listings fall under topic headings such as "Conferences and Symposia," "Safer Sex Information" and "Statistical Reports on the Epidemic."

The Body
http://www.thebody.com/cgi-bin/body.cgi

The Body's (Figure 6.2) disclaimer is that it is designed for educational purposes only; not for rendering medical advice or professional services. It's a service of Body Health Resources Corporation of New York, and perhaps the fact that it is sponsored in part by pharmaceutical companies explains the slick, multimedia experience it is able to deliver. Updated daily, The Body ushers users through "the AIDS Basics" (from "What is AIDS?" to "On Learning You're HIV-Positive"); through treatment and lifestyle issues; and even into the political scene with weekly updates from Washington. It also leads the way to top AIDS organizations and hotlines, enlists experts to answer viewers' questions, and incorporates forums for expression and connections. Quite a package.

Center for AIDS Prevention Studies
http://www.epibiostat.ucsf.edu/capsweb/

The University of California San Francisco Center for AIDS Prevention Studies outlines its activities in prevention and provides an exceptional updated listing of AIDS/HIV Internet sites.

Center for Disease Control
http://www.cdc.gov/

CDC Division of HIV/AIDS Prevention
http://www.cdc.gov/nchstp/hiv_aids/dhap.htm

CDC National AIDS Clearinghouse
http://www.cdcnac.org/

CDC Daily AIDS Summaries
gopher://gopher.niaid.nih.gov:70/11/aids/cdcds

Now in its fiftieth year, "the nation's prevention agency" has plenty to offer in the age of AIDS (though you probably won't want to start looking on its home page). The

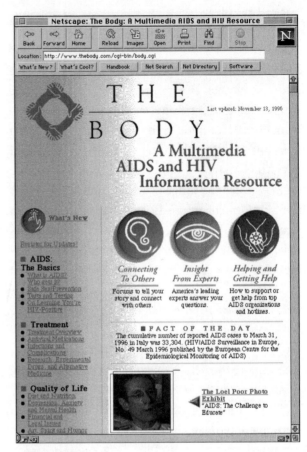

Figure 6.2
The Body

CDC Division of HIV/AIDS Prevention files everything from basic statistics and funding opportunities to slides and software. The organization's National AIDS Clearinghouse (Figure 6.3) makes education and prevention materials easily accessible. Order HIV/AIDS brochures and posters online for free. Both databases are fully searchable. Finally, the CDC makes its AIDS Daily Summaries available for quick call-up via gopher menus. Each day, the summaries round up HIV/AIDS information from hundreds of publications around the world.

Choices for Gay Men who are HIV Positive
http://www.oneworld.org/avert/choices.htm

Written for gay men who have recently tested HIV-positive, this page outlines some of the choices that may

Figure 6.3
CDC National AIDS Clearinghouse

have to be made in the immediate future; from coping with the results to living a healthy lifestyle. It's a service of the U.K.-based AVERT, an AIDS education and research trust.

Critical Path AIDS Project
http://www.critpath.org/

The Philadelphia-based Critical Path Project was founded by people with AIDS to extend information and services to the broad spectrum of the AIDS community, but first and foremost to other PWAs, "who often find themselves in urgent need of information quickly and painlessly." Naturally, the group's Web site offers a range of invaluable services.

Dr. Jim Weinrich's AIDS and Sexology Home Page
http://math.ucsd.edu/~weinrich/

Dr. Weinrich is the Principal Investigator of the Sexology Project at the HIV Neurobehavioral Research Center,

administered through the Department of Psychiatry at the University of California, San Diego. If all that doesn't turn you off, you'll discover sexological studies and scads of science about HIV infection and how it affects the central nervous system within his intriguing Web creation.

Edward King's AIDS Pages
http://www.users.dircon.co.uk/~eking/

Edward King writes a regular AIDS column for Britain's gay and lesbian weekly, *The Pink Paper*. He began writing his AIDS pages "mainly as part of an interest in learning HTML," and he's done an excellent job, in both the HTML and in delivering news and views on HIV treatment and prevention from the U.K.

XI International Conference on AIDS
http://www.interchg.ubc.ca/aids11/aids96.html

The conference happened during July 1996, in Vancouver, Canada; this Web site makes abstracts from the conference available in searchable format. It also looks forward to the next conference in the series, the 12th World AIDS Conference, July 1998, in Geneva.

Glaxo Wellcome HIV/AIDS page
http://www.treathiv.com

A public health service from the National Minority AIDS Council on the National Lesbian and Gay Health Association, in cooperation with Glaxo Wellcome; this infopage explains HIV in four ways: advanced English, simple English, advanced Spanish, and simple Spanish.

Lesbian Safer Sex
http://www.safersex.org/women/lesbianss.html

Yes, lesbians are at risk. This frank page (Figure 6.4)—plucked from the equally frank Safer Sex Pages—defines some guidelines for safer lesbian sex and explains which behaviors are potentially risky.

Figure 6.4
Lesbian Safer Sex

Guide to NIH HIV/AIDS Information Services
http://sis.nlm.nih.gov/aids/index.html

National Institutes of Health
http://www.nih.gov/

U.S. National Library of Medicine
http://www.nlm.nih.gov/

U.S. Public Health Service
http://phs.os.dhhs.gov/phs/phs.html

The National Library of Medicine draws from the National Institutes of Health and various Public Health Service offerings to present a "single, easy-to-use" guide to HIV/AIDS information services (Figure 6.5). It's intended as a tool for everyone—health professionals, caregivers, affected community, and the general public alike—and uses grids and symbols to light the way nicely through an otherwise bureaucratic labyrinth.

Figure 6.5
National Institute of Health AIDS Information Services

Helseutvalget For Homofile
http://www.glnetwork.no/HU/index.html

The Norwegian Gay Health Committee presents this gay-oriented HIV/AIDS information site. In Norwegian only, though English translation is being considered.

HIV Center for Clinical and Behavioral Studies
http://cpmcnet.columbia.edu/dept/pi/hiv/

This postdoctoral fellowship program with the Columbia-Presbyterian Medical Center aims to train research scientists in the determinants of HIV risk behaviors, the evaluation of models of behavioral change, and other mental health aspects of HIV infection. Details and application information available on site.

HIV InfoWeb
http://www.jri.org/infoweb/

Maintained by Boston's JRI Health Information Systems, HIV InfoWeb links the online community with up-to-date information about HIV and AIDS, from treatment to volunteer opportunities and consumer activism.

HIVNet
http://www.hivnet.org

The Amsterdam-based HIVNet points to information on HIV/AIDS—newsgroups, software, the Electronic Quilt—and is available in Dutch and English versions.

Immunet
http://www.immunet.org/

Simply put, Immunet provides easy access to quality information about HIV/AIDS. It's presented in a simple newsletter format and aimed at AIDS-treating medical professionals, though laypersons will no doubt find it an invaluable resource.

Nutrition for Life
http://www.csun.edu/~hbbio016/nfl.html

Find details on this nutritional study for people living with HIV and AIDS.

Poz.com
http://www.poz.com

Poz, the glossy newsstand standard on AIDS culture and politics, makes the expected high-Q mark on the Web (Figure 6.6). Since it was founded in 1994, POZ has documented AIDS politics, art, treatment, and lifestyles with a distinctive style of investigation and reporting. It has also served as a reference guide on such issues as treatment standards of care and drug payment assistance programs. Poz.com makes all of the publication's services that much easier to access with current and archived profiles, news stories, and columns. The reference-guide aspect is also enhanced by a searchable glossary of terms. Without a doubt, a very positive Web experience.

ALTERNATIVE MEDICINE

Acupuncture.com
http://acupuncture.com/

James Knox's AIDS Survivors' Page
http://www.primenet.com/~jknox/

Information on the concentrated herbal formulation known as FGP. This site believes it represents "a major advance in the treatments of AIDS and HIV-related infections, and perhaps many other diseases which effect the immune system."

AIDS Authority
http://www.aidsauthority.org/main.html

Founded on the belief that the prominence of medicine as a social institution is a dangerous trend "toward the use of science to infringe upon fundamental individual rights." Committed to resisting this trend in every way.

Bastyr University AIDS Research Center
http://www.bastyr.edu/research/recruit.html

Bastyr University of Seattle, WA is studying the use of alternative medicine to treat AIDS/HIV. Research information and related links are on site.

The Kombucha Home Page
http://www.sease.com/kombucha/index.html

Devoted to this popular health-promoting beverage made by fermenting tea. Find out about its health benefits and where to get it.

PozForce
http://www.pozforce.com

PozForce bills itself as "your source of complementary treatment for HIV," or alternative holistic medications. The products—detailed in the site's online catalog—are designed to boost natural defenses against HIV and opportunistic infections, and to "promote a sense of well-being and energy." Online ordering is available.

Rethinking AIDS
http://www.xs4all.nl/~raido/index.htm

"A growing group of bio-medical scientists claim the cause of AIDS is still unknown ... This Web site tells you their story."

A Short Introduction to Smart Drugs
http://www.uta.fi/~samu/SMARTS2.html

Originally written for a Belgian rave zine ...

Sumeria—The Immune System
http://www.livelinks.com/sumeria/aids.html

Articles and files by and about those who challenge the conventional wisdom about AIDS.

Yoga for HIV/AIDS
http://www.yogagroup.org/

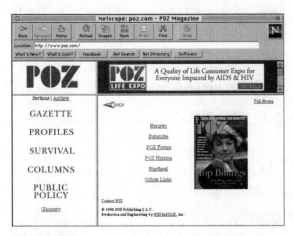

Figure 6.6
Poz.com

Rainbow Mall's AIDS/HIV Information Resource Center

http://www.rainbow-mall.com/mall/
aidsinfo.html

The Rainbow Mall is building what it believes to be "the largest collection of HIV/AIDS resource links anywhere on the Web." It's a lofty claim, considering what all is out there, but the list is reportedly being updated constantly.

Red Ribbon Net

http://www.redribbon.com/

Red Ribbon Net claims to be the world's largest source of information and research on HIV and AIDS. It also features classified ads, live chat (at the Red Ribbon Coffee House), and an online mall for "everything from condoms to clothing, and vitamins to vacations."

12th World AIDS Conference

http://www.aids98.ch/

Looking ahead to July 1998 in Geneva, this official site for the 12th World AIDS Conference files preparatory newsletters and announcements, along with general information about Geneva.

UNAIDS—The Joint United Nations Programme on HIV/AIDS

http://www.unaids.org/

The name pretty much says it all. It's a clunker, and not terribly exciting, but informative enough for those interested in what the UN is doing about AIDS around the world.

University-wide AIDS Research Program

http://www.ucop.edu/srphome/uarp/

The University of California University-wide AIDS Research Program was established to administer and coordinate all aspects of the application and funding process. The Web site includes UARP news briefs, abstracts for download, and online application forms and instructions.

Community Outreach

AIDS Foundation Houston

http://www.powersource.com/afh/default.html

AIDS Project Los Angeles

http://www.gus.net/care/apla/index.html

Asian Pacific AIDS Intervention Team

http://members.aol.com/APXRDS/frapait.html

The Los Angeles-based Asian Pacific AIDS Intervention Team educates Asian Pacific Islander communities on HIV/AIDS infection, promoting hope, support, advocacy, and resources. The Web site gives details on "family" units and volunteer opportunities.

Boy2Boy—Denver

http://www.tde.com/~boy2boy/

Boy2Boy (Figure 6.7) is the response of young gay Denver men to the rise in HIV infection among gay and bi youth. The prevention program targets men ages 15 to 25. Information on events, workshops, and the outreach team is available on site.

Colorado AIDS Project

http://www.coloaids.org/

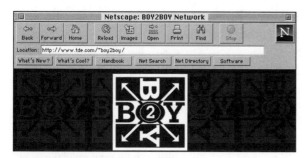

Figure 6.7
Boy2Boy—Denver

Community Health Project— New York City

http://www.chp-health.org/

New York City's only gay and lesbian health center, the Community Health Project provides information on its low-cost, accessible health care services. Details on programs such as Health Outreach to Teens and Lesbian Health are provided.

Community Prescription Service

http://www.prescript.com/

HIV-owned and operated, this 800-number prescription service offers an info package, online ordering, and the latest drug information.

Gay Men's Health Crisis

http://www.gmhc.org/

The nation's oldest and largest nonprofit AIDS org, GMHC (Figure 6.8) provides hands-on services to more than 7,000 people with AIDS each year in New York City. The group's Web presence offers insight as to how your time, money, and voice can fight AIDS, along with the basics on AIDS, HIV testing, and safer sex.

Hermanos de Luna Y Sol—San Francisco

http://www.epibiostat.ucsf.edu/capsweb/
projects/hlsindex.html

This San Francisco-based empowerment HIV program for Spanish-speaking Latino gay and bisexual men approaches the subject in a culturally appropriate fashion.

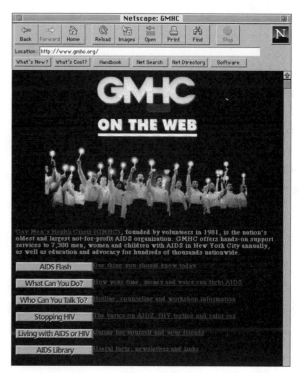

Figure 6.8
Gay Men's Health Crisis

KAIROS Support for Caregivers—San Francisco

http://the-park.com/kairos/

Kairos is a Greek word meaning "This is the moment of life." The San Francisco-based organization with this name provides support for caregivers of HIV-affected people.

The KY Baby Home Page—London

http://www.geocities.com/WestHollywood/
2628/KYBabies.html

The KY Babies are a group of gay and bi Londoners under age 26 who try to reduce the spread of HIV in their communities.

Mouth2Mouth

http://www.aris.org/m2m/

Funded by the California Department of Health Services, Mouth2Mouth is an HIV peer education program for and by gay, lesbian, bi, and questioning youth.

Nebraska AIDS Project
http://www.nap.org/

PAWS—Pets Are Wonderful Support
http://www.qrd.org/qrd/www/usa/maine/paws.html

This Portland, Maine-based nonprofit org works from the premise that pets are extremely helpful in reducing stress, improving health outcomes, and increasing the general well-being of people living with HIV/AIDS. From providing pet food and supplies at no cost, to distributing "safe pet guidelines" to owners, the organization's services are outlined here.

HIVnAlive
http://www.hivnalive.org/

Positively HIV is a volunteer-based nonprofit Pennsylvania org providing services to HIV-positive individuals via the Net. Its vehicle, the splashy HIVnAlive site (Figure 6.9), offers a resource library, rants, and contests, along with special interactive features like "CyberQuilt."

Project Open Hand Atlanta
http://www.gaypride.com/poh/

"We cook. We care. We deliver," is the motto of Project Open Hand Atlanta, which prepares and delivers two fresh, nutritious meals each day to people living with AIDS or HIV-related illnesses in the Atlanta metro area. The organization was originally modeled after San Francisco's Project Open Hand, though the two operate independently. Find out how to volunteer or make donations on site.

Project Open Hand—San Francisco
http://www.openhand.org/

Project Open Hand (Figure 6.10) provides comprehensive nutrition services to more than 3,000 people living with symptomatic HIV and AIDS in San Francisco and Alameda counties in California. Services include daily home delivery of meals and nutrition counseling. The Web site features an online "Positive Nutrition" newsletter and tells how to get involved as a volunteer.

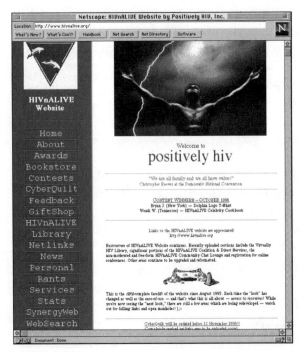

Figure 6.9
HIVnAlive

Figure 6.10
Project Open Hand

Rural Center for AIDS/STD Prevention
http://www.indiana.edu/~aids/

The Rural Center for AIDS/STD Prevention is a joint project of Indiana and Purdue universities. As the title implies, the group promotes prevention of HIV and other STDs in the rural United States. Fact sheets, newsletters, and project details are available on site.

S.W.I.S.H.(Body Positive)—Wales
http://www.cyberstop.net/swishbp/

It all stands for South Wales Immune-deficiency Self Help, and it was formed in 1992 by a group of AIDS- and HIV-positive individuals who found there were few HIV/AIDS services available in the area. The story and the organizational offerings are covered on the S.W.I.S.H. home page.

Toronto People with AIDS Foundation
http://www.gaytoronto.com/pwa/

UCSF AIDS Program
http://sfghaids.ucsf.edu/ucsf.html

Research and Clinical Trials Search
http://sfghaids.ucsf.edu/ucsfresearch.html

The AIDS Program at San Francisco General Hospital cares for more than 2000 people living with HIV. Its excellent Web site covers the services, resources, and people of the program's community, with quick links to high-priority pages for patients and providers. The program's research and clinical trials page offers something truly unique: a searchable database of more than 125 open clinical trials in California. Keyword and personalized searches are available, or users can browse through a list of all open trials.

The Art of Activism

The AIDS Memorial Quilt—NAMES Project
http://www.aidsquilt.org/

A patchwork of lives, the icon of the epidemic, art that heals ... it's the AIDS Memorial Quilt and it now has a place in cyberspace (Figure 6.11). The mission of the NAMES Project Foundation is to use the quilt to help

Figure 6.11
The AIDS Memorial Quilt—NAMES Project

bring an end to the epidemic, and the mission of the organization's Web site is to spread the word about how you can get involved personally. Contacts for local chapters and affiliates are listed and the foundation's quarterly newsletter is on display.

ACT UP—Paris
http://www.gaipied.fr/Associations/actup/

ACT UP—New York
http://www.actupny.org/

ACT UP—Philadelphia
http://www.critpath.org/actup/

The diverse, non-partisan AIDS Coalition to Unleash Power remains united in anger, and is now united by the Net. Chapters in New York, Philadelphia, and Paris advise and inform, demonstrate, and continue to flout "silence" with their dynamic, separate Web presences. New York offers a "What the Board of Education Doesn't Want You to Know" flyer as part of its Youth

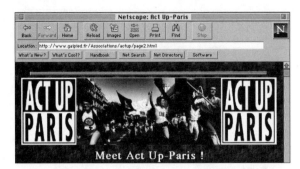

Figure 6.12
ACT-UP, Paris

Education Life Line (YELL). Paris (Figure 6.12) posts an illustrated diary of its action during the XI International Conference on AIDS in Vancouver, Canada. And Philadelphia outlines its women's standard of care and research/treatment agenda.

Gay Men Fighting AIDS—London
http://www.users.dircon.co.uk/~eking/gmfa.htm

Marty Howard's Essential Site
http://www.smartlink.net/~martinjh
Activist Marty Howard hosts this home page/hotspot for links and opinion on HIV/AIDS and related issues. Loads of interesting links.

STOP AIDS—San Francisco
http://www.stopaids.org/

Stop AIDS—San Jose
http://users.aimnet.com/~yamanaka/stop-aids/

United in Anger
http://www.panix.com/~boyfren
Bill Bytsura's exceptional online photographic exhibit introduces activists from ACT UP chapters around the world. Black and white portraits are accompanied by personal histories and statements. "United in Anger" makes for a powerful online experience.

GAI-Q Out Take

The following results from Out.com's August 1996 GAI-Q survey (Figure 6.13) illustrate parallels in the importance respondents place on AIDS funding, education, and drug accessibility programs. A little more than half rate each with extreme importance. A quarter more rate each issue as "very important."

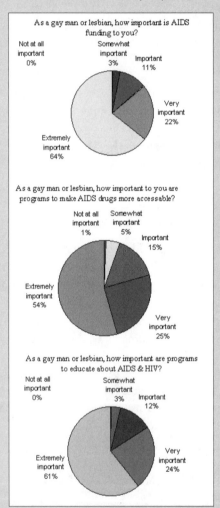

Figure 6.13
Out.com's August 1996 GAI-Q survey

MIND AND BODY

Compared to the expanse of online information available about HIV and AIDS, the rest of the gay and lesbian mind-and-body beat is an anemic contender. Obviously, we've channeled so many resources into fighting the epidemic that we've had to forgo in-depth exploration of the less obvious, or at least the less urgent, aspects of our unique health needs and issues. Despite a lack of holistic healthcare sites specifically addressing gays and lesbians, however, topics such as "chemical dependency" and "coming out" are beginning to register online.

The Association of Gay and Lesbian Psychiatrists
http://members.aol.com/aglpnat/homepage.html

If the thought of a large group of psychiatrists and psychiatry residents semi-creeps you out, take comfort in the fact that all of the ones in this organization serve as a voice for the concerns of gays and lesbians in the profession. The Association is also committed to fostering a more accurate understanding of homosexuality, opposing discriminatory practices against gays and lesbians, and promoting supportive, well-informed psychiatric care for lesbian and gay patients. Nothing creepy about all that. Get the group's history, newsletter, and list of upcoming events on the Web site.

Betty Berzon PhD
http://members.aol.com/bberzon/index.htm

She's been called "a saint of nurturing" and "a first-class writer" by colleagues. She's Dr. Betty, and she has inserted her voice because she knows from experience how hard it can be for gays and lesbians to maintain love and commitment. Dr. Betty's Web page tells more about her, and about the books she has written on meeting the challenge of anti-gay prejudice and achieving long-term success in gay and lesbian intimate relationships.

Fat and Healthy
http://www.fatso.com/fatgirl/health1.html

Impossible? Contradictory? Nah. Lori Ann Selke reports from the trenches for FaT GiRL, the zine that would know. "It's my hope that the information in this column will help you be happy, content, outrageous and healthy dykes, prepared with energy and information to challenge stereotypes and ignorance about fat women and health," Selke writes.

Gay & Bisexuals: Men's Health Issues
http://www.vub.mcgill.ca/clubs/lbgtm/info/men.html

Lesbian Health Issues: We are not immune!
http://www.vub.mcgill.ca/clubs/lbgtm/info/women.html

Lesbian Safer Sex: Think about your risks
http://www.vub.mcgill.ca/clubs/lbgtm/info/lessafe.html

Substance Abuse in the Gay and Lesbian Community
http://www.vub.mcgill.ca/clubs/lbgtm/info/substanc.html

Main LBGTM Index
http://www.vub.mcgill.ca/clubs/lbgtm/info/index.html

Dot Wojakowski wrote these straight-shooting and highly informative articles dealing with oft overlooked aspects of gay and lesbian health. The articles are on file, along with several others of unrelated merit, at the Lesbian, Bisexual, Gay, and Transgender Students of McGill (Montreal) site. For lesbians, Wojakowski covers general hygiene and disease prevention, STDs, and sex toys. For men, she moves over AIDS to hit on less-covered STDs such as Hepatitis A/B and genital warts. Her article on substance abuse is more fleeting, but it does require that readers ask a few tough, and potentially revealing, questions of themselves.

GAI-Q Out Take

Out.com's May 1996 GAI-Q survey on "Health and Fitness" suggests that of the 70 percent of respondents who say they have a regular physician, only about half of them are fully out to their doctors (Figure 6.14).

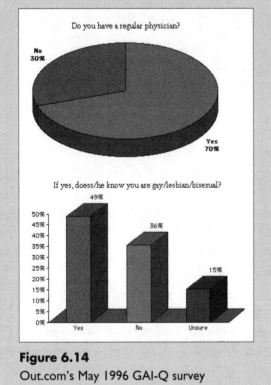

Figure 6.14
Out.com's May 1996 GAI-Q survey

GayZen Meditation Retreat
http://members.aol.com/zenretreat/zen/gayzen.html

"Take a weekend retreat to Satori—that enlightened Zen state ... Metamorphosis." Read about it, see it, hear the chimes on this promotional page.

GriefNet
http://rivendell.org/

Those experiencing loss and working through the grieving process may find value in GriefNet, a free system for connecting to resources related to death, dying, bereavement, and emotional or physical loss. The gopher/Web server provides retrievable information, and discussion and support groups are run through mailing lists. Cendra Lynn, the site's founder, is a psychologist in private practice in Ann Arbor, Michigan.

Lesbian Health—Human Rights Campaign
http://www.hrcusa.org/issues/lesbianh/index.html

The Human Rights Campaign includes this special section on advocacy of health-care policy for lesbians, who "face a medical and scientific establishment that often dismisses the validity of our health concerns and ignores our existence in treatment and education interventions." The info-page explains that results of certain lesbian health behaviors put them at greater risk than heterosexual women for certain diseases like cancer and heart disease; and it outlines what the HRC is doing to combat heterosexism in health care.

Lesbian Health Program
http://www.chp-health.org/lhp.html

One must live in the Big Apple to take full advantage of the Community Health Project's Lesbian Health Program (see Figure 6.15). The rest of the world can gather a good bit of basic information—on lesbian safer sex and breast self-exams, for example—from the program's Web page.

Medical Emergency Cards
http://www.buddybuddy.com/medicard.html

The Seattle-based Partners Task Force for Gay & Lesbian Couples reminds that, under current law, no matter how committed you and your partner are, you may end up being treated as legal strangers; barred from making medical decisions for each other—even barred from the hospital and excluded from medical-condition reports. To help combat these possibilities, this page includes a form for a medical-emergency card, which you can print, fill out, cut out, and carry in your wallet. Such a card doesn't replace a power of attorney (which, the site reminds, you should also have), but it at the very least directs health-care workers to alert the partner in case of emergency.

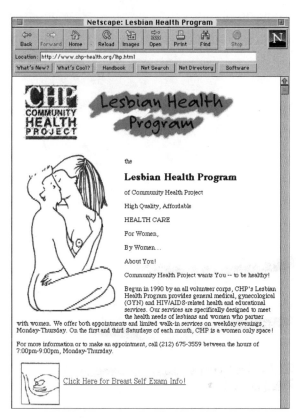

Figure 6.15
Lesbian Health Program

MedWeb: Biomedical Internet Resources
http://www.cc.emory.edu/WHSCL/
medweb.html

It's not gay-specific (and the chicken-scratch graphic design could be a metaphor for doctors' penmanship), but for fast access to general health facts and resources, MedWeb's biomedical Net resources directory is just dandy. A service of Emory University, the MedWeb indexes links by country, region, or keyword. Keywords range from AIDS/HIV to Virtual Reality in Medicine. What a spread.

Montrose Counseling Center Home Page
http://www.NeoSoft.com/~mcc/

Houston's Montrose Counseling Center is a nonprofit community-based org providing "culturally affirming, quality and affordable outpatient mental health and case management services, education and research ... primarily

for and about gay, lesbian, bisexual, and transgender individuals and their significant others." Specific tracks include "Life," "Chemical Dependency," and "HIV/AIDS."

The National Lesbian and Gay Health Association
http://www.serve.com/nlgha/index.htm

Based in Washington, D.C., the National Lesbian and Gay Health Association serves as a single, comprehensive resource for physical and mental health-related issues, advocacy, education, and research. (It was the result of a merger between the National Alliance of Lesbian and Gay Health Clinics and the National Lesbian and Gay Health Foundation in 1994.) With several major gay and lesbian community health centers and tens of thousands of gay and lesbian health-care providers on board, it also lends a powerful voice for educating public health officials of our often unique health needs. The organization's Web presence provides details on NLGHA's activities and its annual National Health Conference. It also lists contact information for and descriptions of member clinics across the country. At press time, NLGHA promised as forthcoming a resource library and clearinghouse on health services provided to the gay, lesbian, bisexual, and transgender communities. Stay tuned for this much-needed service.

The Safer Sex Pages
http://www.safersex.org/

"More stuff about sex than you probably wanted to know" is the tagline on the Safer Sex Pages (Figure 6.16). See how to put on a condom; see how to use a condom; see how a condom is made. (Fun fact: This site is one of the original plaintiffs in *ACLU v. Reno*, the challenge to the unconstitutional Communications Decency Act.)

Women's Health Resources on the World Wide Web
http://cpmcnet.columbia.edu/dept/rosenthal/
Guide5.html

Columbia-Presbyterian Medical Center rolls out this annotated list of the Web's offerings in the way of women's health. Contents cover the academic and the governmental, the conventional, and the alternative.

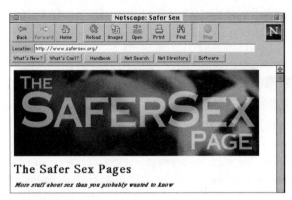

Figure 6.16
Safer Sex Pages

Figure 6.17
Coming out

C'mon ...

Coming Out
http://www.anet-dfw.com/~nemesis/
open.html

The site's Webmaster gives a humorous account of coming out—"an act of survival"—and offers a lighthearted, personalized mini-workshop for those still on the fence (Figure 6.17). Nice graphics, and a ready-made message of explanation for someone to whom you've recently come out.

Gender, Sex and Sexuality
http://www.ccnet.com/~lafond/sex.htm

With his Gender, Sex and Sexuality page, Rod Raffi's mission is simply "to support people that are trying to accept themselves for who they are" and not to advocate any particular gender identity or sexual orientation. He does it with an offering of "cool" articles and links, and gay chat.

The Human Rights Campaign's National Coming Out Project
http://www.hrcusa.org/whowhat/whatwedo/
ncop/index.html

National Coming Out Day (NCOD) only happens once a year, but the Human Rights Campaign's official project for the cause works 'round the clock encouraging gays and lesbians to be upfront about their sexual orientation 365 days a year. The project's Web presence seems more like a buildup to NCOD, but it does file away a worthwhile tip sheet for coming out.

I think I might be gay
http://www.msstate.edu/org/glbf/
gaythink.html

I think I might be a lesbian
http://www.msstate.edu/org/glbf/les.html

Understanding Gay Friends and Roommates
http://www.msstate.edu/org/glbf/Under.html

If you're a young gay man or lesbian in the state of Mississippi (or anywhere, for that matter), resources such as these homegrown online brochures will come in handy. In plainspoken language, Gays, Lesbians, Bisexuals, and Friends of Mississippi State University outlines what it means to be gay or lesbian, and provides some pointers for "learning to like yourself" and eventually coming out. The organization goes one step further to include heterosexual friends of gays and lesbians with the brochure "Understanding Gay Friends and Roommates." It answers to some common het concerns, such as "Now that I know my roommate is gay, I don't feel comfortable about nudity, dressing, showering, etc."

The Out List
http://VTGinc.com/rainbow/Words/
OutList.html

It's not about coming out per se, but this list of more than 500 living famous or distinguished people who have publicly acknowledged that they are lesbian, gay, or bisexual definitely drives home the fact that you are not alone.

Random Posting

OutProud
http://www.cyberspaces.com/outproud/

OutProud Brochures
http://www.cyberspaces.com/outproud/html/
brochures.html

OutProud—the national coalition for gay, lesbian, and bisexual youth in America—offers "the answers you're
looking for regarding sexual orientation" through an assortment of online brochures. Titles include "I Think I
Might Be a Lesbian ... Now What Do I Do?" and "Coming
Out to Your Parents" (developed by PFLAG). Beyond the
brochures, there is plenty to explore on the OutProud
site, which also features a community forum, and a resource library for middle and secondary school teachers.

Young Gay Men Talking
http://www.oneworld.org/avert/ygmt.htm

An offering of the U.K.-based AVERT AIDS education
and research trust, this page delivers exactly what the title promises. The blurbs presented ("Being gay is not a
way of life, it's a part of life") are excerpted from an
AVERT research project ("Young Gay Men & HIV Infection) and are arranged topically ("Coming Out," "Sex:
Fantasy Fear and Fact").

Random Posting

Clean and Sober

Alcoholics Anonymous Meetings for Gay Beginners in New York City
http://www.geocities.com/SoHo/4504/

If you live in NYC or in the tri-state area and are looking
for a gay or gay-friendly Alcoholics Anonymous group,
this "totally unauthorized and sometimes arbitrary" page
of gay (or at least gay-friendly) listings may be just what
you need. It includes a day-by-day breakdown of AA activity, addresses, and contact information. "Experiment!"
the Webmaster encourages. "A meeting is a meeting.
You don't have to stay in the gay ghetto."

The Galano Club—Milwaukee
http://www.execpc.com/~reva/

Galano is Milwaukee's social and support club for gays, lesbians, bisexuals, and transgendered people in substance
abuse and emotional recovery, and its meetings include every 12-step group imaginable. The site features schedules
of meetings and upcoming events, and a "serenity room."

Gay AA/Recovery in Jacksonville, Fla.
http://www.unf.edu/~rcharl1/aa.html

Unified Live and Let Live
http://ourworld.compuserve.com:80/
homepages/John_J_2/unifiedl.htm

This gay AA group is in Rapid City, S.D.

THE SPORTING LIFE

Sports groups can be excellent health maintenance organizations. They keep our minds clear and bodies fit, they enable us to network and make new friends, and they keep us out of the smoke-filled spots where we may otherwise end up getting together. Web sites for gay sports and gay sports organizations reflect a growing trend—if trend is the right word. After all, we have our own Olympics.

Gay Games 1998
http://www.dds.nl/~gaygames/
The fifth Gay Games (Figure 6.18) will be held in Amsterdam in 1998, marking the first time the event has been held outside of North America. The official Web site for the games gives a brief history, ceremony previews, and general information for travelers.

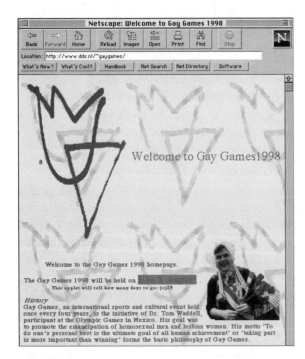

Figure 6.18
Gay Games 1998

Gay and Lesbian Sports Alliance of Greater L.A.
http://www.webcom.com/bkm/sa.html

International Gay and Lesbian Outdoor Organizations (IGLOO)
http://www.chiltern.org/chiltern/igloo.html
International Gay and Lesbian Outdoor Organizations (Figure 6.19) is a worldwide network which fosters communication and interaction between member groups and helps gays and lesbians connect with outdoor sports clubs in their regions. IGLOO's Web site features news from sports groups around the world and a clickable map for generating localized listings.

GaySport—Europe
http://www.gaysport.org/
Europe's proud GaySport is a combined effort of the Gay Integration through Sport and Activities Holland and the European Gay & Lesbian Sport Federation. It promises "all the information on sport you might require" (even if you're not European). Notable site features include an international tourney calendar and a matching service that helps those who register find a "SportMate."

LBG—Sports
http://cybervision.kwnet.on.ca/lgb-sports/
Bookmark the LBG-Sport Home Page, an excellent springboard to organizations, special events, and news articles on the gay sporting life. Devoid of clunky graphics, it's a lightning bolt to everything imaginable on the subject. Inquiring minds will dig the "Out Elite Athletes" file, which lists personal information and links to articles on many more names than the usual Greg, Rudy, Martina, and Billie Jean.

Team Seattle
http://www.teamseattle.org/usa/
Team Seattle organizes the city's offerings for the Gay Games and produces the Northwest Gay/Lesbian Summer and Winter Sports Festivals. The team's Web site covers upcoming events, history, and information on various Seattle sports groups.

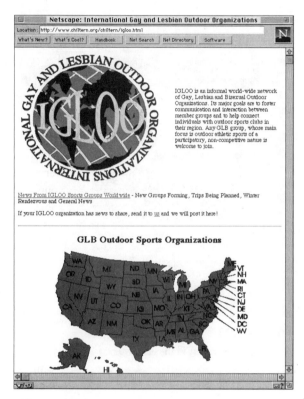

Figure 6.19
International Gay and Lesbian Outdoor
Organizations (IGLOO)

Tijgertje—Amsterdam
http://www.xs4all.nl/~tijgertj/
A gay and lesbian sports club in Amsterdam. The site is
written in Dutch.

The Gaymes We Play

Aquatics

Atlanta Rainbow Trout
http://www.mindspring.com/~atltrout/
Figure 6.20 shows their clever logo.

Bottom Dwellers Scuba Club—Seattle
http://204.137.167.120/bdsc/

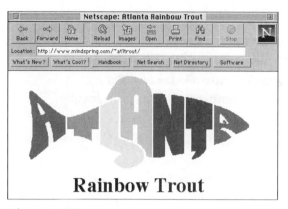

Figure 6.20
Atlanta Rainbow Trout

Gay & Lesbian Windsurfers
http://members.aol.com/glwindsurf/
windsurf.html
A gay windsurfing enthusiast offers general information
on the subject and proposes a network.

Triangle Divers—New England
http://www.tiac.net/users/jmcbride/
triangledivers.htm
New England's gay and lesbian scuba diving club.

West Hollywood Aquatics Swim Club
http://www.kwic.net/lgb-sports/teams/WH2O/
team.html

Basketball

Rainbow Hoops—Toronto
http://www.geocities.com/WestHollywood/
4606/
"Lesbian-positive" basketball league in Toronto.

Bowling

Garden State Gay Bowling Organization—Jersey City
http://members.aol.com/jeffnj/gsgbo/index.html

"New Jersey's most well known gay bowling league."

International Gay Bowling Organization
http://www.igbo.org/

Includes a tournament schedule, membership information and bowling links.

Show Me St. Louis Classic Invitational Bowling Tournament
http://www.artsci.wustl.edu/~rbreese/smcmain.html

Each year, more than 200 gay and lesbian bowlers descend upon St. Louis ....

Halloween Invitational Tournament—Tucson
http://www.indirect.com/www/bamabear/hitt96/hitt96.htm

In Tucson, Halloween means jack-o-lanterns, cacti, and bowling balls.

Cycling

Bicycle Boys From Hell—Denver
http://members.aol.com/bbfhco/

A social organization for gay men who have an active interest in cycling (Figure 6.21). Sounds heavenly.

Different Spokes of Southern California
http://members.aol.com/DSpokesSC/index.html

Rainbow Cyclists—San Diego
http://www.liscom.com/rainbowcyclist/

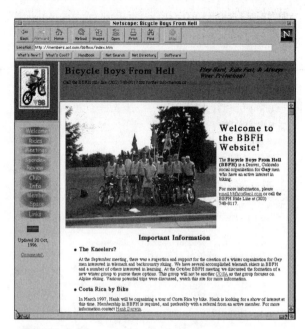

Figure 6.21
Bicycle Boys From Hell—Denver

Frontrunners International
http://www.webcom.com/bkm/if.html

Frontrunners Los Angeles
http://www.webcom.com/bkm/clubs/la/index.html

Frontrunners New York
http://www.tiac.net/users/kaz/frny.html

Shoreline Frontrunners—Long Beach
http://www.webcom.com/~bkm/sfr.html

What started as a jogging class and the title of a popular gay novel now has gays and lesbians running together in major cities around the world. The International Frontrunners home page (Figure 6.22) combines history, a calendar of events and a "family album," while a few of the individual city chapters keep members and potential members informed as to what's happening on their local scenes.

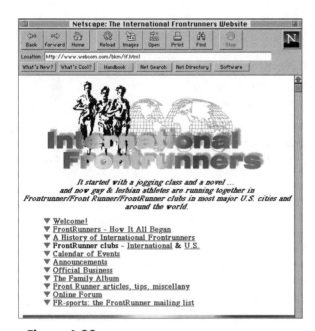

Figure 6.22
Frontrunners International

___

Rodeo

Alberta Rockies Gay Rodeo Association—Calgary
http://www.canuck.com/~argra/

Atlantic States Gay Rodeo Association
http://www2.ari.net/cowboy/asgra.html
The Atlantic States Gay Rodeo Association is a charitable and social organization which promotes "the country/ western lifestyle in the gay and lesbian community." Members come from farms and the inner city alike.

Bay Area Regional Gay Rodeo— San Jose
http://users.aol.com/gsgra/bac.html

Golden State Gay Rodeo Association
http://users.aol.com/gsgra/rodeo.html
California "cowboys, cowgirls, and so much more."

GAI-Q Out Take

Out.com's September 1996 GAI-Q survey reveals that three-fourths of gay male respondents claim to be less interested in sports than their straight male counterparts (Figure 6.23). Nearly half of the lesbian respondents say they're more interested in sports than their straight female counterparts (Figure 6.24). Are we shocked by this?

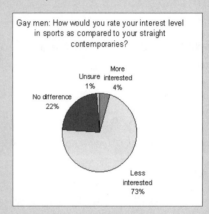

Figure 6.23
Gay males and sports

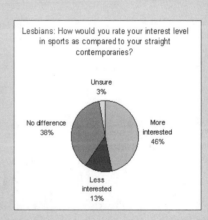

Figure 6.24
Lesbians and sports

Greater Los Angeles Rodeo Association
http://users.aol.com/gsgraglac/rodeo.html

International Gay Rodeo Association
http://www.igra.com/

The Denver-based International Gay Rodeo Association posts a rodeo calendar and features photos and explanations of rough stock, roping, speed and camp (see Figure 6.25) events. That makes it informational and action packed.

Los Angeles Gay Rodeo Association
http://newton.physics.ucla.edu/~rose/rodeo.html

New Mexico Gay Rodeo Association
http://www.swcp.com/~rkmartin/nmgra.html

Texas Gay Rodeo Association
http://home.earthlink.net/~txboots/tgra.html

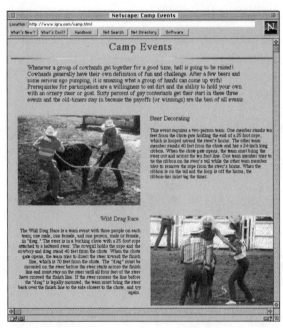

Figure 6.25
International Gay Rodeo Association

Rowing

D.C. Strokes Rowing Club—Washington, D.C.
http://www.clark.net/pub/dcsrc/dcsrc2.htm

Gay Lesbian Bisexual Rowing Page
http://www.geocities.com/TheTropics/1257/

Skiing

Aspen Snowmass OnLine Home Page
http://www.aspenonline.com/

It's the heart of the Colorado Rockies online. Dig deep into the site for details on Aspen's annual gay ski week. It's buried within the annual events calendar.

Colorado Outdoor and Ski Association
http://www.tde.com/~cosa/

Colorado Outdoor and Ski Association is a casual gay and lesbian organization for appreciation and enjoyment of the great Colorado outdoors.

Tennis

Atlanta Team Tennis Association
http://www.atta.org/

San Diego Gay and Lesbian Tennis Alliance
http://members.aol.com/gaytenis/index.htm

Volleyball

Don't Panic
http://www.geocities.com/Colosseum/Field/1787/

North American Gay Volleyball Association
http://qrd.tcp.com/qrd/www/orgs/nagva/

Wrestling

Madison Gay Wrestling Club - Madison, Wisc.
http://tps.stdorg.wisc.edu/MGLRC/Groups/MadisonGayWrestlingClub.html

Metro Gay Wrestling Alliance—New York City
http://plaza.interport.net/wrestle/metro.html

New England Wrestling Club
http://digital.zipnet.net/newc.html

WrestleSpeak!
http://plaza.interport.net/wrestle/

Dedicated to gay and gay-friendly wrestling orgs around the world, WrestleSpeak includes schedules, listings, special events, and contact information.

Grab Bag

Karaboom
http://fglb.qrd.org:8080/fqrd/assocs/karaboom/

Details on this Paris-based karate organization, but only in French.

Pink Pong
http://www.tu-berlin.de/~insi/gol/pinkpong.html

You guessed it: a gay table-tennis club in Berlin. In German, English, and French.

GAI-Q Out Take

A May 1996 GAI-Q survey asked Out.com viewers whether or not they exercise regularly. Sixty-three percent answered yes, and the chart below (Figure 6.26) illustrates the breakdown of their favorite forms of physical activity. Weightlifting is the big winner, while an unspecified "other" strides neck and neck with "Walking." Wonder what "other" could be.

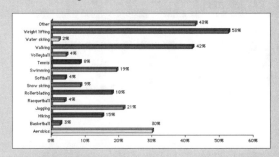

Figure 6.26
May 1996 GAI-Q survey

Chapter 7

ROADS LESS TRAVELED

The InfoSuperHighway is infinitely veined with biways, gravel paths, and roads less traveled. Subculture and underground movements in particular seem to latch on to the Net with unmatched zeal; that, again, thanks to the Net's unmatched networkability. This "Roads Less Traveled" section is a peek into the online antics of all of the pride-parade curiosities that make people who wear Tommy Hilfiger shirts squirm and make the Religious Right's documentaries so incendiary (or is it steamy?). Bears, big girls, drag queens, trans-males, masochists, leather daddies ... they're here, they're queer, and they're painting the Web various shades of pink and black. Happy trails. I think.

GRRR AND BEAR IT

The FAQ on the definitive Resources for Bears site defines "bear" as "a homosexual or bisexual man who is hairy, has facial hair, and a cuddly body ... [though it is] often defined as more of an attitude than anything else—a sense of comfort with our natural masculinity and bodies that is not slavish to the vogues of male attractiveness that is so common in gay circles and the culture at large." Check *American Heritage* and you'll get something else altogether, but suffice to say, the "bear movement" has hit the Web like a big ol' furry sumo wrestler. Do a little surfing on the subject and you'll find there are, literally, bears, bears everywhere. And a smattering of big-boned gals, to boot.

Resources for Bears
http://www.skepsis.com:80/.gblo/bears/

Bear Club Information—International
http://www.skepsis.com:80/.gblo/bears/
CLUBS/

The Papa Bear of all bear sites, Resources for Bears (Figure 7.1) archives details on clubs and businesses on an international scale. A glance at the list of clubs confirms, bears are everywhere: Tel Aviv ... Tokyo ... Toledo. In fact, the site's section for links to the home pages of bears on the Net grew to such an unwieldy size that it had to be broken into three parts. The authors are so enthusiastically bear that they have even come up with a definitive scientific "Natural Bears Classification System," because "classified ad prices are sooooo expensive." Are you a "1" (very slight beard) or a "9" (belt-buckle-grazing long beard; prototype is ZZ Top)? What's your "fur factor?" If you're still confused about the physical aspects of a bear, the site's "Bears in the Movies" page (which seems more like a wish list than anything else) informs that both Kevin Costner and Ed Asner make the cut. Grrr!

Figure 7.1
Resources for Bears

The International Bear Calendar
http://www.zoom.com/personal/aberno/
calendar.shtml

The hot spot for finding out about bear events around the world. The list is a monster, and it includes listings for events from Junction City, KA to Sydney, Australia.

Gen-X Bears
http://www.hockey.net/~gxb/

The idea for Gen-X Bears (Figure 7.2) was born at a Santa Clara, CA pool party in 1995, when founder Randy Stern noticed that he had nothing in common with the majority of "beautiful bears" he saw lounging around the pool. (The generation-gap thing, you know.) These days, Stern's San Diego-based cub-and-bear creation reports more than 200 members in four continents.

Bear Clip Art
http://esther.la.asu.edu/asu_tes/TES_Editor/
PERSONNEL/RAMSEY/bear_ca.html

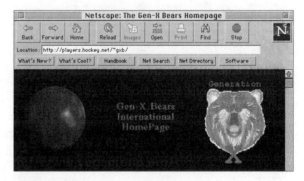

Figure 7.2
Gen-X Bears

 **BOB DONAHUE, RESOURCES FOR BEARS WEBMASTER**

Bob Donahue, of Somerville, MA, is an astronomer, and a post-doctoral research fellow at the Harvard-Smithsonian Center for Astrophysics. He's also the "Grand Poo-bah" over at the honker Resources for Bears site. Donahue took some time out of his busy schedule to answer a few questions about the thriving bear movement in cyberspace.

Q: I'm amazed at how many bear-oriented sites there are on the Web. Why do you think there are so many?

A: I think part of the reason is that there's been an online "bear presence" on the Net for many years, going back to 1988 when Steve Dyer started the "Bears Mailing List." This probably sensitized people towards looking

to handle alone, so I combined my efforts with Kevyn Jacobs who was trying to do something similar. Kevyn has pretty much kept things running since then, and now oversees a handful of other volunteers—Mike, Scott, Michael—keep things up to date and come up with new ideas for the service.

Q: I imagine you've been involved in the bear scene for quite some time. What was networking with others like before the Net caught on?

A: Actually, almost all my contact with the bear community has happened through the Internet. First off, it's a very easy way to keep in touch with friends who are far away. Through online resources, it becomes very easy to

Q: In what ways has the Net changed the international bear scene?

A: It's definitely prevented people from becoming too isolated. Bear Clubs have more opportunity to find out what other groups are doing. In any month there are events happening all over the U.S. that attract participants from all over.

Q: Any misconceptions about bears or the bear movement that you'd like to clear up?

A: Heh. I don't think that any one person can do that. There's some misconception surrounding what criteria define someone as a "bear"—where the dividing lines are. After Jeff Stoner and I had dreamed up the NBCS ("bearcode") we real-

> **"Actually, almost all my contact with the bear community has happened through the Internet."**

for and using online resources, like the Web.

Q: How has the Resources for Bears site changed since you started it in 1994?

A: I first put up a few meager pages in 1994, and at the time had the naive idea that I'd be able to keep up with all the bear clubs and bear home pages. It very quickly became too much for me

meet people in other cities or countries, or to connect with people when traveling. So, what's happened in "Network times" is that we are able to seek out like-minded people very easily. And for people just coming out, or realizing that things like bears really exist, it's a wonderful way to find out that no matter where you live, you're not alone.

ized that it could be applied to anyone—and some lesbians jokingly proved this to us! The bear movement started because people were looking for an identity within mainstream gay culture. I think we have to be careful to remember why this happened, and to be as open and welcoming as possible.

Clip Art for Bears

http://www.skepsis.com:80/.gblo/bears/
CLIPART/

Leather bears, bear cubs, Far Side bears, "Just Say Woof!" signs, the R.E.M. Monster tour shirt ... something for everyone's bear-art needs between these two sites.

Bears around the World

Asia

Tel Aviv, Israel—Israeli Bears

http://www.geocities.com/WestHollywood/
2243

Tokyo, Japan—Bear Club Japan

http://www.st.rim.or.jp/~lonestar/bcj/

Australia

Bears Down Under

http://www.skepsis.com:80/.gblo/bears/
CLUBS/BEARS.DOWN.UNDER/

Sydney—Harbour City Bears

http://www.geocities.com/WestHollywood/
1498/

Canada

Toronto, Ontario—Bear Buddies Toronto

http://www.torque.net/~bill/bbt/bbthome.htm

Vancouver, B.C.—BC Bears Online

http://www.bcbears.com/

Calgary, Alberta—Bearback Clagary

http://www.geocities.com/WestHollywood/
3469

Europe

Belgium—Girth & Mirth Belgium

http://www.planete.net/~nounours/

London, England—BearHug Home Page

http://www.bearhug.demon.co.uk/

Cologne, Germany—Bears Cologne

http://www.skepsis.com:80/.gblo/bears/
CLUBS/BEARS.COLOGNE/bmkln96.html

Italy—Orsi Italiani Home Page

http://www.geocities.com/WestHollywood/
2703/

Milan, Italy—Magnum Club

http://www.geocities.com/Paris/2645

Amsterdam, Netherlands—Girth & Mirth Amsterdam

http://www.xs4all.nl/~bubble

Spain—Gorditos

http://www.geocities.com/WestHollywood/
2062/gorditos.html

Sweden—Viking Bears

http://www.abc.se/~m8135/viking_b.html

United States

Phoenix, Arizona—Phoenix Bears

http://www.swlink.net/~phxbears/

**Tucson, Arizona—
Bears of the Ol' Pueblo**

http://www.csn.net/~jls2/bop/

Fresno, Calif.—Golden State Bears

http://www.cybergate.com/~gsbears

Los Angeles, Calif.—Bears LA Home Page
http://www.bearsla.org/

Sacramento, Calif.—Sacramento Valley Bears
http://www.geocities.com/WestHollywood/1700/

San Diego, Calif.—Bears SD Home Page
http://www.bear.net/clubs/bears.sd/

San Francisco, Calif.—Bears of San Francisco Home Page
http://www.q.com/bosf/

San Jose, Calif.—South Bay Bears
http://www.rahul.net/rhollis/sbb/

Denver, Colo.—Front Range Bears
http://www.spintheweb.com/~wburdine/

Florida—Bears of Central Florida
http://members.aol.com/bocf/

Florida—South Florida Bears
http://users.icanect.net/~mikebear//sfb.htm

Florida—Bears of Southwest Florida
http://members.aol.com/boswf/

Florida—West Florida Growlers
http://members.aol.com/wfghome/index.htm

Florida—Girth & Mirth of Florida Online
http://members.aol.com/gmfla/index.htm

Gainsville, Fla.—GatorBears
http://gnv.fdt.net/~gwydion/bears/

Atlanta, Ga.—Southern Bears
http://www.mindspring.com/~bryon/sbears.html

Idaho—Bears of Idaho
http://members.aol.com/bearsboi/bearsboi.html

Chicago, Ill.—Great Lakes Bears
http://www.marketplaza.com/spec/glb/glb.html

Indianapolis, Indiana—Hoosier Bears
http://www.win.net/~indy/hoosier.html

Iowa City, Iowa—The Ursine Group
http://www.avalon.net/~iowabears/tug/TheUrsineGroup.html

Wichita, Kan.—Hirsute Pursuit
http://www.fn.net/~awes/hp/

Cambridge, Mass.—New England Bears
http://www.bearsoft.com/neb/

St. Louis, Mo.—Show Me Bears
http://www.i1.net/~sek/smb/smb.htm

Detroit, Mich.—Motor City Bears
http://members.aol.com/mcbinfo/

Minneapolis, Mn.—Nash County Bears
http://www.wavefront.com:80/~kraklite/ncb96/ncbears.htm

Las Vegas, Nevada—BlackJack Bears
http://www.wizard.com/~topbear/bjbindex.htm

Reno, Nevada—Silver Bears
http://www.greatbasin.net/~nevadab/sbrindex.htm

Albuquerque, New Mexico—Bears of Mañana
http://www.thuntek.net/~kbear/bom/bom.htm

New York, N.Y.—Bergenfield Bears Lodge
http://www.panix.com/~carpen/bbl.html

New York, N.Y.—Metro Bears
http://www.wkeys.com/metrobears/

Toledo, Ohio—Black Swamp Bears
http://www.glasscity.net/users/yogibubu/

Philadelphia, Pa.—Delaware Valley Bears
http://www.early.com/~dvbears/

Rhode Island—Rhode Island Grizzlies
http://www.ici.net/cust_pages/bearfurr/
rigrizz.htm

Austin, Texas—Heart of Texas Bears
http://spdcc.com/home/hotb/index.html

Dallas, Texas—Dallas Bears
http://www.ecnet.com/home/tzank/cvbears/

San Antonio, Texas—Bexar County Bears
http://members.aol.com/bcobears/index.htm

Washington, D.C.—Chesapeake Bay Bears Home Page
http://members.aol.com/chbaybears/cbb.htm

Wisconsin—The Backwoods Bears
http://www.primenet.com/~rstbear/
bwbears.html

Eau Claire, Wisc.—Chippewa Valley Bears
http://www.ecnet.com/home/tzank/cvbear

Milwaukee, Wisc.—Brew City Bears
http://www.execpc.com/bcb

Subject: nacho
hello
Sat Apr 6 11:22:22 EST 1996 - ()
anonymous

FaT GiRL
http://www.fatgirl.com/fatgirl/

Meant to serve as both a representation of the paper version of *FaT GiRL* and an e-zine all on its own, FaT GiRL (Figure 7.3) is the creation of Max Airborne: a zine for "fat dykes and the women who want them." The site includes an action page, which highlights such events as the "International No Diet Day" and boycotts of Lane Bryant stores. (Don't miss the Fat Girl Revenge Cocktail recipe.) You'll also find interviews, or fat-chewing sessions, with people like Judy Freespirit, foremother of the fat liberation movement, and "difficult seductress" Dorothy Allison. For some comic relief, check out Airborne's personal comic-strip creations like "True Tales from Life in the Fat Lane." Big fun.

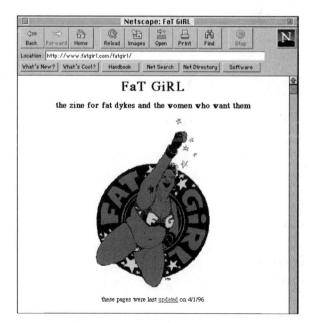

Figure 7.3
FaT GiRL

THE BI WAY

As you've probably already noticed, most gay-and-lesbian oriented sites are inclusive of bisexual resources; hence monikers including umbrella words like "lesbigay" or "queer." A few decidedly bi sites, however, warrant pulling out the bifocals and taking a look. Go ahead, live bicariously.

Anything That Moves
http://www.hooked.net/users/jonesey/atm.html

If you're a card-carrying bisexual, the zine *Anything that Moves* (Figure 7.4) is probably an essential. This electronic extension of the paper product asserts, no, screams: "We will write or print or say anything that moves us beyond the limiting stereotypes that are displaced onto us." The underlying message is that bisexuality is a whole, fluid identity—and don't mistake fluidity for confusion, irresponsibility, or an inability to commit, dammit. (That said, the zine's title should not be subjected to literal interpretation.) Items fished out of the editorial well are provocative: an article about "class" by Betty Rose Dudley, a self-described "fat, white, working-class bitch," for example. Elsewhere, you'll find poetry, fiction, and comics appealing to the bi sensibility.

Australian Bisexual Network
http://www.rainbow.net.au/~ausbinet/

This good-time Aussie network is devoted to serving "bisexual women, transsexuals, and men; partners and friends of bi people and bisexuals; and bi-friendly groups and services." Think they left anyone out?

Bi Day, Bi Night
http://www.kirstens.com/bipages/bipage.html

Webmaster Kirsten inherited these pages for bisexuals from a character named Pirate Queen, who sounds like a hoot in addition to being "very thoughtful (and always helpful)." Visitors are treated to an assortment of BiLinks, BiStories, and BiSpots of interest.

Figure 7.4
Anything That Moves

Bisexual Hell
http://www.tiac.net/users/danam/bisexual.HTML

Based on Woody Allen's observation that being bisexual would most likely double one's chances for a date on Saturday night, Bisexual Hell sounds like an oxymoron. What's so hellish about being bi? Besides the fact that one would have to spend several Saturday nights indoors online exploring the spread of sites to which this one points, that answer remains shrouded in ambiguity.

Bisexual Options
http://www.bisexual.org/

We all suspected that bisexuals had options, and this page is the clincher. From bi resources on the Net to "biographies of people to meet," San Diego-based Fritz Klein, M.D., slaps 'em down.

GAI-Q Out Take

According to the response to this March 1996 GAI-Q survey question (Figure 7.5), nearly 40 percent of gays and lesbians don't take individuals' identification as bisexual seriously.

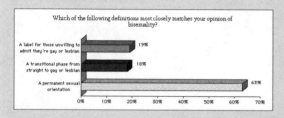

Figure 7.5
March 1996 GAI-Q survey

The Bisexual Test
http://www.mcs.com/%7elunde/web/bi/bi-test.html

This test has not decided what it wants to measure. However, it is designed to be taken by bisexuals to tickle their fancy. (Either alone or in groups.) Pencils ready, class.

Hapless Romantic's Bi Page
http://www.geocities.com/WestHollywood/1117/

Yes, that's hapless. Ed, the talented twentysomething Webmaster and student at West Virginia Wesleyan College, has not given up hope yet. With this page, he strives for exposure, and begins to tell the story of "a good Christian boy" who is not straight and not gay, but bisexual. After reading the story, one can only hope that Ed's Web creation will help him find someone else who enjoys Tori Amos, Japanese animation, and Nintendo 64 as much as he does.

THE T* FILES

Pop-culturally speaking, the transgender movement has successfully played to the masses. Witness the multifaceted career of RuPaul, the number-one box office business of Hollywood films like *The Birdcage* and *To Wong Foo....* Each flirts with the essence of transgender and presents it in a cuddly, star-studded spotlight. In reality, however—as site after site on the Web illustrates—the transgender movement is a caged fledgling at best, grappling with its own private rainbow of identities, misunderstandings, and misgivings. Terms range from transsexual (often spelled transexual) to gender dysphoric. Sexual orientations prance across the board. Perhaps it is the transitioning and non-specific nature of the transgender population at large that makes it difficult for even some of the most open-minded individuals to "get it." From a transgender support group in Central Texas to a personal page documenting the experience of transition, the Web is playing host to the transgender movement and is getting its many messages, lessons, and pleas out there.

The Androgyny RAQ (Rarely Asked Questions)
http://www.wavefront.com/~raphael/raq/raq.html

"Brothersister" Raphael Carter serves up all of what no one is necessarily asking but what he in particular wants you to know about androgyny. Begin with "The Angel's Dictionary" for demystification of words like "homovestite" and some gender-free pronouns. From there, work through "M. Manners' Guide to Androgyne Etiquette" and "The Murk Manual," which will help you understand medical writing on intersex. RAQ on, brothersister.

Boychicks

http://www.e-zines.com/boychicks/

We learn that "boychicks" are many things, and that the only constant that they share is that there is no one set definition of them. Get an education on this page of topical links ranging from a "Butch/Femme FAQ" to a "Stone Butch Blues Discussion."

Christian Crossdresser's Confession

http://www.engr.ucdavis.edu/~jsdevlin/
glorygod.html

A Christian and a crossdresser? Thou hadst better believe it. And one with "22% less evil than the average human being," to boot. With its lighthearted-but-earnest readings ("Christ in a nutshell," "Transition and salvation"), The Christian Crossdresser's Confession is well worth a look.

Creative Design Services Bookstand

http://www.cdspub.com/AAA.html

Creative Design Services publishes self-help titles such as "Crossdressers and Those Who Share their Lives" and *LadyLike* magazine. The CDS transgender resource guide promotes its titles by category groupings and, surprise, provides for online ordering.

CyberBitch

http://www.cyberbitch.com

"Artificially enhanced" and "unsocially called for," the CyberBitch, aka Charlie Brown (Figure 7.6), extends a warm welcome to "heterosexuals, homosexuals, asexuals, bisexuals, trisexuals, and [expletive] freaks." Check out the site's online show, "Dragscape," featuring entertainers from Charlie Brown's X-rated Cabaret in Atlanta.

Drag Hag

http://www.geocities.com/WestHollywood/
1814/

At long last, it's the "dragazine" for drag queens and the grrls who love them.

Figure 7.6
CyberBitch

ETVC

http://www.transgender.org/tg/etvc/etvc1.html

San Francisco's nonprofit Educational TV Channel was created in 1982 to provide support for transgender people and educational material to the transgender community and general public. Its programs and activities include monthly socials, an annual cotillion, and a speakers bureau. Information on ETVC membership is available on this info page.

GenderTalk

http://www.gendertalk.com/

A weekly talk-radio show in Boston, GenderTalk (Figure 7.7) serves a much larger audience on the Web. "Diversity begins at home, with family and friends" is the site's motto, and the show's executive producer/hostal entity

Figure 7.7
GenderTalk

Figure 7.8
GenderWeb

Nancy Nangeroni is "personally to blame" for it. Besides information on the show, the site hosts some interesting feature stories ("'Hermaphrodites with Attitude' Call for Demonstration") and an irresistibly titled "Twisted Nasty News Archive."

Gender 3
http://199.171.16.53/gender3.html
Devoted to abolition of the "2 sex system," Gender 3 utilizes two consciousness-raising vehicles—a book and a slideshow. Each deals with "the apartheid of sex." Preview the slideshow and read up on the book at this organizational site.

GenderWeb
http://www.GenderWeb.org/
Virginian Julia Case created the GenderWeb (Figure 7.8) to help educate people on the transgendered community. She does so in a fun and informative fashion, utilizing real-time chat, Java and a discussion forum along with medical and legal information, and personal experiences.

FTM International
http://www.ftm-intl.org/
Women probing their gender identity will find a safe and serious place for further exploration of issues, options, and potentials at the FTM International site. The San Francisco-based peer support group for female-to-male transvestites and transsexuals was founded by trans-male activist Louis Sullivan in 1986. The site provides details on memberships, meetings, and the mailing list, which currently includes some 600 subscribers.

Hedda Lettuce WorldWide
http://www.hedda.com/
Fats, femmes, and druggies are welcomed and the cosmetically challenged are encouraged to check out New York's Hedda Lettuce (Figure 7.9) online, where HTML stands for "Hedda's Tips & Make-Up Lessons." Flip

Figure 7.9
Hedda Lettuce WorldWide

through some trouble-twisted bedtime stories ("Heather's Mommy is a Closet Case") and get up close and personal with our heroine via her "Hedda Files" editorials ("I know Debbie Boone is not Rock 'n Roll, but I really feel that deep underneath Debbie's conservative, sickeningly sweet exterior lies a she-bitch waiting to emerge"). Elsewhere, eye Hedda's sketches, ogle the glam shots in her photo album, or do as good queens do and dish the dish in her Java-based chat room. With this site, Hedda proves to the world that "doing drag is more than just running around in a wig and a print dress and lipsynching Barbara."

Intersex Society of North America
http://www.isna.org/

The Intersex Society of North America is a peer support, education and advocacy group operated by and for intersexuals, those born with "anatomy or physiology which differs from cultural ideals of male and female." Three professional sexologists serve on the board of directors, and visitors will find recommendations for and positions on medical and treatment issues, and can flip through back issues of the newsletter, "Hermaphrodites with Attitude."

Journeys: A Nexus of Personal Transition
http://www.well.com/user/melanie/journeys.html

The Subversive
http://www.well.com/user/melanie/subversive.html

"Transition is not a state but a process," explains Webmaster Melanie Anne. "To deny one's past is to lose the victory of one's transformations." With this intriguing site, she documents experiences in transition—her own and those of others. Features include a step-by-step guide to developing a female manner of speaking, along with transgender fiction and real-life stories of transformation. Melanie also publishes a technologically enhanced gender zine, *The Subversive*, accessible here.

Julie Waters's Gender Issues Page
http://soong.club.cc.cmu.edu/~julie/gender.html

Gender to Julie Waters has always been a complicated issue. "I know a lot of people who feel that their own gender is something fixed and unchangeable," Waters writes, "but I believe them to be wrong in this regard." If this sounds like someone you'd like to see walking up your alley, check out the Gender Issues Page, and explore with Julie Waters the "smorgasbord of gender and sexuality" that is humanity through excellent links, mailing lists, and archived articles.

The Phoenix Project
http://www.abmall.com/tss/tss.html

The Phoenix Project provides transition support services by way of information and products for achievement of "gender congruity." Order online products such as Evanesce, a non-prescription herbal-estrogen capsule, or "The Employer's Guide to Transition."

Renaissance Education Association
http://www.ren.org/

Renaissance provides safe spaces for transgendered people and education on the subject via four chapters and 12 affiliates in 10 states. Get contact information and check out the organization's educational publications on site.

Sex Change Indigo Pages

http://www.servtech.com/public/perette/Sc/
sexchange.html

"Let your mouse do the walking" through the Indigo Pages, which lists surgeons who perform FTM and MTF sex change operations. Maintained by Perette, a post-op MTF transsexual and software engineer.

Sexual Identity and Gender Identity Glossary

http://ezinfo.ucs.indiana.edu/~mberz/ttt/faqs/
glossary

This no-frills, text-only page defines the common terms associated with the language of gender and sexual identity communities. If you don't know transvestites from transsexuals, you'd best start here.

Tampa Gender Identity Program

http://www.nu-woman.com:80/tgip.htm

The Tampa Gender Identity Program attempts to put a new spin on the transgender clinic by offering "a friendly and professional setting for a new concept in transgender care." The clinic's gender team provides counseling, medical and hormonal treatment, and electrology. This promotional site includes details about the team and the program.

Transgender Forum

http://www.tgforum.com/

The award-winning Transgender Forum claims to be the largest such resource on the Net. Its goal is to provide crossdressers, transvestites, and transsexuals with up-to-the-minute news, accurate resource information and a top-notch selection of vendor services. It accomplishes all of those goals, and with its friendly, colorful format, visitors will probably want to hang out for a while. Site segments include a weekly news magazine, a community center, and an online mall. The contact listing of transgender support groups around the world is first rate.

Transgendered Magazine

http://www.tiac.net/users/dba/menu.shtml

All of the material within *Transgendered Magazine* is "informative, upbeat, insightful, and designed to educate everyone about our often misunderstood lifestyle." Download a free copy on site. Elsewhere, visit the Gender Mall for online shopping, or become a member and gain access to the TG Suite, where message boards and real-time chat await. They're all services of DB Associates Publishing, which produces "an ever growing product line of transgendered related material."

Transgendered Officers Protect and Serve (TOPS)

http://www.greatbasin.net/~kuryakin/tops/

The Florida-based organization for current and past enforcement officers, fire fighters, and military personnel who happen to be transgendered (Figure 7.10) promotes and supports the emotional, professional, and legal needs of those in these "target professions." The site features a newsletter, membership information, and extras like the "CIA Report on Sexual Behavior."

The TransMale Task Force

http://www.azstarnet.com/~goodrum/
tmtf.html

This national grassroots org of transsexual and transgendered men focuses on educating FTMs—as well as the general public—on the major issues affecting the community; especially on legal and medical issues. Membership is open to all those who were born female but identify as male.

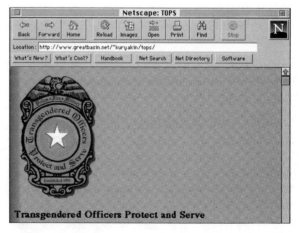

Figure 7.10
Transgendered Officers Protect and Serve (TOPS)

Subject: It's me again.... the raving homosexual.
For now ya'll can call me ultra violet. The reason I can't give you my e-mail address is because I don't bloody well know it. But not to worry ladies I'll find it out soon enough. Until then........
Wed Jul 31 9:35:22 EDT 1996 - ()
anonymous

Transvestite, Transsexual, Transgendered Home Page
http://ezinfo.ucs.indiana.edu/~mberz/ttt.html

From "Lola" lyrics to "lots o' lots of information on hormones," the TTT page runs the gamut of what's available online for the T* crowd. Articles ("My Son My Daughter"), regional resources (Iowa Artistry), and major Web sites dot the hot sheet.

TStar
http://travesti.geophys.mcgill.ca/~tstar/

TStar points to an international spread of nonprofit orgs and groups which serve the transgendered community. Webmaster Olivia Jensen also provides personal information on herself, her family, and her "T-friendly" colleagues.

Wigstock
http://www.at-beam.com/wigstock/ default.html

Tragic news last year was that Wigstock (Figure 7.11), the incomparable New York drag festival founded by the "Lady" Bunny, was canceled due to lack of funds, and also because of opposition from an NYC council member. (It was replaced by "Wig-Not," a benefit for Wigstock '97.) Fortunately, some of the spirit of the fest lives on online. Visitors are treated to a history of Wigstock, hot shots, and "hair extensions." It's outdated, but hopefully the organization will find the funds to get the show on for 1997 and get back to work on its delightful Web presence.

Figure 7.11
Wigstock

Zen and the Art of Post-Operative Maintenance
http://www.pcnet.com/~elspeth/zen1.html

Not nearly as trendy as the title makes it sound, "Zen and the Art of Post-Operative Maintenance" runs through the areas of pre-surgical preparation, post-surgical responses, hygiene, and dilating. It's dedicated to "anyone who has ever helped someone find their way."

The Essentials

H.E.R.S. Home Page
http://userwww.sfsu.edu/~tlewis/hers.html

Health Education Research Services is one of the largest West Coast retailers of breast forms. Survey and order the company's "mystique forms" on site.

The Lipstick Page
http://www.users.wineasy.se/bjornt/lip.html

Webmaster Madeleine Endre invites you to "put some style in your smile." Her page of all things lipstick (Figure

7.12) covers tips and consumer issues ("'Berries Flam-bée' is a great lipstick"), a cosmetics exchange network, and lipsticks of the stars (Ricki Lake: Aveda "Shizandra"). Gotta love this.

Nu-Woman Transgender Cabaret
http://www.nu-woman.com/

Kimberly Westwood realized years ago that the secret to beauty is "creating the illusion of perfect skin." She wanted to learn all she could. Trained first as an electrologist and then in skin care and makeup, she has since launched Nu-Woman, which sells cosmetics, wigs, and related beauty products with the transgendered in mind. Appropriately enough, Westwood presents her online boutique as a cabaret. Inside, you can download free transgender software, or consider purchasing designer wigs ("beautiful hair is a woman's crowning glory"), a premium makeup kit, or a video about "the operation." Available in English, French, and Spanish.

Shoecraft
http://www.best.com/~djr/shoecraft/

Ultra heels, pumps, flats, sandals, boots, and sneakers—Shoecraft specializes in sizes 11 through 14 and probably has just what you're looking for.

Wig Outlet
http://www.wigs.com/

Besides a stunning array of wigs (including the longest one on earth—named "Cher," wouldn't you know), the Wig Outlet hosts what has to be to the longest list of links to transgendered personal pages on earth.

Figure 7.12
The Lipstick Page

Trans-Continental Resources

Australia

The Australasian Good Tranny Guide
http://host2.mbcomms.net.au/austg/

The Tranny Guide started out as a simple contact list distributed by e-mail. Now it is a full-blown Web presence, with details on support groups, doctors, and trans-friendly businesses throughout Australia and New Zealand.

Europe

The Austrian Transgender Pages
http://www.oeh.uni-linz.ac.at/~transgen/

Maintained by Webmistresses Andrea and Anita, the Austrian Transgender Pages (also called Positive Change) make up sections on Internet resources and transgender life in Europe. Most of the writing is in German, though some English translations are available.

The Scandanavian Transgender Page
http://home.sn.no/~jane/

IFGE International Transgender Resource Guide
http://home.sn.no/~jane/intlist.html

This personal creation includes a section on legal issues for transgendered people (especially for Europeans) and "Dragmania," which features photos, news, and gossip about drag. The host's major attraction, however, is the International Foundation for Gender Education International Transgender Resource Guide, which provides contact information and organizational summaries for transgender resource groups around the world.

Scotland—The Plaid
http://www.wintermute.co.uk/users/snuffles/The_Plaid/

It's Scotland's first (and so far only) transgendered information server.

U.K.—The Gender Trust
http://www3.mistral.co.uk/gentrust/
index.html

The only registered charity in the U.K. specifically helping people who are "transsexual, gender dysphoric, or
transgenderist."

U.K.—The Northern Concord TV/TS Support Group
http://www.u-net.com/~nconcord/

The Manchester-based Northern Concord transvestite
and transsexual support group presents a site of support,
creativity, and just plain fun.

U.S.

Transexual Menace International
http://www.echonyc.com/~degrey/
Menace.html

Don't be afraid of the Transexual Menace (Figure 7.13).
The activist group standing up for the rights of transgendered people around the world confronts with love, and
asks only that you enter its domain with an open mind
and a compassionate heart. The group was founded first
to focus on transgender inclusion in Stonewall 25.
Strange the effort had to be made, considering it was the
bashing of T* types that triggered the riots in the first
place. But those who identify as transgendered are no
strangers to exclusion, even from relatively liberal pockets of the gay community. The group's international
headquarters is in New York, and its site is an eye-open-
er, listing accounts of "targets of prejudice" and "fighting
back," and lots of information on members. The Menace
now boasts chapters in North Carolina, Pittsburgh,
Washington, D.C., and Toronto. Chapters are also beginning in Boston, Portland, and Atlanta. Membership is
"just a willingness to stick your neck out and stand up
against prejudice; no violence, only peace."

Transexual Menace North Carolina
http://www.lava.net/~dewilson/menace/

Transexual Menace of Toronto, Canada
http://www.interlog.com/~sarah/menace.htm

Figure 7.13
Transexual Menace International

Transexual Menace of Western Pennsylvania
http://www3.pgh.net/~dscott/menace.html

Transexual Menace of Washington, D.C.
http://www.clark.net/pub/tsmdc/

California—Bay Area Transgender Resources
http://www.transgender.org/tg/people/jff/
tgrg.html

A quick rundown of what's out there for transgendered
folks fortunate enough to live in the San Francisco Bay
Area.

California—Diablo Valley Girls
http://www.best.com/~rwr13/.dvg/

Diablo Valley Girls is a nonprofit, non-sexual support
group for transgendered people and their families and
friends. The group mostly services the needs of those in
the East Bay Area of Northern California, though membership spans six states. Get all the details on what the
group is and what it is not.

California—Rainbow Gender Association
http://www.transgender.org/tg/rga/
rgapage.html

This social and support group for transgendered people in the South San Francisco Bay Area provides details on its activities and runs down the schedule of the social events calendar.

Illinois—Chicago Gender Society
http://www.transgender.org/tg/cgs/
cgsmain.html

The Chicago Gender Society is a social and educational nonprofit org for crossdressers, transsexuals, and their supporters.

Missouri—St. Louis Gender Foundation
http://members.aol.com/stlgf1/index.html

The St. Louis Gender Foundation's corner on the Web provides an organizational overview and extended calendar, along with some practical goodies like a "Gender Bill of Rights" and a safe guide to crossdressing in St. Louis.

Nevada—Silver Rose Gender Association
http://www.transgender.org/tg/slvrse/
index.html

This nonprofit, non-sexual support group for transgendered people and their families and friends serves the populations of Northern Nevada and Northeastern California.

New Jersey—Jumpstart
http://haven.ios.com/~chatchka/jumpstrt.html

New Jersey's "fastest growing transgendered support group," Jumpstart deals with the value of empowerment, especially on the personal level.

Ohio—Cleveland Transgender Information
http://www.en.com/users/audrie/clevtgnd/
clevtgnd.htm

Pictures, stories, and poetry are thick on this personal page intending to bring those in the Cleveland area "the information they need to explore and live their second lives."

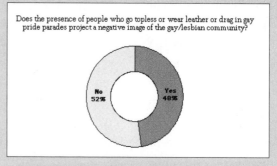

GAI-Q Out Take

The results of this question from Out.com's April 1996 GAI-Q survey (Figure 7.14) suggest that we are only about half way there when it comes to full acceptance of the diversity within the gay and lesbian community—at least when it comes to full community participation and representation in pride parades.

Does the presence of people who go topless or wear leather or drag in gay pride parades project a negative image of the gay/lesbian community?

No 52%   Yes 48%

Figure 7.14
Out.com's April 1996 GAI-Q survey

Tennessee Vals
http://www.transgender.org/tg/tvals/

The transgender social and support group of Nashville and the rest of the Southeast provides information on the group and on community resources available in Tennessee.

Central Texas Gender Society
http://www.ccsi.com/~george/index.html

Most don't associate crossdressers, transvestites, and transsexuals with the heart of Texas, but this society and its Web site lend support to these individuals and other transgendered Texans.

Washington—Ingersoll Gender Center
http://www.halcyon.com/ingersol/
iiihome.html

Washington State's nonprofit Ingersoll Center offers a range of services to the gender dysphoric, including therapy referrals, and counseling as it pertains to preparation for surgery and post-operative recovery.

100 PERCENT GERM-FREE RADICAL-SEX ROUNDUP

In the words of rad feminist Pat Califia, from her book "Public Sex," being a sex radical means "being defiant as well as deviant ... questioning the way our society assigns privilege based on adherence to its moral codes [and believing] that these inequities can be addressed only through extreme social change."

It's interesting to note that most radical-sex-group organizational platforms (if that's what you want to call them) seem to relate more to the idea of pansexuality and yawn at the limitations of gay/straight/bi identities. And, believe it or not, compiling a definitive list of radical sexuality sites on the Web turns out to be a real snooze. The vast majority of these sites—most of which celebrate variations on imaginative, sport-like sex—are surprisingly unimaginative in content and design. Besides that, there are plenty of sites lurking in the ether that all but one or two on the planet would just as soon forgo. Think of this section, then, as a small sampler of what's available. The run-of-the-mill leather-n-Lycra shopping holes and sticky minutae have been passed over for sites which strive to contribute insight and informed opinion on the defiant ones who inhabit and incite the wild side of sex.

Alternative Sexuality Resource List
http://www.phantom.com/~reive/altsex2.html
Not that the Webmaster here has anything against smut, but the Alternative Sexuality Resource List is just what it claims to be—not a page of links to porn archives. Between the many pointers to newsgroups and mailing lists, visitors will find Web documents on body art ("Historical Information about Lip Plates"), political files ("Sex,

Censorship, and the Internet"), and general queer listings. Pretty much everything but tips on the straight missionary position.

Black Rose
http://www.br.org/
A pansexual nonprofit org providing a forum for the many different expressions of power and love and play in Arlington, VA. Why? Why not? Get general information on the group and its telephone hotline number right here.

The BootMaster
http://www.geocities.com/WestHollywood/1211/
In order to enter the BootMaster's Domain, you have to get past a bare-bootied photo, service his boots (Figure 7.15) and read a few thoughts about him ("I drink my coffee black, like my leathers, in the morning with a smoke"). Still interested in the BootMaster? Well, he lives actually in Boston and virtually in Geocities's West Hollywood. He wears leather pants to brunch at Geoffrey's, and he displays his very own erotic poetic creations online. Boot up and boot out.

Brat Attack
http://fnord.tlg.net/brat/
Brat Attack was a "highly unprofessional and irreverent dyke SM zine" from 1991 to 1994. Now that the project has ended and the last of the back issues has gone out to lucky fans, the trademark "fun articles" and comics linger eternally in deep, dark cyberspace. Articles on file include "99 Cent Sex Toys" and "An Extremely Unofficial timeline of Dyke SM." Better hurry: Inflation has set in on those sex toys, and the timeline becomes more and more outdated each day.

Figure 7.15
The BootMaster

Charles Haynes's Radical Sex
http://www.fifth-mountain.com/radical_sex/

Charles Haynes offers a thoughtful, gay-oriented look at what's available within the realm of radical sex. Pointers go to places like a goddess-worship church and the Deaf Leather Resources page. Haynes also archives a selection of text documents and images of interest.

Cuir Underground
http://www.black-rose.com/cuiru.html

Cuir Underground is a San Francisco-based zine aimed at the "pansexual kink communities," or people of all genders and orientations who enjoy radical sexuality. News, reviews, and kinky fiction make up the pages (whip through back issues if you've got time). And the zine's Kinky Events Calendar makes sure that readers don't miss out on popular favorites like Rubber Blowout Weekend in Chicago and the Chicks with Dicks Workshop.

The Deviants' Dictionary
http://www.geocities.com/WestHollywood/1879/dictintr.htm

Londoner Dirks Hoekje compiled and wrote most of the definitions for the terms in the Deviant's Dictionary (Figure 7.16)—or the "encyclopervia of the Net." Spend hours enhancing your vocabulary with terms like "algolagnia" ("love of pain, from the Greeks"), "signal whip" ("as used with dog teams") and "enforced chastity" (look it up).

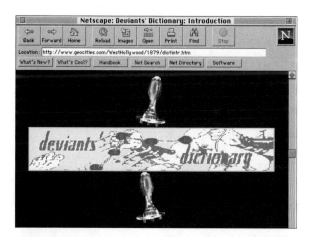

Figure 7.16
The Deviants' Dictionary

Adult Children of Heterosexuals
http://www.tiac.net/users/danam/acoh.HTML

What started as a mixed-gender cabaret/political theater-rock band in Boston has registered in the virtual realm with a "sex-positive, queer cultural" experience like no other. Basically, Adult Children of Heterosexuals (Figure 7.17) is a guided tour of the "glorious colorful musings of bisexuals, transsexuals, dykes, fags, and freaks" on the Net. And if any of that language offends you, don't bother pulling up the site, which features a weekly "fab three," queer resources links for days, and even an indepth look at bisexual hell.

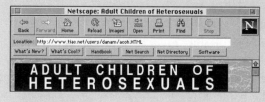

Figure 7.17
Adult Children of Heterosexuals

The Fetish Fashion Page
http://login.dknet.dk/~pg/fetish/

Slaves to fashion won't want to miss the spread here (Figure 7.18). From DJ's Fantastic High Heels Gallery to Rubbererotic tailors, the bases are covered in style.

Frankfurter Leder Club (Frankfurt, Germany)
http://ourworld.compuserve.com/homepages/flc_ffm/

"The FLC is a german leatherclub who set himself the target to increase the acceptance for gay men (especially leathermen). In this pages the FLC will gradually inform you about his or general actions, meetings etc." Pretty much says it all. In English and German.

Figure 7.18
The Fetish Fashion Page

International Mr. Leather
http://www.IMrL.com/#intro

The largest leather event in the world approaches its 19th year in the Windy City. Get all the details on the official International Mr. Leather site, which packs in hotel and travel information, a day-by-day events planner, and the essential hankie code.

Leather Navigator
http://www.leathernavigator.com/

The membership-supported Leather Navigator (Figure 7.19) wants to be your link to the "queer leather & bear community" on the Web. Follow the leads between color, original content and photographs, and the Navigator will turn you on to rodeo and rubber clubs; leathermen and leatherwomyn on the Web; erotica, political activism, and much more.

LeatherNexus
http://members.aol.com/nitestick/links0.htm

A strapping compilation of leather-oriented pointers—from an AOL member! An automatic "LeatherBOT" checks the links regularly to make sure they squeak. For sure, he's prompted by floggings from the Webmaster.

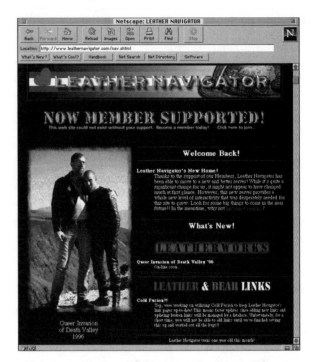

Figure 7.19
Leather Navigator

LeatherWeb
http://www.lainet.com/~leather/home.htm

LeatherWeb's Global Leather Village reaches around the world with news from "the Leather News Bureau," education (for keeping things "safe, sane, and consensual"), and an international events calendar. Separate entrances are available for gays, lesbians, bisexuals, and straight folks (whew!), and the site incorporates a Clintonesque "Town Council" forum for discussion and feedback. Don't miss the randy selection of "caverns" for exploring distinctive appetites in fetishism. Yes, hit the Shoes cavern for fun, passion, and shines.

Mon Cherie
http://www.moncherie.com/

Mon Cherie is "The American Leather Woman '95-'96" and the butt-tanning scourge of the Atlanta Pride parade. (You may have read about her in *Skin Two, A Taste of Latex,* or *Details.*) Ms. Cherie also hosts "a myriad of fetish performances amidst a very regular yet eclectic dance crowd" at The Chamber, which is basically Atlanta's enthusiastic answer to the Vault. Read all about her here, and flip for her new online zine, "Chain Links."

The 100-point BDSM Purity Test
http://www.lungfish.com/friday/bdsm_purity.html

Assuming you have passed Bondage/Dominance/Sadism/Masochism 101, you can leap right into action on this "purity test," checking off boxes—and diminishing your purity factor—as the answer is "yes." (If you're not all that familiar with the BDSM scene, a crash course is provided on site.) The questions range from "Bought/read pornographic periodicals?" to "Been restrained inside a body bag?" The test's scientific quality is questionable, since one loses the same percentage of purity for having worn a chastity belt as for having been flogged with a hard loaf of bread.

Powerhouse
http://www.powerhouse.co.uk/powerhouse/

The British Powerhouse spread includes Gummi, a men-only rubber-only club, and SM Gays, a social and educational group for gay men into SM. Yummi.

Sandmutopian Guardian : a Journal of BDSM Realities
http://catalog.com/utopian/www/guardian.html

The Sandmutopian Guardian describes itself as a practical guide to safe and enjoyable exotic eroticism, or "the Popular Mechanics of kinky sex." You won't find any of the kinky practicality online, but you can check out table-of-contents highlights from past issues and, if you're so moved, purchase a subscription.

Slakker's Leather Page
http://www.intnet.net/public/slakker/SM.html

This Slakker is no slacker, and the stellar Slakker's Leather Page (Figure 7.20)—a kind of BDSM 101—is virtual proof. While many sites on the subject of sadomasochism take the lurid route, Slakker's Leather Page, with an innocent schoolbook design, asserts "there is little to nothing which would appeal to the prurient interest, and none of the documents contained herein were written or designed with that intention." The intention, rather, is to inform and

Figure 7.20
Slakker's Leather Page

advise anyone interested in the practice of safe, sane, and consensual sadomasochism—from the vantage point of a Slakker on the scene. The site's wordy intro to SM sets the tone: "People outside the SM community (the vanilla crowd) have some rather odd ideas about us.... We have voices and we can speak for ourselves—and with the advent of the Net, we can speak to more people than ever before!" Slakker uses an authoritative tone and samples heavily from other sources to compile this exhaustive, ultimately enlightening course for beginners, practitioners, and inquiring minds. Slakker gets an A.

QSM
http://www.qualitysm.com/

The Q stands for quality, and the SM stands for, well, you know. This mail-order business is dedicated to bringing quality written material and education to the worldwide SM community, extending open arms to all sexual orientations and all fetishes. Browse the bookshelf for titles like "The Bitch Witch" and "Consensual Sadomasochism," or consider the unique offering of classes ("Playing as a Femme Top") available to people in the San Francisco Bay Area who are 21 years and older.

Without Restraint
http://www.mcsp.com/smcop/toc.html

The NYC-based SM/Leather/Fetish Community Outreach Project presents this regularly updated information page (Figure 7.21). Features include news, columns, opinions,

Figure 7.21
Without Restraint

Figure 7.22
Loving More

and reviews of current events and recent happenings in the BDSM scene.

Polyamory

Loving More
http://www.lovemore.com

It's love, love, and more love at Loving More (Figure 7.22), a quarterly publication and Web site which takes "a fresh look at relationships." That means discussion boards, chat, news, and an "amazingly popular survey"— all about "evolving sustainable relationships and new relationship options." Articles online include a school-of-hard-knocks look at how to have an unsuccessful non-monogamous relationship, and "Christians Loving More," a biblical perspective on polyamory.

The Open Hearts Project
http://world.std.com/~bearpaw/bp-poly.html

The Open Hearts Project provides a place where people who have decided "to step outside the standard two-person, sexually fidelitous and romantically fidelitous relationship" can share their experiences. Read the autobiographical stories of polyamorous folks like "Wolfie," "Stef," and "Bearpaw MacDonald." The site's polyamory pamphlet—"A Brief Introduction to Polyamory"—delivers the language of love on the run via a vocabulary tipsheet. Bet you can't guess what "triad" means.

Group Marriage Alliance
http://www.aracnet.com/~beattie/gma/

The Group Marriage Alliance is a Portland, OR-based group which meets once a month to socialize and discuss issues related to "polyfidelity." Find details on the term and the alliance here, along with pointers to other "poly organizations."

FINDING RELIGION AND SEEKING SPIRITUALITY ONLINE

Around Christmas time last year, a *Time* magazine cover glowed from the newsstand with a haloed Christ and the words "Jesus Online." Considering *Time*'s track record of covering Internet issues (see the notorious July 3, 1995 *Time* cover, displaying a child at a keyboard with the word "Cyberporn" printed in neon below his chin), it could have been hysteria, it could have been hype, or maybe, just maybe, it would turn out to be a well-researched piece on a provocative subject.

Lo and behold, those who made it past the creepy cover and actually read the article were treated to a fascinating look at how the Internet is shaping our views of faith and religion. One of the article's academic sources was even quoted as saying that "people see the Net as a new metaphor for God."

Huh?

Before your eyes start rolling back and your head starts spinning, think about it: a world of its own, apart from earthly reality, man-made, but growing beyond human control ....

Whether that's hyperbole or not, there's no denying that Baptists, Buddhists, Quakers, Jews, the Vatican, and most any other religious or spiritual organization one can call to mind (yes, even the Amish) are taking to the Net—the Web, in particular—as a bold new way to spread The

Word. The *Time* article suggested that, "Just as ur-banization brought people together for worship in cities—and ultimately led to the construction of larg-er and larger cathedrals—so the electronic gathering of millions of faithful could someday lead to online entities that might be thought of as cyberchurches."

Of the moment, it also keenly noted, "For Funda-mentalists prohibited from openly discussing such social issues as homosexuality and abortion, the Net has become the best—and sometimes the only—way to get exposed to a wide range of religious opin-ion." And just as the Net may allow those who hold fundamentalist viewpoints to consider thoughts from the rest of the world, it also makes an excellent networking and support backbone for gay and lesbi-an people in need of spiritual guidance that actually applies to their lives. What a concept. Gay residents of large urban areas enjoy their Metropolitan Com-munity Churches and other increasingly gay-friend-ly (and exclusively gay) congregations. But those in small and remote burgs aren't so lucky; they may be (and most likely are) faced with direct homophobia even as they seek sanctuary in a local congregation.

What you may expect to find in the way of gay re-ligious issues—Gay Male Tantric Massage and Bodywork; the Gay Pagan Heaven—is out there on-line. It's the stuff you wouldn't expect to find that drives home the fact that "Jesus Online" was not only an eyepopper of a magazine cover, but a per-ceptive editorial choice for a cover story, as well. Re-ligion is all over the Net.

Witness the Lesbian, Gay, and Bisexual Catholic Handbook; a page from a gay and lesbian Jewish congregation in Georgia; the Christian Science Les-bian Connection; the National Gay Pentecostal Alli-ance; Association of Welcoming and Affirming Baptist Churches. Nothing radical, nothing revolu-tionary and nothing outrageous, really. Just a grow-ing mass of religious resources. And a mass of religious resources that are a hell of a lot more civi-lized than what we're used to seeing.

The Interfaith Working Group
http://www.libertynet.org/~iwg/
The Interfaith Working Group believes that the charac-terization of religion as inherently conservative—and the portrayal of social debates as disagreements between the religious and the irreligious—undermines faith and "the ideal of religious diversity." The group expresses the di-versity of religious opinion on social issues where it is not widely recognized; mainly by providing a voice and a fo-rum for religious organizations who favor gay rights, re-productive freedom, and separation of church and state. Its activities include writing letters of support for gay teachers, protesting censorship, upholding marriage for same-sex couples, and argument against the policies of the "Radical Religious Right." Though Interfaith is based in and predominately serves Philadelphia, its Web site enables visitors from all around to search for a local re-ligious organization whose policies are compatible with their own beliefs.

Queer-Friendly Religious Links
http://world.std.com/~rice/q-light/links.html
You can never have too many of these. Arranged as "more-or-less denominational" and "more-or-less non-denominational," the site points to dozens of links; from the Radical Catholic Page and Gay Pagan Heaven to Walk Away, a page for ex-fundamentalists. Affirming churches, temples and meetings are also listed.

Rainbow Spirituality Ring Homepage
http://www.geocities.com/WestHollywood/3528/rainbow.html
If you produce a gay spirituality- or religion-themed site, you might want to step with it into the ring. The Rainbow Spirituality Ring (Figure 8.1) is a part of the "Webring," a free service that connects sites to one another and en-ables surfers to move from one site in a ring to the next. Hundreds of interest-specific rings are available, from *Star Wars* to Egyptology to body piercing. And there's this one, for Spirituality. (Think of the sites connected here as people holding hands in the pews.) The Spirituality Ring

Figure 8.1
Rainbow Spirituality Ring Homepage

home page gives information on the ring, tips for preserving ring integrity, and content guidelines. If you'd like to join, an online form makes it easy.

MEET THE GAY CYBERCHRISTIANS

Gay congregations and organizations from Catholic to Baptist to—gasp!—Christian Science denominations have begun to set up gay shrines online. Predictably, many of these sites dwell on "What the Bible Says about Homosexuality." Others are getting active. Witness Ontario, Canada's Center on Religious Tolerance; or the Phoenix Evangelical Bible Institute, which trains and prepares gay and lesbian Christians for responsible full- or part-time ministry. To see what the other side is up to, one can always drop in on a site like the dubiously titled "Gay Dilemma" for a loving, Christian stand against homosexuality. For the kinder flip side, check out folks like the Reverend Jerry, of Rochester, N.Y.,

who delivers via the Web one of the most gay-friendly and affirming sermons you're likely to read.

Ark's Home Page
http://www.geocities.com/Heartland/1184/
Revs Ricki Richards and Susan Kliebenstein welcome you to the Ark, a Christian resource center which proudly waves the rainbow flag (Figure 8.2). The goal is to minister to Brevard County, Florida, and eventually expand outreach to "go into all the world." The site features hot links to places such as "a hypertext edition of the Word," along with detailed information on Ricki and Susan ("In 1991, the Lord blessed us with a place to call home and a facility which we have called the ARK"). Perhaps the highlight is the electronic "Prayer Request Log," which allows visitors to send prayer requests via e-mail, and to read the requests of others.

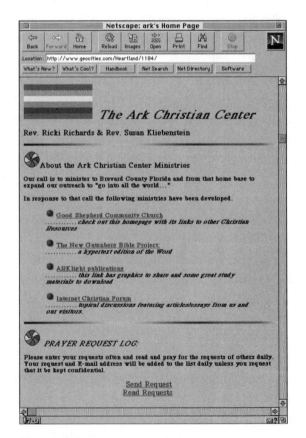

Figure 8.2
Ark's Home Page

Brian's Gay Christian Page

http://www.geocities.com/WestHollywood/
2002/gc.html

Brian delivers what the title of his site promises. Random items of interest include a sermon on homosexual unions within the Anglican Church of Canada by the Bishop of New Westminster, and a list of books Brian has read (along with a few he hasn't gotten to yet). He also points to a handful of personal home pages of gay and lesbian Christians.

Evangelical Network

http://www.xroads.com/~ten_net/home.html

Leaving absolutely nobody out, the Evangelical Network of Bible Churches and Christians describes itself as a "positive resource and support network for Christian and non-Christian gays, lesbians, bisexuals, transgenders, and whosoever." Founded in 1988 by Fred L. Pattison, a former Baptist minister, it is not a denomination, but a "fellowship of believers" who desire to carry forth the gospel of Jesus Christ. Get all the details here, along with links to Web sites ranging from The Bible to GayWeb to Weather.

Gay Christian Listservers— Online Discussion/Mailing Lists

http://www.geocities.com/WestHollywood/
2002/lists3.html

This page is a brief introduction to three curiously named resources, Crux, KAIROS-L, and Luti. Crux is a mailing list for the discussion of sexuality, spirituality, faith, and social justice. KAIROS-L is a mailing list for gay, lesbian, bisexual, and transgendered Christians. Last but not least, Luti is "an electronic catacomb of lesbigay Christians" and friends.

GLORY—Gay and Lesbian Organization of spiRitual Youth

http://www.toronto.anglican.ca/MoosWeb/
glory/

The Gay and Lesbian Organization of spiRitual Youth declares it's time to "break the silence and recognize that there are youth in the Church who are lesbian or gay." The Toronto-based group works with youth 25 and younger who are struggling with their sexual orientation and conflicting religious beliefs. Within a spiritual or reli-

gious setting, GLORY explores the role of gays and lesbians in mainstream Christian settings. The group leaders include Russell Walker, a Diaconal Minister with the United Church of Canada, and Sam Moffat-Schaffner, a lesbian working towards her Masters of Divinity within the Anglican Church of Canada. More information on GLORY is available on site.

God's Judgement on Heterosexuals and the Church's Caring Response

http://web.csd.sc.edu/bgla/education/humor_
judgement.html

This work of irony from one Tobias S. Haller is laced with pesky heterosexuals seeking to justify their behavior. It covers heterosexual behavior vs. the heterosexual condition, the ordination of heterosexuals, the heterosexual agenda, and is hard pressed to find a faithful, loving, life-long, monogamous heterosexual relationship in the whole of Scripture. But when all is said and done, it urges viewers to "affirm that heterosexuals, despite the sinfulness of their behavior, are children of God, and worthy of our care and pastoral concern."

Homosexuality and Bisexuality— Ontario Center on Religious Tolerance

http://web.canlink.com/ocrt/homosexu.htm

"The fact that more people have been slaughtered in the name of religion than for any other single reason. That, that my friends, is true perversion." Harvey Milk spoke those words in 1978, and it is to him that this section of essays from the Ontario Center on Religious Tolerance is dedicated. Topics covered here include "'Healing' Homosexuality," "Same-Sex Marriages," and "Homophobia: Its Causes, Incidence, and Cost."

Christ Evangelical Bible Institute, Phoenix

http://www.xroads.com/~ten_net/phebi.htm

Used to be, Christian gays and lesbians who wanted to study the Bible had only two choices: go to a school that accepted them while it watered down Scripture; or go to a school which threatened expulsion if they were honest about who they really are. Now there's another choice. The primary purpose of the Phoenix, AZ-based Christ

Evangelical Institute is to train and equip gay and lesbian Christians for responsible full- and part-time ministries. It also strives to spread the word to nonbelievers—especially those who have been disenfranchised and outcast because of sexual orientation or sexual identity. Learn about the institute's prices, academic standards, and available courses (offered both on-site and via correspondence).

"When 'Gay' Means Hurting"—a Sermon by Rev. Jerry Alan Smith
http://www2.rpa.net/~revjas/rtf_031096.html

Rev. Jerry Alan Smith, of Rochester, N.Y., was complimented by an adult-education speaker for being daring enough one week to preach about addiction to his congregation. To Smith, "that was easy" compared to the "much more difficult" issue of the gay and lesbian community and "how the church might relate to them." And that's exactly the issue he tackles in this sermon, "When 'Gay' Means Hurting," which he has archived on his very own server. Refreshingly, it's not anti-gay propaganda wrapped in a thin veil. In fact, it turns out to be one of the most gay-friendly, affirming sermons you're likely to read. Amen.

What the Bible Says about Homosexuality
http://web.canlink.com/ocrt/hom_bibl.htm

This mostly text page delivers a gay-positive version of "what the Bible says about homosexuality." In other words, it offers the flip side to the anti-gay Leviticus interpretations and points out that the Bible says "almost nothing about homosexual feelings" and that the concept of sexual orientation was not even developed until the 19th century. Which means the concept of homosexuality would most likely have been lost on the Bible scribes who were supposedly running down gays whenever they got a chance. The page gives specific verses from the Hebrew and Christian scriptures along with tips for interpretation.

Whosoever: a News Journal for Gay and Lesbian Christians
http://www.mindspring.com/~sagecomm/whosoever/

The Religious Right may say that you can't be both gay and Christian, but the Atlanta-based "Whosoever" news journal (Figure 8.3)—available in both paper and electronic versions—is determined to set the record straight. The bi-monthly publication promises a "first hand look at how gay and lesbian Christians look at our world." Typical feature stories include "Queering the Congregation: How Gay and Lesbian Christians are Breathing New Life into the Church" and "Same Sex Marriage—the Unholy Battle over Matrimony." Subscription information is available online, as are highlights from recent issues.

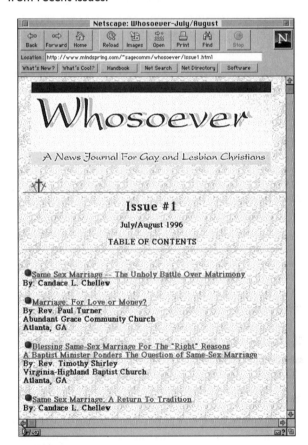

Figure 8.3
Whosoever: a News Journal for Gay and Lesbian Christians

Anglican

AGLO (Action for Gay and Lesbian Ordination)

http://www.dircon.co.uk/aglo/

The U.K.-based Action for Gay & Lesbian Ordination organization is something to be aglow about, indeed. "It's time for the Church of England to be honest about its gay clergy and to stop discriminating against them," the site proclaims. This single-issue pressure group campaigns for lesbians, gay men, and bisexuals who want to be equal with heterosexuals in the Anglican priesthood. Get information on what AGLO has and what AGLO needs on site.

Good Shepherd Anglican Church

http://ecuvax.cis.ecu.edu/~rllucier/church.html

A parish of the Evangelical Anglican Church in America, the Good Shepherd Anglican Church meets every Sunday at the Unitarian Universalist Congregation in Greenville, N.C. The parish home page features pictures of the Bishop's visit, along with snaps of the recent Down East Pride Festival.

Baptist

Association of Welcoming and Affirming Baptist Churches

http://members.aol.com/wabaptists/index.html

Surprise. It's an association committed to actively affirming the inclusion of gay, lesbian, bisexual, and transgendered persons into the full life and mission of local congregations, as well as the regional and national offices of the American Baptist Churches in the U.S. The association sets out to "create a community in solidarity, empowerment, and reconstruction committed to true peace and justice." Get a brief history of the association, a list of member churches and organizations, and information on how to join.

Catholic

The Christians Gay and Lesbian Association

http://aleph.pangea.org/org/cgl/cristiae.htm

The Christian Gay and Lesbian Association is a Barcelona-based group related to the Catholic Church which serves as a meeting place and "the first step for many gays and lesbians who want to share their faith and live their sexual orientation without links or traumas" (well, the site does contain a few links ...). Get details on the group's activities and theological workshops on the home page.

Lesbian, Gay, and Bisexual Catholic Handbook

http://www.bway.net/~halsall/lgbh.html

The Lesbian and Gay Catholic Handbook is author and maintainer Paul Halsall's online "attempt to organize and present a great deal of information, discussion, and argumentation that will be helpful to lesbian, gay, and bisexual Catholics." The book is structured as 10 chapters which range from "Basic Bibliographical Guides" to "Writings in Support of Lesbian, Gay, and Bisexual Catholics," and the number of meticulously arranged hyperlinks within each chapter is impressive. Halsall invites dissenters to his party, as well. He writes: "To people who are hostile to gay people, or to those who wonder what is the point or 'agenda' of a site like this, please read on." What you'll find here will keep you busy for a long time.

Mike's Homopage

http://www.geocities.com/WestHollywood/3528/index.html

Welcome to Mike's Homopage, the gay side of his world, on which he links out to sites that will be of interest to most gays and lesbians, and particularly to those who are fellow Catholics. "If you are offended or disturbed by the idea that gay people are normal," Mike warns, "do us both a favor and return to whence you came."

Dignity/USA
http://www.dignityusa.org

Dignity Canada Dignité
http://www.odyssee.net/~prince/dcd.html

Dignity/USA (Figure 8.4) is an organization of gay, lesbian, bisexual, and transgendered Catholics and their friends in more than 80 chapters across the U.S.—many of which have made homes online. "We believe that gay, lesbian, bisexual, and transgendered Catholics in our diversity are members of Christ's mystical body, numbered among the people of God," the group's Statement of Position and Purpose explains. This main site for Dignity in the U.S. (which is headquartered in Washington, D.C.) provides contact information for chapters across the country. It also archives the monthly newsletter, "Dignity Dateline." The Canadian version, Dignity Canada Dignité, adds that "We are not a mission of the Catholic Church to the gay and lesbian people, rather we are the mission of gay and lesbian people to the church. For Dignity, there is no conflict between being gay or lesbian and being Roman Catholic." Canada's site also points to information on local chapters and national executives, along with links to progressive Catholic sites around the world.

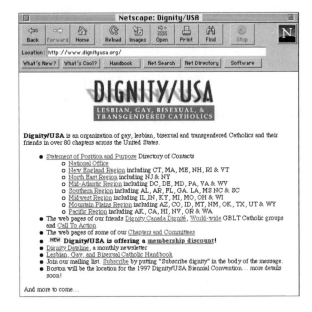

Figure 8.4
Dignity/USA

Dignity Chapters in the U.S.

Dignity Los Angeles
http://www.geocities.com/WestHollywood/1009/index.html

Dignity New Mexico
http://www.swcp.com/~dignity/

Dignity New York
http://www.bway.net/~halsall/lgbh/lgbh-digny.html

Dignity Phoenix
http://www.netzone.com/~diginphx/

Dignity San Diego
http://www.lanz.com/dignity/

Dignity San Fernando Valley
http://www.geocities.com/WestHollywood/2356/

Dignity Chapters in Canada

Dignity Montreal Dignité
http://www.odyssee.net/~prince/dmd.html

Dignity Ottawa Dignité
http://www.odyssee.net/~prince/dod.html

Dignity Toronto Dignité
http://www.arcos.org/aduddin/dtd.html

Defenders
http://www.blackiris.com/SFLeatherMC/SFLClubs/Defenders/DefNational.html

Defenders San Francisco
http://www.blackiris.com/SFLeatherMC/SFLclubs/Defenders/Defenders.html

Let's face it: An organization for the gay Catholic leather and Levi scene had to happen sooner or later. And here you have it. The "Defenders of Dignity" was founded in 1981 as a leather/Levi club in association with Dignity/USA (the gay and lesbian Catholic organization). The Defenders aim to "work for the acceptance of the leather/Levi community as full and equal members of the one Christ." Contact information for local chapters (in Boston, Denver, Florida, Los Angeles, D.C., and New York City) is available, as is a link to Defenders/San Francisco, which gives its own spiel with a page on the Web.

Christian Science

Christian Science Lesbian Connection
http://www.geocities.com/WestHollywood/1892/lesbian.html

Now here's something you don't see every day (Figure 8.5). This "loose network" of lesbians met through ads placed by Kathelen Johnson, a lifelong student of Christian Science, in the magazine *Lesbian Connection*. The women are teachers, bus drivers, foresters, etc.; some accepted by their branch churches, others shunned by them; some out of the closet, some still in. The common bond is simply that of being lesbian and a student (or former student) of Christian Science. The site is loaded with Bible lessons (mostly from the *Christian Science Quarterly*) and information on various organizations for gay, bisexual, and transgendered Christian Scientists. Connected to such pages as Gay and Lesbian Principians, it turns out to be an excellent connection for men and women alike.

Church of Jesus Christ of Latter Day Saints (Mormon)

Affirmation: the Official Web Site
http://ng.netgate.net/~jfirth/affirmation/

Affirmation (Figure 8.6) is a nonprofit educational fellowship group serving gay, lesbian, and bisexual Latter-day Saints and their families and friends ("It's all about love"). It was organized in 1977 and has served as a network for open, honest dialogue and support. The official Web site for the worldwide organization gives background information, and there is a "fun & games" area, where you can "learn more about the gay/lesbian experience while having fun." An area dedicated to chapter and group leader development is promised for the future.

Figure 8.5
Christian Science Lesbian Connection

Affirmation Los Angeles
http://www.westworld.com/~tiburon/lasaints/

AffirmationNYC
http://www.columbia.edu/~fs94/affnyc.html

Affirmation—Chapter At large
http://members.aol.com/affirmchlg/index.html

AffirmationNYC and Los Angeles serve their respective metropolitan populations of people who are gay, lesbian, bisexual, or transgendered with an interest in Mormonism. The groups comprise active, inactive, resigned, or excommunicated Mormons, and supportive family and friends. Check out localized Affirmation news and events on each of the coasts. The Chapter at Large serves members who are not affiliated with any of the other various Affirmation groups and chapters throughout the U.S. Chapters outside of the U.S. are also included here. Site features for the "at large" group include chapter and group maps, news, and gay, lesbian, and Mormon links.

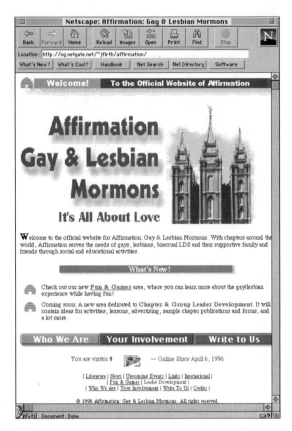

Figure 8.6
Affirmation: the Official Web Site

Episcopal

Bishop's Commission on Gay and Lesbian Ministry
http://www.primenet.com/~bcglm/

Your online source of information about the Episcopal Church—and about the Episcopal Church in the Diocese of Los Angeles, in particular. Site features include basic information about the Episcopal Church and welcoming parishes, a bibliography on Christian spirituality for gays and lesbians, and a calendar of events. All that, plus a gay pride photo album.

The Oasis
http://www.princeton.edu/~meneghin/oasis/oasis.html

The Oasis is a mission and ministry of the Episcopal Diocese of Newark, N.J., with gays, lesbians, and their families and friends. The ministry promotes reconciliation between the gay community and the church. The site includes a listing of sponsoring churches, and details on upcoming events.

Integrity
http://members.aol.com/natlinteg/index.html

Integrity is a nationwide association of lesbian and gay Episcopalians and their families and friends. This unofficial Web site for the organization (which actually seems official enough) explains that the primary Integrity focuses are worship in a supportive environment, emotional support and counseling, spiritual nourishment and Christian education, and service to the church and to the gay and lesbian community. The site includes a form for national membership, and an area with information on forming a new chapter. It also archives press releases, historical information, and Integrity clip art. Integrity chapters in Minnesota, New York, Northern California, Tampa Bay, FL, Toronto, and Washington, D.C. all have official organizational pages up, as well.

Integrity/Minnesota
http://members.aol.com/bridgemn/index.html

Integrity/New York
http://members.aol.com/IntegriNYC/index.html

Integrity/Northern California
http://www.gvn.net/~barb/

Integrity/Tampa Bay
http://www.cftnet.com/members/integtb/home.html

Integrity/Toronto
http://www.kapn.tap.net/integrity/

Integrity/Washington, D.C.
http://members.aol.com/integwash/index.html

Lutheran

Gay, Lesbian and Bisexual Concerns Group
http://www.bloomington.in.us/socserv/mit/GAY.html

Just a quick fact sheet on this supper club consisting of gay, lesbian, and bisexual members and friends of St. Thomas Lutheran Church in Bloomington, IN.

Lutherans Concerned/North America
http://www.lcna.org/

The official gay Lutheran organization, Lutherans Concerned helps people to reconcile their spirituality and sexuality in an uplifting way. It also seeks to lead the church by example. "We cannot wait for everyone in the church to understand how acute the need is," the site explains. "We are called to minister to the people now." Find information here on local LC chapters (including Northeast Ohio and San Francisco, which each have their own Web presences), and the "Reconciled in Christ Program."

Lutherans Concerned Northeast Ohio
http://members.aol.com/lcneo/lcneo.htm

Lutherans Concerned San Francisco
http://www.crl.com/~malarak/lcsf/lcsf.html

Mennonite

Brethren/Mennonite Council for Lesbian and Gay Concerns
http://www.webcom.com/bmc/welcome.html

The Brethren/Mennonite Council for Lesbian and Gay Concerns provides support for Mennonite and Church of the Brethren gay, lesbian, and bisexual people, and their friends and families. It also works to foster dialogue between gay and nongay people in churches, and attempts to provide accurate information about homosexuality from the social sciences, biblical studies, and theology. The organizational site provides details on congregations which support the council, an events schedule, and more.

Universal Fellowship of the Metropolitan Community Churches (MCC)

UFMCC Global Headquarters
http://www.ufmcc.com/

The Universal Fellowship of the Metropolitan Community Churches, a.k.a. MCC (Figure 8.7), is an "inclusive worldwide fellowship of Christian congregations, with a special outreach to the world's gay and lesbian community." It has also become commonly recognized as the gay denomination. Naturally, its global headquarters is the primo starting point for finding out all there is to know about UFMCC, which, founded in 1968 by the Rev. Troy Perry, is now a denomination of some 300 churches in 18 countries around the world. From "how UFMCC began" to "Metropolitan Community Churches today," the site covers the basics, also incorporating online features such as "Lesbians and Gay Men in the Bible." And check out the impressive line of MCCs around the world which have their own sites up on the Web.

Figure 8.7
UFMCC Global Headquarters

Canadian UFMCC Sites

Universal Fellowship of Metropolitan Community Churches

http://www.ualberta.ca/~cbidwell/UFMCC/
uf-home.htm

Another fine general resource on UFMCC, this Canadian site offers background information and details on service units (AIDS Ministry Resources; the Commission on Faith, Fellowship, and Order). It's not as extensive as the site from global headquarters.

Universal Fellowship of Metropolitan Community Churches

http://www.trends.ca/~ufmcc/

Yet another Canadian site focusing on the UFMCC denomination as a whole, with a focus on Canadian churches.

Metropolitan Community Church of Edmonton

http://gpu.srv.ualberta.ca/~cbidwell/UFMCC/
mcc-ed.htm

European UFMCC Sites

Metropolitcan Community Church of Copenhagen

http://qrd.tcp.com/qrd/www/orgs/mcc/cph/

Metropolitan Community Church of Hamburg

http://qrd.tcp.com/qrd/www/orgs/mcc/cph/
6hambg1.html

Metropolitan Community Church of London

http://www.bluenet.co.uk/blue/christmas/
pages/mcc.htm

New Zealand

Metropolitan Community Church of New Zealand

http://nz.com/NZ/Queer/MCCChristchurch/

U.S. UFMCC Sites

Metropolitan Community Church of Boise (Idaho)

http://members.aol.com/MCCBoise/
mccboise.htm

Metropolitan Community Church of Central Texas (in Waco)

http://www.creative.net/~thepark/shelters/
ctmccfth.html

Metropolitan Community Church of Charlotte (North Carolina)

http://www.geocities.com/WestHollywood/
2326/links.html

Metropolitan Community Church of Columbia (South Carolina)

http://www.geocities.com/WestHollywood/
3622/

Metropolitan Community Church of Dallas

http://www.cohmcc.org/

See Figure 8.8.

Metropolitan Community Church of Fort Collins (Colorado)

http://people.delphi.com/mark_lee/

Metropolitan Community Church of Greensboro (North Carolina)

http://www.uncg.edu/~jrervin/stmarys.html

Metropolitan Community Church of Hickory (North Carolina)

http://www.geocities.com/WestHollywood/
3758/

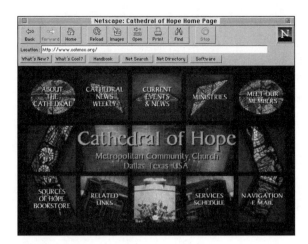

Figure 8.8
Metropolitan Community Church of Dallas

Metropolitan Community Church of Houston (Texas)
http://www.neosoft.com/~mccr/mccr.html

Metropolitan Community Church of Huntsville (Alabama)
http://www.dink.com/qr/mcch.html

Metropolitan Community Church of Jacksonville (Florida)
http://members.aol.com/smcguinn/stlukes.htm

Metropolitan Community Church of Kansas City
http://www.cris.com/~Brynda/souls.htm

Metropolitan Community Church of Nashville
http://www.geocities.com/WestHollywood/1099/nashmcc.html

Metropolitan Community Church of Orlando (Florida)
http://www.hway.net/joymcc/

Metropolitan Community Church of Omaha (Nebraska)
http://www.radiks.net/mccomaha/

Metropolitan Community Church of Phoenix
http://www.primenet.com/~victorv/gsmcc.html

Metropolitan Community Church of Pittsburgh
http://www3.pgh.net/~dscott/mcc.html

Metropolitan Community Church of Rapid City (South Dakota)
http://www.Rapidcity.com/~jjohn/mcc.htm

Metropolitan Community Church of Richmond (Virginia)
http://www.mccrich.spectek.com/

Metropolitan Community Church of Seattle
http://www.serv.net/~johnl/mcc.html

See Figure 8.9.

Figure 8.9
Metropolitan Community Church of Seattle

Metropolitan Community Church of Tacoma (Washington)
http://www.interinc.com/Allfaiths/NHMCC/

Metropolitan Community Church of Washington, D.C.
http://www.nicom.com/~mccwash/mcc.html

Metropolitan Community Church of Winston-Salem (North Carolina)
http://members.aol.com/mccwsnc/
mccwsnc.html

Metropolitan Community Church of Washington, D.C.
http://www.geocities.com/WestHollywood/
4881/

Pentecostal

National Gay Pentecostal Alliance
http://www.cris.com/~Ngpa/
The National Gay Pentecostal Alliance was formed in the early eighties when William H. Carey, a 22-year-old man studying for the ministry in a United Pentecostal church, was forced to leave when he was discovered to be homosexual. "Sister Schwarz" decided to leave at the same time, and the two began to search for a church that would allow them to worship in the Pentecostal manner without making judgments based on sexual orientation. "Finding none, and feeling the hand of God," they formed their own. Today, the National Gay Pentecostal Alliance is recognized by the federal government as its own denomination. The church's home page offers plenty of background and current news, and it gives contact information for NGPA churches across the U.S. and in Russia. Despite the word "gay" in the name, the site explains that NGPA is not a "gay church," but that by including the word in the name, "those who are not welcome in the other Pentecostal churches will know that they are welcome here," where "Jesus loves you no matter what."

Presbyterian

Presbyterian Lesbian and Gay Concerns
http://www.epp.cmu.edu/~riley/PLGC.html
This hot spot for "Presbyqueerians" and "Lysbyterians" (their terms) lists pointers to accepting congregations and other topical resources.

More Light
The following congregations are all part of the Presbyterian Church U.S.A. They call themselves "More Light Congregations" to indicate that they warmly welcome and encourage participation and membership to Christians regardless of "worldly condition," notably sexual orientation.

Downtown United Presbyterian Church (Rochester, N.Y.)
http://www.tamfs.org/htmfiles/dupc.htm
See Figure 8.10.

Lincoln Park Presbyterian Church (Chicago)
http://www.suba.com/~barry/

Northside Presbyterian Church (Ann Arbor, MI)
http://www-personal.umich.edu/~laustin/
NorthsidePC.html

St. Luke Presbyterian Church (Wayzata, MN)
http://www.churchnet.org/churchnet/
stlukepres/

Tabernacle United Church (Philadelphia)
http://www.libertynet.org/~iwg/tab.html

Westminster Presbyterian Church (Washington, D.C.)
http://www.radix.net/~ncpby/0432/wpc1.html

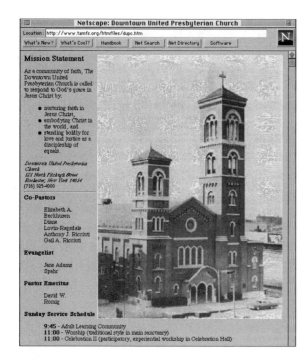

Figure 8.10
Downtown United Presbyterian Church
(Rochester, N.Y.)

Reorganized Church of Jesus Christ of Latter Day Saints

Gay and Lesbian Acceptance
http://www.angelfire.com/pages1/GALA/index.html

Gay and Lesbian Acceptance (or GALA) is an association of gays, lesbians, bisexuals, and their families and friends within the Reorganized Church of Latter Day Saints community. Dedicated to the celebration of diversity and committed to exploring issues of spirituality and justice through dialogue, education and action, the group supports "self actualization in an atmosphere of love, understanding, and confidentiality." Site features include suggested readings, "what the Bible says about homosexuality," information on GALA retreats, and more.

Seventh-Day Adventist

SDA Kinship International, Inc.
http://www.qrd.org/qrd/www/orgs/sda-kinship/

Seventh-Day Adventist Kinship International is a support group ministering to "the spiritual, emotional, social and physical well-being" of the church's gay, lesbian, and bisexual members. The organization includes more than 1000 people in 16 countries. Its home page reaches out to inform and educate—with statements of purpose, contact information, etc.—and to further network gay Seventh-Day Adventists.

Society of Friends (Quaker)

Friends for Lesbian and Gay Concerns
http://tps.stdorg.wisc.edu/MGLRC/Groups/FriendsforLesbianGayConc.html

This is the official page for Friends for Lesbian and Gay Concerns (FLGC), an association of lesbian, gay and non-gay Quakers seeking to "know that of God within ourselves and others and to express God's truth in both the Quaker and lesbian/gay communities, as it is made clear to us."

Friends for Lesbian and Gay Concerns
http://www.geocities.com/WestHollywood/2473/flgc.html

... and here's the unofficial page for Friends for Lesbian and Gay Concerns.

Q-Light Home Page
http://world.std.com/~rice/q-light/

Q-Light is a mailing list for discussion of topics of interest to gay, lesbian, bisexual, and transgender Quakers. This Web page for Q-Light gives an introduction to and subscription information for the list, in addition to resources such as a list of LGBT Quaker orgs.

Non-Denominational

City of Refuge Home Page
http://www.sfrefuge.org/

City of Refuge (Figure 8.11) was founded in 1991 in San Francisco by people "committed to a ministry of restoration and reconciliation." Through the gospel of Christ, the church strives to "bring relevance to a changing community which has traditionally been unresponsive to a steady Church presence." The home page gives more details on the church's history, mission and programs, including an HIV/AIDS ministry. Select sermons from Reverend Yvette Flunder are also archived.

Community Church of Hope
http://www.CommunityHope.com

Meet the staff and learn about special events at Phoenix, Arizona's Community Church of Hope, "the valley's largest gay and lesbian non-denominational Christian church."

Figure 8.11
City of Refuge Home Page

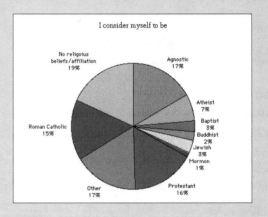
Holy Trinity Community Church
http://www.geocities.com/WestHollywood/4525/

Reverend Glenn E. Hammett welcomes visitors to the home page of his Holy Trinity Community Church, the only independent gay-oriented church between Abilene and Phoenix. And the only gay-oriented church in the Odessa/Midland, Texas area. Learn about the church's Bible study groups, substance abuse counseling, and same-sex holy unions.

Trinity River Church
http://WWW1.Minn.Net/~robina/

This Minneapolis-based nondenominational Christian church reaches out and is open to all people, regardless of race, creed, color, sexual identity or orientation.

Universal Light Ministries
http://www.ulm.ilion.ny.us/

Organized exclusively for charitable, religious, and educational purposes, and located in Ilion, N.Y., Universal Light Ministries sets out to "spread the Christian word ... save souls and enrich lives" regardless of race, gender, background, sexual orientation, or other church affiliations.

BUDDHISM

dharma-dykes
http://www.cpsc.suu.edu/users/henderso/lzg.htm

dharma-dykes is a mailing list for lesbians who study and practice Buddhism of any tradition. Subscribe to the list from this page.

Gay Buddhist Fellowship
http://www.vidaviz.com/~geewhiz/adpages/gbf/gbf.html

The Gay Buddhist Fellowship, located in San Francisco (Figure 8.13), exists to support Buddhist practice and its growing network in the gay community. This organizational site offers news of interest to GBF members and serves as a forum where gay Buddhist practitioners address spiritual concerns. Visitors will find an ongoing calendar of events, and a directory of Dharma centers in the Bay Area. Feature articles of interest are also archived.

GayZen Meditation Retreat
http://members.aol.com/zenretreat/zen/gayzen.html

"Take a weekend retreat to Satori—that enlightened Zen state ... Metamorphosis." Read about it, see it, hear the chimes on this promotional page.

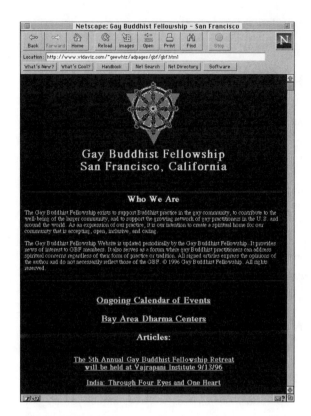

Figure 8.13
Gay Buddhist Fellowship

Introduction to Meditation
http://ourworld.compuserve.com/homepages/brenda/meditate.htm

As a large portion of her personal home page, CompuServe member "Brenda" offers instruction to meditation, which she explains is not constrained by gender, transgender, or orientation issues. "The basic good heart of friendliness is the only foundation needed," she writes, and goes on to provide a list of 21 tips for what will hopefully be "pleasurable yet fierce" daily meditation.

JUDAISM

Home Page of Sharon Silverstein
http://www.nyu.edu/pages/sls/silverst/
sshome.html

Sharon's Jewish Home Page
http://www.nyu.edu/pages/sls/jewish/
jewhome.html

Sharon Silverstein is co-author of the recent book "Straight Jobs, Gay Lives." Along with educational and personal information, her home page includes a "Jewish Interests" section, with numerous links to organizations and resources, many specifically aimed at gays, lesbians, and bisexuals.

Nice Jewish Girls Mailing List
http://www.zoom.com/personal/staci/njg.htm

Nice Jewish bisexual and lesbian girls, that is. Learn how to subscribe to the list (Figure 8.14) here, or link out to the personal home pages of a bevy of nice Jewish girls. Queer links, Jewish links, and pointers to sites dealing with women's issues are also featured.

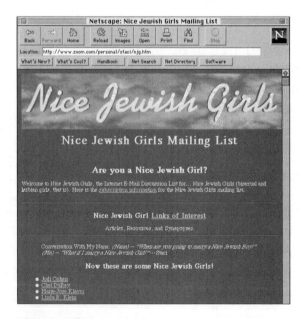

Figure 8.14
Nice Jewish Girls Mailing List

Twice Blessed—Jewish GLBT Archives
http://www.magic.ca/~faygelah/Index.html

Bursting with twice the pride of most sites, this Canadian one promises "everything gay/lesbian/bisexual/transgender and Jewish." Webmaster Johnny Abush (faygelah@astral.magic.ca) has been collecting and cataloging sites of interest to his community since 1991. The fruits of his labor are online for the world, from "some of our rabbis" to novels to a joke page.

Gay Jewish Organizations

Gayava
http://www.columbia.edu/cu/jsu/web_page/
backup/orgs/jsu/gayava.html

Gayava is the Columbia University Jewish Student Union's group for gay and lesbian Jews and their friends. Get details and contacts on this info-page.

Jewish Activist Gays and Lesbians
http://www.actwin.com/stonewall/handouts/
JAGL.html

For those "sick and tired of discrimination," the Jewish Activist Gays and Lesbians organization comprises young gay, lesbian, and bisexual Jews "who struggle against homophobia in the Jewish community and anti-Semitism in the gay world." The page includes contact information, and not much else.

Sjalhomo (Netherlands)
http://www.worldaccess.nl/~lodewykz/
#English

This is the English language page for Sjalhomo, an organization for Jewish gays and bisexuals of the Netherlands. Current News and a list of events are among the site features.

Yakhdav (Montreal)
http://www2.accent.net/yakhdav/

The Montreal-based Jewish organization Yakhdav is committed to providing gay and lesbian Jews of all affiliations with a safe and comfortable environment in which to socialize and learn about and experience Judaism.

World Congess of Gay and Lesbian Jewish Organizations

http://www.wcgljo.org/wcgljo/

Founded in 1990, the World Congress of Gay and Lesbian Jewish Organizations (Figure 8.15) now includes more than 65 member organizations. The congress conducts workshops and conferences, and represents the interests of gay and lesbian Jews around the globe. The organization's growing Web presence gives a brief history, lists member organizations, and runs down upcoming events. It also includes activism items such as a copy of a letter sent to Ezer Weizman, the president of the state of Israel, to protest against derogatory remarks he made about gays and lesbians.

Jewish Congregations

Beit Ha Chidush (Amsterdam)

http://huizen.dds.nl/~chidush/

The name means "House of Renewal," and Beit Ha Chidush strives to renew a sense of community, purpose, spirit, and joy to Jewish life in Amsterdam.

Beth El Binah (Dallas)

http://oaklawn.global.org/beth.el.binah/

Beth El Binah ("house of an understanding God") is the Reform Jewish congregation with outreach to the gay and lesbian community of the Dallas/Fort Worth area. The site includes a Shabbat service schedule, a monthly Jewish calendar, and more.

Congregation Keshet Shalom (Toronto)

http://www.magic.ca/~faygelah/
Keshet.Shalom.html

This progressive congregation is dedicated to meeting the needs of the gay and lesbian Jewish community of Greater Toronto. Congregational activities and a calendar are available on site.

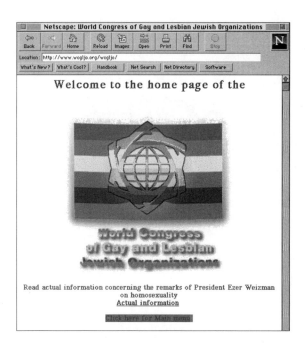

Figure 8.15
World Congress of Gay and Lesbian Jewish Organizations

Congregation Or Chadash (Chicago)

http://www.shalom.com/coc.htm

Congregation or Chadash is Chicago's synagogue serving gay and lesbian Jews, and their families and friends. Sabbath service times and details on events and education are available.

Etz Chaim (South Florida)

http://members.gnn.com/etzchaim/index.htm

Established as a gay and lesbian synagogue in 1974, Congregation Etz Chaim (Figure 8.16) provides religious, social and educational programming for the South Florida gay and lesbian Jewish community. Information on its programs, services, social events, and rabbi are available on the home page.

Havurah Shalom l'Chem (San Antonio)

http://www.shalom.com/havurah.htm

Havurah Shalom l'Chem extends a Texas-sized "Hello y'all" to gay, lesbian, and bisexual Jews in San Antonio.

Figure 8.16
Etz Chaim (South Florida)

Congregation Bet Haverim (Atlanta)
http://www.mindspring.com/~cbh/

Congregation Bet Haverim ("the house of friends") is a Reconstructionist Synagogue serving the lesbian and gay community of Atlanta. The Web site provides details on worship and liturgy, the rabbi, committees and activities, and on the Reconstructionist Movement.

Congregation Bet Mishpachah (Washington, D.C.)
http://www.betmishpachah.org

Bet Mishpachah was founded in 1975 for gay and lesbian Jews and all others who want to participate in "an inclusive, egalitarian and mutually supportive community." Members represent a variety of Jewish backgrounds.

Out.com—Religious Concerns
http://www.out.com

For an archive of perspectives and reports on religious issues related to gays and lesbians, visit Out.com's "News" section and click on "Religious Concerns" (Figure 8.17). Articles on file range from "Transsexual Minister Allowed to Retain Ordination" to "New Christian Group Boycotts Disney Over Gay Issues."

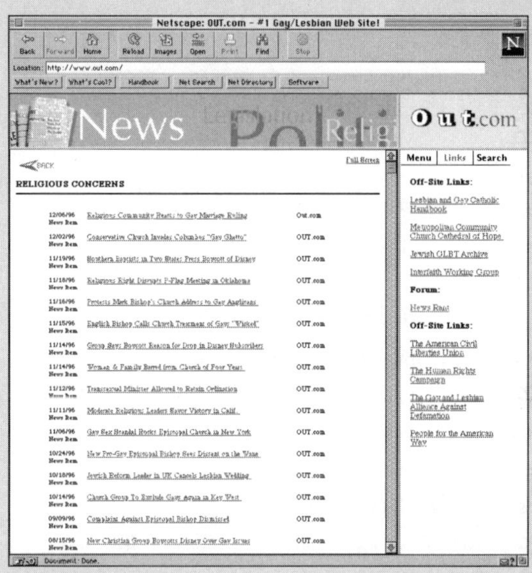

Figure 8.17
Out.com—Religious Concerns

The Lesbian and Gay Havurah (Long Beach, Calif.)
http://www.compupix.com/gay/havurah.htm

The Lesbian and Gay Havurah of the Long Beach Jewish Community Center reaches out to the community and offers a variety of programs. "Involvement opportunities" and the newsletter *Gay Spirit* are but a few of the site's offerings.

PAGANISM

The Gay Pagan Haven
http://www.goodnet.com/~mcavoy/

If your modem's less than 28.8 bps, don't go diving in to the Gay Pagan Haven for a quick fix. The graphics-heavy site is painfully slow on the download. When it's finally in front of your eyes, however, you'll be greeted with intriguing options, such as the Pagan Site of the Week, Pagan Chants and Songs, and "Pagan Web Mania."

Mariposa's Wings
http://www.tezcat.com/~mariposa/

Welcome to "a place for the gay pagan." Webmaster Dean Barthuly does a fine job of pointing to gay texts, rituals and stories, gay pagan e-mail pals, and a variety of general spiritual, magical, and occult pages.

Radical Faeries
http://www.eskimo.com/~davidk/faeries/faeries.html

Straight from the Radical Faeries FQA file (frequently questioned answers), the "fellowship is a diverse and unorganized group of gay men who center their spiritual lives around various and sundry pagan doctrines." The movement is deeply rooted in Native American spirituality, though members create pagan rituals that validate and celebrate their lives; embracing life in its entirety, "yin and yang, drag and mufti." The Web site is crawling with Faerie contacts and "hiss-tory," along with links to "sanctuaries, funny farms, and gathering venues" of interest.

Rainbow Wind Home Page
http://users.aol.com/RainboWind/rbwintr.htm

"The Constitution of the United States protects the civil and religious rights of all citizens," the Rainbow Wind page (Figure 8.18) explains. "Yet, queers and pagans have found that instead of receiving support for their right to live and worship according to their beliefs, they are under attack." The organization is a political group for U.S.-based gay, lesbian, and bisexual pagans and their friends. The goals include working with those who are interested in securing the constitutional freedoms of gays and pagans, and education of the public about paganism.

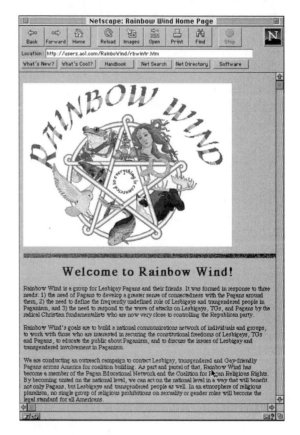

Figure 8.18
Rainbow Wind Home Page

Chapter 9

U.S. PRIDE AND ACTIVISM

While most of the sites covered in this book can be neatly filed away in a by-subject chapter, many defy the pinpoint classification; they prefer a grab bag. The terms "pride" and "activism" work well to facilitate the grab-bag feeling that this chapter attempts to achieve.

Not unlike the spread you might expect to find in a pride parade, this virtual lottery samples the United States gay community, which, as we all know, is less like a community and more like a country. It's a reflection of what's going on in the gay communities across the United States. (The next chapter takes on the rest of the world.)

Take in the pages as if you are eyeing a map. Check out the special sections on African American, Asian American, youth, student, deaf, and PFLAG organizations. And if you happen to be using the CD-ROM (definitely not a bad idea here), enjoy linking out at will. As is true with the best of the pride parades, you'll see all of the things you'd hope to see. And hopefully you'll encounter a few things you never dreamed existed.

NATIONWIDE ACTION AND INFORMATION SOURCES

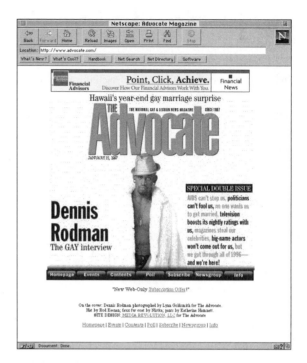

Figure 9.1
The Advocate

ACLU Gay and Lesbian Rights

http://www.aclu.org/issues/gay/hmgl.html

"At no time in our nation's history have gay men and lesbians been more visible, fighting for their rights in Congress, in the courts, in the workplaces, in the community," the American Civil Liberties Union summarizes in its impressive nod to the cause. After all, the ACLU should know as well as anybody. Anyone interested in court cases and briefing papers won't want to miss what the ACLU has done with this Gay and Lesbian Rights section within the massive ACLU site—searchable by keyword or concept.

The Advocate

http://www.advocate.com/

The popular American gay and lesbian news magazine uses the Web as a teaser for what readers will find on the newsstand. (An electronic subscription form is on hand.) You can view the cover of the current issue and read the table of contents here, but don't expect to find any in-depth features (Figure 9.1).

Community Lesbian and Gay Resource Institute

http://www.users.interport.net/~clgri/

This New York-based "community educational and development incubator" creates programs to "help meet the challenges of today and nurture dreams for a better tomorrow." The Web site contains details on such programs as the Wall Street Project (for elimination of workplace discrimination based on sexual orientation) and the Art Group (for creating venues to promote the diversity of gay expression and creativity).

Digital Queers

http://www.dq.org/dq

The legendary Digital Queers, a good-time group of queer computer professionals and technology aficionados, arrived on the scene in 1992 with a vision of equipping gay rights groups with the "silicon horsepower" necessary to organize and communicate more effectively, or digitally. Look around; obviously the DQs were on to something. The volunteer organization has performed its trademark "computer beauty makeovers" on such worthy recipients as NGLTF, GLAAD, P-FLAG, and the Lambda Legal Defense. The founders have more recently gone big time with PlanetOut, but individual city chapters (notably Digital Queers in New England and D.C.) rage on.

Digital Queers in D.C.

http://www.dc.dq.org

Digital Queers New England

http://www.actwin.com/DQ/index.html

Gay, Lesbian & Straight Teachers Network
http://www.glstn.org/freedom/

"Teaching respect for all" is top curriculum for the Gay, Lesbian & Straight Teachers Network, a coalition of parents, teachers, students, and concerned citizens working to create schools where everyone is valued. The group's impressive Web site lists directions for organizing a regional GLSTN chapter, sample letter excerpts for a school letter-writing campaign, and professional tools for educators and community leaders. The site's vast array of files includes pieces on "Understanding the experience of openly gay and lesbian educators," "Ideas for educators addressing homophobia in schools," and "Breaking the Silence: a Resource Guide for Independent Schools." It's a real learning experience.

Gay and Lesbian National Hotline
http://www.glnh.org/

The hotline (888-THE-GLNH) is a nonprofit org which provides nationwide toll-free peer counseling, information, and referrals. Callers speak directly to a trained volunteer who has access to a national database of referrals specific to the gay and lesbian community. More information, including a summary of the various services, is available online.

Gay and Lesbian Think Tank
http://www.buzznyc.com/gaythink/

"A sign of intelligent life," the Gay and Lesbian Think Tank (Figure 9.2) is a discussion group for "intelligent and discerning gay individuals" who want to explore social and political issues affecting the gay and lesbian community. Queer brainiacs can post thoughts on a given topic ("Discrimination within the Gay Community"), or pick one of their own for the "Open Discussion" board.

Genre Magazine
http://www.genremagazine.com/

Genre, the popular gay men's magazine, gets Web treatment from the folks at Southern California Gay Wired. Visitors will find a sampling of features from the current newsstand issue—perhaps just enough to make you want to go buy it—and other attractions like a circuit-party preview and classified advertising.

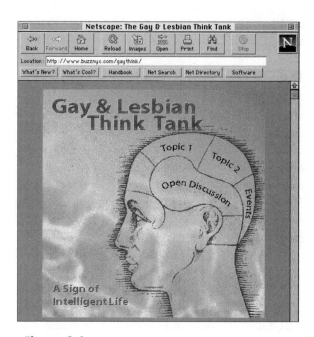

Figure 9.2
Gay and Lesbian Think Tank

GLAAD
http://www.glaad.org

GLAAD Lines
http://www.glaad.org/glaad/glaad-lines/index.html

GLAADAlert
http://www.glaad.org/glaad/alert/index.html

For dish with an activist's slant, the Gay & Lesbian Alliance Against Defamation makes a strong showing with its reports about homophobia attacks and positive portrayals of gay images in the mass media. (Chastity Bono heads up GLAAD's Entertainment Industry Relations, FYI.) More than just the poop, GLAAD gives you tips and information about what you can do to help combat the perpetrators of homophobia, and to thank the media sources which handle gay and lesbian issues responsibly. The GLAAD Lines page will keep you informed when gay-positive billboards are defaced in Texas, or when PBS gives a gay television show a near-perfect time slot. The GLAADAlert section provides background information on gay issues in the media and allows you to send instant messages to columnists, editors, producers, and those on whom your words will have the most impact. Read about the issues, but don't just get mad. Get GLAAD.

The Guide
http://www.guidemag.com/

The Guide magazine claims a readership of "tens of thousands of gay men" and it offers some of its offline content online. The publication is notable for its gay travel writing and gay-destination maps, but it also runs articles on sex, culture, and politics (with the emphasis being on sex). The Web site is fully searchable.

Human Rights Campaign
http://www.hrcusa.org/

The Washington, D.C.-based Human Rights Campaign (Figure 9.3) is the nation's largest lesbian and gay political org. With a national staff and volunteers across the U.S., it lobbies the federal government on gay, lesbian, and AIDS issues; educates the general public; participates in election campaigns; and provides expertise and training at the state and local levels. In short, the campaign "envisions an America where lesbian and gay people are ensured of their basic equal rights—and can be open, honest and safe at home, at work, at work, and in the community." With its exemplary, action-oriented Web

Figure 9.3
Human Rights Campaign

presence, visitors get to help make the vision a reality. As it concisely outlines and explains the major issues affecting our community (HIV/AIDS, workplace issues, marriage, lesbian health), the HRC site includes pointers for those who want to get active; from sending e-mail messages to Congress, to contacting the organizers of an HRC event in your area.

Log Cabin Republicans
http://www.lcr.org

Honest Abe greets visitors to the conservatively designed home page of the Log Cabin Republicans. Learn the history of the nearly 20-year-old organization for gay conservatives, locate a local chapter, and become a member online.

National Gay and Lesbian Task Force
http://www.ngltf.org/ngltf

This front-line activist organization in the U.S. gay and lesbian rights movement serves as a resource center (in Washington, D.C.) for grassroots gay, lesbian, bisexual, and transgender organizations facing battles at the state and local levels (Figure 9.4). Its home on the Web sports a striking design, and allows the Force to transmit breaking news and press releases (the press releases are traceable by search). A publications section was still in development at press time, but was shaping up to be an impressive online library of NGLTF research and studies publications dealing with issues such as violence, health, the workplace, and the media.

People for the American Way Equal Rights Page
http://www.pfaw.org/equalrt.htm

If you're ready to "stand up to the Religious Right's Political agenda of division and fearmongering ... willing to stand up for fundamental American values like opportunity, equal justice under the law, and individual liberty" then People for the American Way requests your assistance in its mission to build a national community that offers opportunity, respect, and hope to all. The PFAW Web site provides details on lawsuits and legal action in which the organization is involved, as well as a meticulous section all about the Religious Right (in case you need to

Figure 9.4
National Gay and Lesbian Task Force

know more). There's even a section for responding to the Right-Wing via "American Way Action Line." That means, for $5 a month, the action line will monitor the issues you care about and will contact you (by e-mail, fax, phone, or beeper) to let you know when your voice will make the most difference.

Queer CyberCenter
http://www.qcc.org/

The Queer CyberCenter started as a University of Southern California research project (to study the "Definition of Community in the Digital Age") in conjunction with the Los Angeles Gay and Lesbian Community Services Center. The funding ended in December 1996, but the Los Angeles Center decided to continue operating the service, allocating the operational and staffing funds to keep the "community" alive. Registration is required (it's free), and members get in on chat, opinion surveys, e-mail service, and more.

QueerNet
http://queernet.org/

San Francisco's QueerNet provides dozens of unique mailing lists for the gay, lesbian, bisexual, and transgendered communities. Find the list of lists here (including titles like cyberdykes, boychicks, queerarabs, and handball-digest), and learn how to subscribe.

Stonewall 25
http://www.mps.org/~rainbow/Images/s25/

Missed the March? Never fear, memories of the legendary Stonewall 25 celebration and Gay Games IV are alive and in color online. Find photographs, logos, and background information here.

AVENGERS, COLLECTORS, GIRLJOCKS: THE LESBIAN HOT SPOTS

Amazon Online
http://www.amazon.org/amzonline/amzonl.shtml

This "little hideaway on the information superhighway" houses info and pointers of interest to lesbian and bisexual women; particularly those in the San Francisco Bay Area, where the site is produced. "Things to Do in SF," "Politics and Activism," and "Guilty Pleasures" are among the sections.

Astraea Foundation
http://www.imageinc.com/astraea/

This multi-racial, multi-class feminist group, "the first lesbian foundation" (Figure 9.5), has been in development for nearly two decades. Based in New York City, the national group intends to build "not just a house, but a whole community with institutions" that represents and serve its diverse needs. Find out how to become a part of the action by calling up the foundation's informative Web site.

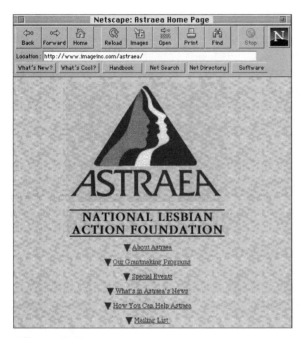

Figure 9.5
Astraea Foundation

Bay Area CyberDykes
http://www.best.com/~agoodloe/lists/
bacd.html

If you're a Bay Area Lesbian with a modem, this organization wants you—for friendly online discussions and "lots of fun events offline." Get the info here, and get on the list.

Echo Lesbians Page
http://www.echonyc.com/~lesbians

New York's online hipster community, Echo, gives visitors the opportunity to "construct an archive" by participating in a collective cyberspace biography ("memory is corruptible," you know). The kind-of-abstract interactive experience has you click on the letters in the word "lesbian" (l is for dreams; e is for style ...) which lead you to feedback forms in which you're asked to add personal information to the archives. Appropriately enough, Barbara Hammer's e-mail address is also on hand.

Girljock
http://www.tezcat.com/~ksbrooks/Gj/
Gj-front.html

It's the online sister of the paper zine whose pages are filled with articles such as "Muffin Spencer-Devlin's Emergence from the Golfing Closet," "The Joy of Cycling," and "Am I Stuck Up?: The Test." Online, its more of a promotion for paper (Figure 9.6), but the slim selection of offerings—pieces like "Nation of Jogbras" and "Farrow to Solve Nation's Orphan Problem"—make this a mandatory squat for office-chair girljocks.

The Isle of Lesbos
http://www.sappho.com/

The online "home of Sappho" is a place of art, culture and learning—and, naturally, women. Features include first rate sections on poetry, classic art, and a developing collection of quotes by, about, and of interest to lesbians.

June L. Mazer Lesbian Collection (Los Angeles)
http://www.lesbian.org/mazer/index.html

Located in Los Angeles, the Mazer Collection gathers and preserves materials by and about lesbians of all classes, ethnicities, races and experiences. It has been doing

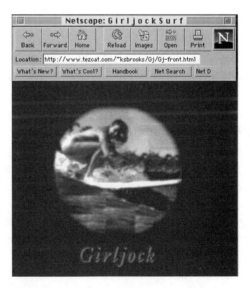

Figure 9.6
Girljock

so since 1981. "Imagine yourself in a room surrounded by almost a century of lesbian artwork, manuscripts, books, records ...."

Lesbian Avengers Chicago
http://www.lesbian.org/chicago-avengers/index.html

Lesbian Avengers of San Francisco
http://www-dept.cs.ucl.ac.uk/students/S.Stumpf/LA.html

The direct action group with a killer name comprises lesbian, bisexual, and transgendered women focused on issues vital to survival and visibility. The San Francisco chapter site features sections on coalition building and Avenger actions from 1993 to '95. The Chicago site throws "The Lesbian Avengers Handbook" into the mix.

Lesbian Herstory Archives
http://www.intac.com/~kgs/lha/

The Lesbian Herstory Archives originally opened in a New York City apartment pantry in 1974, a response to the failure of mainstream publishers, libraries, and archives to collect and value lesbian culture. Information on arranging a visit and making a donation accompany an on-line sampling of resources from the permanent collection.

Lesbian History Project
http://www-lib.usc.edu/~retter/archives.html/

This text page lists and, whenever possible, links to archives and oral history collections which contain lesbian

materials; from the Gerber/Hart Library in Chicago to the Shango Project, the national archives for black lesbians and gay men, in Bloomington, IN.

Lesbian Organizations
http://www.lesbian.org/

Amy Goodloe started collecting lesbian links in early 1995. By mid-year, she decided to devote an entire site to promoting lesbian visibility on the Net. The result is Lesbian.org, a well-organized and user-friendly collection—allegedly the oldest and largest—of lesbian-specific information on the Net. Thanks, Amy.

National Lesbian Political Action Committee
http://www.lesbian.org/nlpac/index.html

This non-partisan, non-connected political action committee gives money to candidates, male or female, who meet its criteria and have actively supported lesbian issues.

STATE OF THE STATES

Alabama

Gay and Lesbian Alliance of Alabama
http://members.aol.com/GALAA1/index.html
Working to end discrimination against gays and lesbians in Alabama, GALAA extends a page of links to invaluable resources, most of which are national organizations. Local contact information and details on becoming a member are included.

Alaska

Southeast Alaska Gay and Lesbian Alliance
http://www.ptialaska.net/~seagla/
This nonprofit organization provides a support network for gays, lesbians, and bisexuals in Southeast Alaska. Its Web site includes sections on politics and activism, local resources, events, and membership.

Arizona

Arizona's Pride Site
http://www.azpridesite.com/

Arizona's gay and lesbian online resource directory contains links for news, business, health, and fun.

Valley of the Sun Gay and Lesbian Community Center (Phoenix)
http://www.swlink.net/~vsglcc/

The Web site for the Phoenix-based Valley of the Sun Gay and Lesbian Community Center provides information on current and upcoming events, youth programs, and more.

Women's Central News of Arizona
http://www.swlink.net/~wcnews/

This "daughter organization" of the Women's Center, Inc., endorses aspects of women connecting with women by announcing community events, and health, political, religious resources, and more.

California

Asian/Pacific Crossroads (Orange County)
http://members.aol.com/APXRDS/frapc.html

The social activities of this Orange County-based organization for gay Asians and friends attracts people from the San Fernando Valley to San Diego. On site, check out the organization's Gay Asian Pages, the Web clearing house for information relating to the gay Asian experience in L.A. and Orange County.

Billy DeFrank Lesbian and Gay Community Center (San Jose)
http://www.rahul.net/rhollis/bdf/

The Billy DeFrank Center is a 10,000 square-foot facility, one of the largest in the U.S. It serves "the diverse and unique needs" of the South Bay community. The Center's Web site gives details on programs and meetings, and information on gay and lesbian events happening within the community.

Community United Against Violence (San Francisco)
http://www.xq.com/cuav/index.html

This long-standing San Francisco-based nonprofit agency addresses and prevents hate violence directed at gays, lesbians, bisexuals, and transgendered people. Among its services: crisis intervention, short-term counseling, advocacy with the criminal justice system, support groups, and a 24-hour crisis line.

GayLA
http://www.GayLA.net/

With business listings for health & fitness, hotels & travel, and food & drink, this site is totally L.A. and totally gay. Special features include a map of West Hollywood and "Starwalk," your guide to the Hollywood stars.

Gay Los Angeles Guide
http://www.gayla.com/

Consider it a "safe and discreet way" to learn about the myriad gay-friendly businesses in the City of Angels. Free personal-ad placement and live chat, too.

The Lavender Pages (San Francisco)
http://www.lavenderpages.com/

Updated and printed twice yearly, the Lavender Pages is a comprehensive business and professional directory by and for the San Francisco Bay Area gay, lesbian, and bisexual community. Order a copy of the printed version, search the Lavender Pages database for resources in other cities, or link out to an "absolutely fabulous" Bay Area guide to fine dining, love and laughs, accommodations, and more.

Long Beach Gay and Lesbian Community Center
http://millenia.com/~center

The Center Post
http://millenia.com/~center/post.htm

Information on the Center's many counseling and support services (including HIV services and a youth program) is featured along with a nightlife bar guide and an online version of "The Center Post," a monthly paper for the gay and lesbian community of Long Beach.

Long Beach Lesbian and Gay Pride, Inc.

http://members.aol.com/lblgpinc/home.html

Get the facts on the annual Long Beach pride celebration in May.

OutNOW! Alive

http://www.outnow.com/

"The Internet's gay newspaper since 1994," OutNOW! Alive is the electronic extension of the biweekly San Jose paper, OutNOW!. Editorial coverage includes national and international reports, in addition to news and views from Silicon Valley and the Bay Area.

Pacific Center for Human Growth (Berkeley)

http://www.ccnet.com/~nikki/pac_cntr.htm

Peers and professionals from the Bay Area gay community offer information, speakers, support groups, counseling, and HIV advocacy from the Pacific Center for Human Growth. The center's Web site provides full information about the various services.

Q San Francisco

http://www.qsanfrancisco.com/

Get the latest on restaurants, bars, and Bay Area happenings with Q San Francisco, which also extends coverage to New York City and "London's Hottest Clubs."

San Diego Career Women

http://www.sdcw.org/

The social and business group of—you guessed it—promotes professional networking, educational, recreational, social, and cultural events for all gay women. The goal: "to provide a safe and confidential environment for quality opportunities within the community." Find out about the group's monthly dance mixers, or learn how to join one of its special interest groups (Coffee House, Golden Girls, Traveling Dinner Club).

Santa Cruz Lesbian, Gay, Bisexual and Transgendered Community Center

http://www.scruz.net/~fez/sclgbtcc/

This volunteer-driven org for the Santa Cruz community exists to "educate, enlighten, inform, instigate, and facili-

tate a better understanding for ourselves and our allies" of what it means to be gay, lesbian, bisexual, or transgendered. Operational information, a map, and details on Pure Pride, a social group from queers under 25, are available on site.

Southern California Gay Wired

http://www.gaywired.com/

"For all your entertainment needs" this top-notch SoCal online service (Figure 9.7) contains news features, arts and entertainment listings, and suggestions for sports and recreation, among its many attractions. The fully searchable site is also the home of *Genre* magazine's electronic version.

Spectrum (San Anselmo)

http://www.fish.com/~lizd/spectrum/

Spectrum is Marin County's center for gay, lesbian, and bisexual concerns. Its various programs and activities serve nearly 5,000 people each year. Newsletter excerpts and details on activities at the center are included on the Web site.

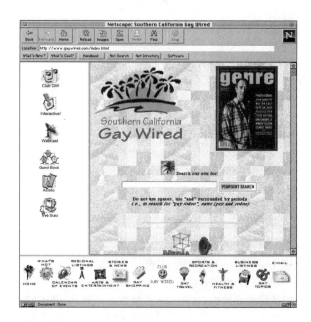

Figure 9.7
Southern California Gay Wired

WebCastro (San Francisco)
http://www.webcastro.com/

WebCastro (Figure 9.8) is an online magazine and "virtual community" highlighting the businesses and people of San Francisco's very gay Castro district. Hosts Ron and Dwight take visitors on a personalized clicking tour of the Castro's history and present state.

Connecticut

Out in Connecticut
http://www.outinct.com/

Groups and organizations, bars and restaurants, and special events make up this gay and lesbian guide to Connecticut, New England, and beyond.

Triangle Community Center (Norwalk)
http://members.aol.com/TCCenter/index.html

The Triangle Community Center serves the gay, lesbian, bisexual, and transgendered community of Southwestern

Connecticut. Visitors will find a center calendar and the monthly newsletter.

Florida

Gay Guide to Florida
http://gay-guide.com/

Florida's "ultimate Web site" for the gay and lesbian community (Figure 9.9) is loaded with information on things to do when in the sunny state. It also lists (and, whenever possible, links to) Florida businesses and services, from hotels and cafes to shops and synagogues. The database is fully searchable.

The Gay and Lesbian Community of Greater Ft. Lauderdale
http://www.terastar.com/glcc/

A community calendar, details on events and meetings, and information on becoming a volunteer are just a few of the online offerings of the Gay and Lesbian Community Center of Greater Ft. Lauderdale, which provides a "safe and nurturing environment" for individuals, groups, and organizations.

Figure 9.9
Gay Guide to Florida

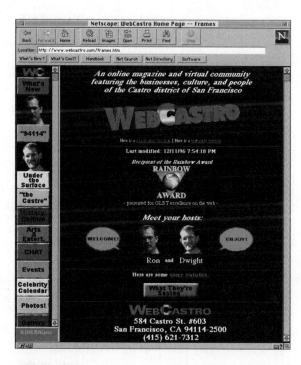

Figure 9.8
WebCastro (San Francisco)

Gay and Lesbian Community Services of Central Florida (Orlando)
http://www.flamingopark.com/glcs/

Gay and Lesbian Community Services of Central Florida provides peer counseling and promotes social interaction between gays and lesbians in Orlando. It leads such programs as the Delta Youth Alliance, and publishes *The Triangle*, a gay and lesbian newspaper. The group also has perhaps the easiest access to gay day at Disney World.

The Key West Business Guild
http://www.gaykeywestfl.com/kwbgpage.html

Since 1978, the Key West Business Guild has been promoting Florida's little jewel to domestic and international gay markets. Today, the guild is 400 members strong, and, obviously, doing a bang-up job.

Stonewall Library & Archives (Ft. Lauderdale)
http://members.gnn.com/StoneLib/index.htm

This nonprofit group is dedicated to providing a library and archive of literary, scientific, and historical materials

ASIAN AMERICAN RESOURCES

Asian/Pacific Crossroads (Orange County, Calif.)
http://members.aol.com/APXRDS/frapc.html

The social activities of this Orange County-based organization for gay Asians and friends attracts people from the San Fernando Valley to San Diego. On site, check out the organization's Gay Asian Pages, the Web clearing house for information relating to the gay Asian experience in L.A. and Orange County, along with pages for a variety of other gay Asian organizations.

The Boston Queer Asian Pacific Alliance
http://www.tufts.edu/~stai/QAPA/qapa.html

Queer Asian Pacific Resources
http://www.tufts.edu/~stai/QAPA/resources.html

Asian/Pacific Gay, Bi, Lesbian Groups in the United States
http://www.tufts.edu/~stai/QAPA/Groups/usa.html

The Boston Queer Asian Pacific Alliance is committed to providing a supportive social, political, and educational environment for gay, lesbian, bisexual, and questioning Asian and Pacific Islander Americans. The group's Web site reaches far outside the Boston area, though. In addition to info on the group's e-mail lists, it offers an extensive collection of pointers to other topical online resources and groups, broken down by state and hyperlinked to contacts when possible.

The Florasian—Asians and Friends of Florida
http://ally.ios.com/~jnp19/

Unlike many of the other U.S. chapters of Asians and Friends, the Ft. Lauderdale-based Florasian specifically promotes friendship and understanding among Asian and non-Asian gay people. It does so through social, cultural, and educational activities. Details are available on the Web site.

Gay Asian Pacific Alliance
http://www.slip.net/~gapa/

Based in San Francisco, the Gay Asian Pacific Alliance (Figure 9.10) serves the interests of gay and bisexual Asian/Pacific Islanders by creating awareness, developing a positive collective identity and by establishing a supportive community. Find out about GAPA's many services and events online, and read the current *Lavender Godzilla Newsletter*.

for and about the gay and lesbian community. Located on the second floor of the Ft. Lauderdale Metropolitan Community Church, it currently has the largest such collection in the South. Its Web site incorporates book reviews, a column by Shelly Roberts, and gay literary links.

Georgia

Atlanta Pride Committee
http://www.atlantapride.org/

The Atlanta Pride Festival attracts more than 300,00 participants each June. It's the largest of its kind in the southeast, and one of the largest in the country. The Web site

contains updates, details on the annual logo competition, volunteer info, and more.

Gay Atlanta
http://www.gayatlanta.org/

Your guide to nightlife, the arts, sports, and everything else that's gay in Atlanta (Figure 9.11).

Greater Atlanta Business Coalition
http://www.gaypride.com/gabc/

The Greater Atlanta Business Coalition is a nonprofit org dedicated to the development and growth of businesses

Figure 9.10
Gay Asian Pacific Alliance

Gay Asian Pacifically Islander Men of New York
http://207.10.38.2/~gapimny/

Based in New York City, this group provides a safe and supportive social, political, and educational forum

for gay, bisexual, transgendered, and questioning men. Read the newsletter online, and don't forget to check out the "totally useless link of the month."

Malaysian Gay and Lesbian Club
http://www.best.com/~aloha/mglc/

This "non-political, participatory, voluntary and social support club" for gay, lesbian, bisexual, and transgendered Malaysians living in the United States provides social and cultural support. It's headquartered in San Francisco, though membership includes people from around the world. The Web site includes an events calendar, a resource guide, and a photo album.

VN-GBLF
http://www.viet.net/Gallery/vietgal/vn-gblf/

VN-GBLF is a mailing list for Vietnamese Gays, Bisexuals, Lesbians, and Friends, providing information to promote better understanding and compassion for the experience of Viet GBLFs, mainly those in the U.S. The Web page offers subscription information and pointers to resources ranging from safe sex to the Boston Gay and Lesbian Film Festival.

Figure 9.11
Gay Atlanta

that support the gay and lesbian community. Specific purposes include education and training to empower gays and lesbians to start and expand their own businesses. Get information here on GABC officers, members, and news.

Hotlanta River Expo (Atlanta)
http://www.mindspring.com/~hotlanta/

The "granddaddy of circuit parties," Hotlanta River Expo is a four-day celebration held each August in Atlanta, featuring music, dance, theater, and physique events (not to mention a river raft race) for gays and lesbians. The promotional site features an online registration form.

Hawaii

GayHawaii.com
http://gayhawaii.com/

GayHawaii.com covers travel, entertainment, and community information. The site includes a "pocket guide to Hawaii online."

Out in Maui: Both Sides Now
http://maui.net/~pattie/glom.html

Find out what's happening in Maui's large gay community by way of this nonprofit org composed of Maui gays, lesbians, and bisexuals. Besides the Web site (Figure 9.12), the group supports a 24-hour recorded hotline.

Illinois

Chicago Area Gay and Lesbian Chamber of Commerce
http://www.glchamber.org/

Chicago's gay and lesbian business community shows that it has its act together with its own private Chamber of

Figure 9.12
Out in Maui: Both Sides Now

Commerce. The Chamber strengthens the gay business community and the city alike through networking, promotions, marketing, and tourist attractions. The group's Web site provides membership information and a directory of supportive area businesses.

Gerber/Hart Library
http://www.gerberhart.org/

The Gerber/Hart Library (Figure 9.13) was founded in Chicago in 1981 and is now "the Midwest's leading lesbian and gay archive." In addition to the library, it also offers cultural and educational programs "aimed at the goal of dispelling homophobia through knowledge." Get information on the actual library, and check out the virtual research collections on the Web site.

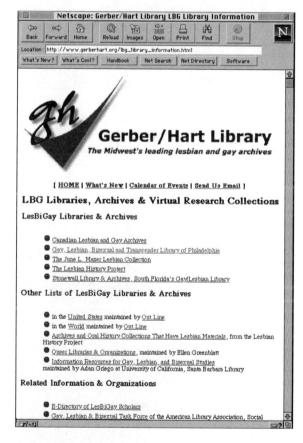

Figure 9.13
Gerber/Hart Library

Lesbian Chicago
http://pinky.interaccess.com/maggy/chicago/

The purpose of Lesbian Chicago is—you guessed it—to bring together Chicago lesbians and provide a one-stop link and information resource to all things lesbian in Chicago and its suburbs. Social and political groups, hangouts, Chicago lesbians on the Web ... they're all waiting online.

OutChicago
http://www.outchicago.org/

Developed and maintained by the Chicagoland LesBiGay Electronic Resources Consortium, OutChicago is a "collaborative, community-based effort to comprehensively index the expanding number of queer Internet sites" in the Chicago area. Visitors will find listings for community organizations, nightlife and entertainment, businesses, community calendars, and more.

Out! Resource Guide
http://www.suba.com/~outlines/adverts.html

Whether it's florists, futons, or financial services you seek in the Windy City, let Out! Resources be your guide to gay supportive businesses, professionals, and organizations. It's a service of Outlines, the online voice of the gay and lesbian community in Chicago.

Indiana

Gay and Lesbian Indianapolis
http://www.gayindy.org/

Get all the details here on supportive local businesses, bars and restaurants, youth groups, and general gay Indy pride.

Indy Pride Home Page
http://home.earthlink.net/~jeffreyalan/indy96/

It's all about Pride in Indianapolis. Call up the official site for information on events, Pride passports, and sponsors for the annual fall celebration.

Justice, Inc.
http://www.intersource.com/~dmcneely/
justice.html

Justice, Inc. fosters the consolidation of the many diverse gay and lesbian organizations throughout Indiana. It's also committed to political action and public awareness on gay and lesbian issues. The site contains action alerts, a membership form, and a phone number for up-to-the-minute information on upcoming events and issues.

Louisiana

Gay New Orleans
http://www.gayneworleans.com/

Gay Mardi Gras
http://www.gaymardigras.com/

Southern Decadence
http://www.southerndecadence.com/

New Orleans Does Becky Allen
http://www.gayneworleans.com/becky/

The Gay New Orleans goal is to use cutting-edge technology and international resources to bring you the definitive source of every detail available in gay and lesbian New Orleans, "the City that Care Forgot." No small undertaking, that; but tour guides Rip and Marsha Naquin-Delain do a bang-up job with this electronic extension of the paper publication *AMbush Mag 2000*, which authoritatively covers gay and lesbian entertainment throughout Louisiana. Bars, travel and lodging, restaurants, and more bars make up this festive online party, which also connects to special features on such standards as Southern Decadence and Gay Mardi Gras. For a guided tour of the gay Big Easy, "just click on Miss Becky Allen" (Figure 9.14). You'll be in good hands, because Allen was not only born there, but also works there as a "female, female impersonator" (she's really a girl). Why a gay tour, Becky? "Because that's where the action is." Drop in on hot spots like Petunias, a restaurant famous for the world's biggest crepes, and & ToTo, Too, the pet shop with the biggest snake in town.

Figure 9.14
New Orleans Does Becky Allen

Lesbian and Gay Community Center of New Orleans
http://www.gayneworleans.com/acc.html

The Center facilitates and assists in providing counseling, and cultural and social services to the greater New Orleans gay, lesbian, bisexual, and transgender community. The Web page is simply a page of facts.

Maryland

The Gay and Lesbian Interests Consortium of Montgomery County
http://www.his.com/~glic/

The Consortium educates Montgomery County citizens about the issues and concerns of the county's lesbian, gay, bisexual, and transgender citizens. It also promotes cultural activities within the community. Contact information and links to local resources are available on the site.

Massachusetts

Alliance for Gays, Lesbians and Supporters (AGLAS)
http://home.aol.com/AGLAS

The home page for AGLAS provides information on the social and support group, including when it meets and where.

BGL Advertising (Gay Boston)
http://www.bgladco.com/

Blowing in to Boston and need a limousine? A place to stay? A hair salon? BGL Advertising's guide to gay Boston businesses and services seems to be the place to start.

The Pink Web (Boston)
http://www.pinkweb.com/

Surrender to the Pink, a regularly updated guide to gay- and lesbian-owned and gay-friendly businesses in the Boston area. The site includes a travel section to assist you in vacation travel, free online referrals to any place in the world, and thousands of business listings.

Michigan

Affirmations Lesbian/Gay Community Center (Detroit)
http://www.webspace.com/pub/tcc/affirmations/

Detroit's gay and lesbian community center, which is actually located in Ferndale, serves the community with a helpline, youth and mentor programs, an art gallery, and a variety of other social and support services.

Triangle Foundation (Detroit)
http://tri.org/

Detroit's Triangle Foundation strives to promote equality and secure freedom from violence, intimidation, and discrimination for gays and lesbians throughout Michigan. The organization's home page attempts to bring the community together with current Triangle news and other topical information on the Web.

Random | Posting

```
Subject: Provincetown - July 4th
Weekend
I am bored in Boston! Looking for other
guys who may want to round up a group
and go over to Provincetown this
weekend (I don't have car).
I am from CA so the beach is my second
home, although never been to P-town
(heard it's absolutely FABulous!)
Was going to go to D.C. but plans were
changed last minute.
Am willing to leave as late as Friday
afternoon. Anyone interested, please
let me know by Fri. @ 3:00...... Let's
go!
Wed Jul 3 16:30:09 EDT 1996 - ()
```

New JerseyJersey Pride
http://members.aol.com/jrsypride

The producer of New Jersey's Gay, Lesbian, Bisexual, and Transgendered Pride parades and National Coming Out Day festivals provides details on upcoming events, highlights from past events, and info on how to get involved.

The Rainbow Place (Woodbury)
http://www.quantumleap.com/homepgs/rainbow.htm

The Rainbow Place, located in Woodbury, is the gay and lesbian community center for Southern New Jersey. The group provides meeting space and information services for a broad range of interests. "If you want to connect with sports clubs, professional networks, reading groups, senior adult groups or youth activities, you'll find it at Rainbow Place." An events calendar and information for joining a committee are provided on site.

New York

Empire State Pride Agenda
http://www.espany.org/

New York's statewide gay and lesbian political organization moves its agenda in four ways: lobbying the state legislature and governor; electing supportive candidates to office through financial and campaign assistance; organizing gay constituent pressure at the local level; and educating the public about gays and lesbians. Check out the organization's Web site for a calendar, and board membership and volunteer information on the "political voice of over 1,000,000 gay and lesbian New Yorkers."

Gay.Guide New York
http://www.gayguidenewyork.com/main.html

"*Gay.Guide New York* is not an online magazine and will not become one," asserts the editor of this useful site. Rather, it's an information source regarding products, service providers, and entertainment options relevant to the big, gay apple. Beyond the hot links and classifieds, the Gay.Guide also throws out some pointed star-rating

AFRICAN AMERICAN RESOURCES

Black Homie Pages
http://www.blk.com/BLK/blkhome.htm

BLK Family of Publications
http://www.blk.com/BLK/blkmag.htm

BLK, "the world's most honored black lesbian and gay publishing company," developed the Black Homie Pages (Figure 9.15) to provide news and information about the black gay and lesbian community and to list information about activities related to its publications. Feature articles, classifieds, and a "worldwide directory of fun places" are all in the mix. For descriptions of the various BLK magazines—titles include "Black Lace" (lesbian erotica); "Kuumba" (poetry); and "B-MAX" (free bar rag featuring pictures of "hot black men").— Check out the BLK Family of Publications page.

The Blacklist
http://www.udel.edu/nero/lists/
blacklist.html

This site has the distinction of being, perhaps, the only blacklist on which being included is a good thing. The list of gay, lesbian, bisexual, and transgendered people includes names, biographical information, and often related hyperlinks.

The BlackStripe
http://qrd.tcp.com/qrd/www/culture/black/

"The rainbow's black stripe," this site represents the cooperative efforts of gays, lesbians, bisexuals, and

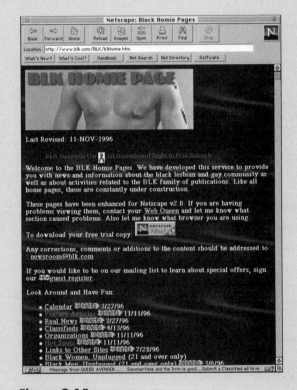

Figure 9.15
BLK Family of Publications

transgendered people of African Descent. "We are claimed by two communities—the black community and the gay community," the site explains. "Neither community fully accepts, appreciates, or understands us." BlackStripe's various online resource segments—

reviews on places like Barney's ("the only cool department store in the city") and The Gap ("every other block").

Lambda Independent Democrats of Brooklyn
http://www.nycnet.com/lid/

Founded by a group of activists in Boerum Hill in 1978, L.I.D. is Brooklyn's oldest and largest gay and lesbian organization—and one of the largest in the state of New York.

New York City Gay and Lesbian Anti-Violence Project
http://www.avp.org/

The Anti-Violence Project serves gay crime victims through counseling, advocacy, and referrals. It also works to change public attitudes "that tolerate, insulate, or instigate hate-motivated crime," and to reform government policy and practices affecting survivors of gay crime. Brochures, community alerts, and volunteer information are available on site.

including articles, books, discussion, and notable people—invite guests to explore, experience, and learn.

Da BrothaHood 2000
http://www.wam.umd.edu/~street/

Da Brotha, a.k.a. Michael Everett Street, Jr., is a poet, a music fan, and an intense admirer of Janet Jackson. The sections on his Web creation for black gays and lesbians reflect these interests as they entertain and inform.

Out in Black
http://www4.ncsu.edu/eos/users/j/jdhardy/public/OIB.html

This bi-monthly publication is published to provide the community with news and information related to black issues. The goal: "to educate and motivate the African American community and to bridge gaps in understanding." It does so with public service announcements and feature stories like "Black on Black Crime" and "Toys for Poor and Sick Kids." Readers are encouraged to submit writing and art for publication.

SBC Online
http://www.sbc-online.com/

"For the Africentric homosexual you," *SBC* magazine brings some of its contents to the Web (Figure 9.16). Fashion features, music reviews, and *SBC*'s men of choice are among the online offerings of the popular monthly magazine for men.

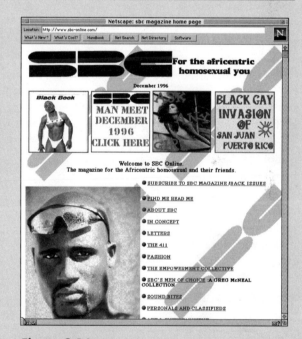

Figure 9.16
SBC Online

New York City Lesbian and Gay Community Services Center

http://www.gaycenter.org/

Located in the heart of Greenwich Village, the New York City Lesbian and Gay Community Services Center (Figure 9.17) has been serving its population since 1983. Center history, meeting schedules, and employment opportunities are just a few of the features of this extensive site.

New York CyberQueers

http://www.nycq.org/

Much like Digital Queers, New York CyberQueers come from computer and technology fields and are concerned about queer community issues. Among its many purposes, the organization helps community organizations get the most out of technology, and makes technology-oriented companies aware of the contributions of their queer employees. Learn more about the organization, download newsletters, or find out how to become a member online.

Figure 9.17
New York City Lesbian and Gay Community Services Center

Oregon

Pride NorthWest

http://pridenw.vservers.com/pridenw.htm

With individual sections for Oregon, Seattle, and Vancouver, Pride NorthWest covers the essential area gay and lesbian restaurants, bars, and shops.

Pennsylvania

Erie Gay Community News

http://www.ncinter.net/~egcn/

Erie's gay community has a concise "community news" guide which covers entertainment, local events and resources, and news reports from Erie and the rest of the country.

Gay, Lesbian, Bisexual & Transgendered Library/Archives of Philadelphia

http://wanda.pond.com/~stevecap/la000001.htm

Philadelphia's gay and lesbian library and research center was established in 1975. Today it serves as an excellent source of research information and reading on topics of interest to the gay community. Read about the archival collections, the library's speakers bureau, and more at the Web site.

Philadelphia Gay News

http://epgn.com/

The Philadelphia Gay News (Figure 9.18) covers the national and local scenes, and the arts online, "with 20 years of honesty, integrity, [and] professionalism" as a backbone.

Texas

The Austin Gay-Friendly Directory

http://www.webcom.com/austin/welcome.html

Central Texas's only comprehensive guide for gay and lesbian consumers. Browse the massive services and retail index. Other features include a detailed list of orga-

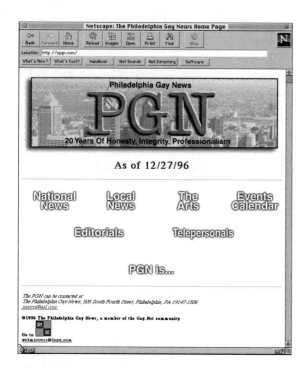

Figure 9.18
Philadelphia Gay News

nizations, bar and club listings, and an entertainment section. Makes you want to get lost in Austin.

Dallas Gay and Lesbian Community Center
http://web.fhu.org/fhu/glcc.htm

The Dallas Gay and Lesbian Community Center provides information on its wide range of education programs, publications, and social events.

Dallas-Fort Worth Lambda Pages
http://www.lambdapages.com/lambdapages/home.html

Gay Yellow Pages-type business directory for the Dallas-Fort Worth area lists its advertisers by category and provides a nice breakdown of the city's bars and some gay-friendly restaurants.

Gay and Lesbian Alliance of Central Texas
http://www.creative.net/~thepark/shelters/GLACT.html

The Gay and Lesbian Alliance of Central Texas was formed in 1993 when "several members of the hetero-sexual community met with several gays and lesbians ... and decided that gays and lesbians needed a social forum to air relevant issues." Within a year, GLACT helped bring the Quilt to Waco, and became the driving force for Gay Pride Week in Central Texas.

Gay and Lesbian Community Center of San Antonio
http://home.earthlink.net/~trottski/

Gay, lesbian, bisexual, and transgendered people in South Central Texas have a home at the Gay and Lesbian Community Center of San Antonio. This Web site outlines the center's mission, philosophy, and programs.

Utah

Utah Stonewall Center (Salt Lake City)
http://www.saff.utah.edu/bennion/stonewal/swchome.html

The Utah Stonewall Center in Salt Lake City is a supportive environment and regional information source on gay community resources, culture, and history. Details on programs, activities, and the facility library are covered on the center's Web site.

Washington

Gay and Lesbian Social Services in Seattle
http://www.pan.ci.seattle.wa.us/seattle/owr/gaylesbs.htm

This text list provides contact information and brief descriptions (no links, however) for local support groups, programs, and organizations.

Pride NorthWest

http://pridenw.vservers.com/pridenw.htm

With individual sections for Oregon, Seattle, and Vancouver, Pride NorthWest covers the essential area gay and lesbian restaurants, bars, and shops.

Safe Schools Anti-Violence Documentation Project

http://members.tripod.com/~claytoly/ssp_home

The Safe Schools project is a public-private partnership of 35 agencies and several individuals who strive to make Washington State schools safe places "where every family can belong, where every educator can teach, and where every child can learn, regardless of gender identity or sexual orientation." The organization's Web site contains several reports and strategies.

Seattle Gay News Online

http://electra.cortland.com:80/sgn/

Seattle Gay News (Figure 9.19) claims to be the nation's third oldest gay publication. Its online version is short on frills and long on excellent coverage of local and national gay news and entertainment. Back issues—both hypertext and plain text—are archived on the site.

Washington, D.C.

Gay and Lesbian Activists Alliance

http://www.glaa.org/

This all-volunteer, non-partisan, nonprofit political org works to advance the equal rights of gays and lesbians in D.C. It claims to be the nation's oldest continuously active gay civil rights organization. Current news and details on GLAA projects are included on the home page.

GayDC

http://www.gaydc.com/

GayDC lists businesses, organizations, bars, and clubs of interest. The site offers free chat, and links for adults only.

Jame's Guide to Gay Washington, D.C.

http://www.alliance.net/~jame/wash-dc.htm

You won't miss a coffee shop, a B&B, or a hotline with Jame as your online guide to D.C.

QUEER KIDS IN AMERICA

LesBiGay Youth Orgs and Resources

Bisexual, Lesbian and Gay Youth of New York

http://www.gaycenter.org/bigltyny.html

This New York City youth-run group for young people, ages 13 to 21, seeks to provide "a sense of belonging" in a drug- and alcohol-free and supportive environment. Details on weekly meetings and location are available on site.

Boston Alliance of Gay and Lesbian Youth

http://www.pride.net/bagly/

BAGLY is a youth-led, adult-supervised support group for gay, lesbian, bisexual, transgendered, and questioning youth, ages 22 and younger. It is "pressure free, violence free, weapons free, alcohol free, drug free, and sex free." Get details on meetings, special events, and youth outreach at the home page.

Boy2Boy (Denver)

http://www.tde.com/~boy2boy/

Boy2Boy is the response of young gay Denver men to the rise in HIV infection among gay and bi youth. The

Figure 9.19
Seattle Gay News Online

prevention program targets men ages 15 to 25. Information on events, workshops, and the outreach team is available on site.

District 202 (Minneapolis)
http://206.9.170.168/cgi-shl/
dbml.exe?template=/202/index.dbm

District 202 is a Minneapolis-based community center by and for gay, lesbian, bisexual, and transgender youth (with an emphasis on the words "by and for"). The District works with young gay people to create opportunities, build strengths, and foster empowerment.

Lavender Youth Recreation & Information Center (San Francisco)
http://thecity.sfsu.edu/~lyric/

The Lavender Youth Recreation & Information Center (LYRIC) provides peer support, and social, recreational, and educational opportunities to gay, lesbian, bisexual, transgender, and questioning youth, age 23 and younger. The center is located in San Francisco.

Long Island Lesbian and Gay Youth
http://www.ligaly.com/

Find out online about this well-rounded organization's support, discussion, and social groups, counseling services, and speakers bureau. The site also leads the way to other helpful gay youth points of interest.

Oasis
http://www.oasismag.com

As any gay, lesbian, bisexual, transgender, or questioning youth knows, it's a desert out there. "So come to the Oasis!" invites this online monthly magazine written by and about gay youth. Editorial coverage includes current events, arts and entertainment, "profiles in courage," and regular columns.

OutProud
http://www.cyberspaces.com/outproud/

OutProud, the national coalition for gay, lesbian, and bisexual youth (Figure 9.20), provides advocacy, information, resources, and support—and an excellent Web site to assist in execution. Visitors will find youth-only chat,

```
Subject: Hi
Help, Anyone that can give me any
advice on being gay, I think I am, but
I am not sure or can you give me
anywhere else I can go to find out
Sat Sep 9 16:24:11 1995 - ()
anonymous
```

and the straight dope on issues such as HIV and violence. But OutProud isn't just for young people; educators will find information on teaching positive values regarding homosexuality, and resources such as a "Lesbian, Gay, Bisexual, and Transgender Bill of Educational Rights."

Youth Assistance Organization
http://www.youth.org/

Youth Assistance Organization is a volunteer-run service, created to help self-identifying gay, lesbian, bisexual, and questioning youth. The site exists to provide young people with "a safe space online to be themselves." Site features include Elight!, a zine for and by gay youth in cyberspace; informative sections such as "I might be gay, what do I do?"; and forums ("Porn on the Internet and its relation to gay youth").

PRIDE ON CAMPUS

LesBiGay Student Orgs

Auburn
http://www.auburn.edu/~aglassn/

With a hot flash of red, the Auburn Gay and Lesbian Association provides online bulletins, classifieds, and "other stuff in and about Alabama."

Figure 9.20
OutProud

Figure 9.21
cmuOUT

California Institute of Technology
http://www.cco.caltech.edu/~clu/

Caltech's LesBiGay Union is a social group which organizes activities and raises awareness on campus. Details on the site.

Carnegie Mellon
http://wwwcontrib.andrew.cmu.edu/org/out/

cmuOUT (Figure 9.21), the gay, lesbian, and bisexual student organization of Carnegie Mellon University in Pittsburgh, sponsors educational and social activities throughout the year. Its Web site also includes loads of information on gay Pittsburgh.

Cornell
http://www.Cornell-Iowa.edu/CornellDocs/Students/Org/LBGA/

The Lesbian Bisexual and Gay Alliance of Cornell dedicates its efforts to promoting awareness and support for different sexual orientations on campus and in the surrounding communities.

Duke
http://www.duke.edu/lgb/

The Duke University Queer Infoserver includes an events calendar and sections for undergrads, graduate students, and alumni.

Emporia State (Kansas)

**http://www.emporia.edu/s/www/asg/groups/
glare/glare.htm**

The Gay/Lesbian Alliance for Resource and Education (or GLARE) is a recognized student organization at Emporia State. Find out about its "Safe Zone" project and campus speaker panels.

Georgia Tech

**http://www.gatech.edu/std_org/gala/gala/
welcome.html**

The Georgia Tech Gay and Lesbian Alliance provides its community with education, support, a positive gay awareness, AIDS information, and more on the Web.

Harvard

http://www.actwin.com/hglc/

The Harvard Gay & Lesbian Caucus includes more than 1,700 members and wants to be "your link to Harvard's gay family." Who's Who in the Caucus, Upcoming Events and News, and History of the Caucus help make up the site.

New York University

http://pages.nyu.edu/clubs/QU/

New York University Queer Union is a campuswide social, support and political organization for gay, lesbian, bisexual, and transgendered students. Contact information, hot links, and a portraits gallery ("the faces of Queer NYU") are site features.

North Carolina State University

http://www2.ncsu.edu/ncsu/stud_orgs/lgsu/

The Bisexuals, Gays, Lesbians, and Allies organization of North Carolina State serves the campus community with support, educational outreach, and activism.

Pennsylvania State

http://128.118.50.35:80/psupride/

The Penn State Pride Page provides information specific to the gay, lesbian, bisexual, and transgendered community at the university.

Princeton

http://www.princeton.edu/~lgba/index.shtml

The Lesbian Gay Bisexual Alliance (Figure 9.22) is the social and political organization for gay, lesbian, bisexual, and transgendered students (and faculty and staff) at Princeton University. Its colorful Web presence tells you all you could possibly want to know about the alliance—from the mission statement to means of communication—and includes extras such as the monthly newsletter, *The Gaily Princetonian*.

Stanford

**http://www-leland.stanford.edu/group/QR/
qg94.html**

Stanford's Gradnet Lambda—a student organization of queer grad students—developed the Queer Guide (much of which is excerpted online) to give Stanford students an insider's view of the university and an overview of Bay Area resources that may be of interest. "We've gone and danced in all the clubs, stood defiantly at the bars, lain provocatively on the beaches, wandered the streets alone at night," the site explains. Might as well

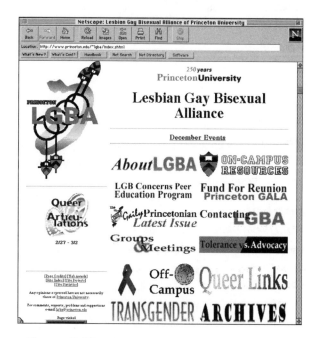

Figure 9.22
Princeton Lesbian Gay Bisexual Alliance

follow the leads to neighborhoods and cities, book-stores, cafes, volunteer organizations, and more. Dated 1994-'95, some of the information may be a bit moldy.

State University of New York (Brockport)
http://www.acs.brockport.edu/~glbsfa/glbsfa.html

The Gay/Lesbian/Bisexual Students and Friends Association is funded by the students of SUNY Brockport. Contact information and details on upcoming events are available in "discrete" (text) and "flamboyant" (graphical) formats.

University of Alabama
http://ua1vm.ua.edu/~glba/glba.html

The University of Alabama's Gay Lesbian Bisexual Alliance covers upcoming events, local and regional resources, and more.

University of Alaska—Fairbanks
http://icecube.acf-lab.alaska.edu/~fbagla/

The home page of the Alaska Gay and Lesbian Association at the University of Alaska—Fairbanks features details on events, political discussion, and the minutes of previous meetings.

University at Buffalo
http://wings.buffalo.edu/sa/lgba/

The Lesbian Gay Bisexual Alliance of the University at Buffalo, N.Y., is an undergraduate student organization which creates "a safe space on campus" and educates the community on issues surrounding homosexuality. The site includes such features as a "heterosexual question-naire" and a section about gay symbols and culture.

University of California—San Diego
http://sdcc13.ucsd.edu/~ucsdlgba

The University of California at San Diego's Lesbian, Gay, and Bisexual Association provides students and the local community with an educational and social forum for gay issues and a support network for those in need. The Web site includes information about meetings, social events, and community resources.

University of Kansas
http://www.ukans.edu/~qanda/

Les/Bi/Gay/Trans Services of Kansas is a "friendly all-pur-pose organization" for queer students at the University of Kansas. Minutes from past meetings are on file here, as is information on "Campaign Gayhawk," an effort to provide scholarships to KU students who make significant contributions to the LesBiGayTrans community.

University of Nebraska-Lincoln
http://www.unl.edu:80/lambda/

The UNL Gay, Lesbian, Bisexual, and Transgender Resource Center provides information and support to students who are coming to terms with their sexual identities. The organization also offers a safe environment for discussion of relevant issues. It's the only resource of its kind in Nebraska.

University of Michigan
http://www.umich.edu/~inqueery

The Lesbian Gay Bisexual Programs Office at the University of Michigan (Figure 9.23), Ann Arbor, provides programming, educational services, and leadership training. It also acts as a coordinator for various LesBiGay student, faculty, and staff groups at the university. Its Web site includes a bi-weekly newsletter, a monthly listing of local events and meetings, and links to other area resources.

University of Pennsylvania
http://dolphin.upenn.edu:80/~lgba/

The Penn Lesbian, Gay, and Bisexual Alliance holds weekly meetings and discussion groups, in addition to trips and other social activities. The site includes campus, national and world news reports, and a features archive of various points of interest on the Web.

University of South Carolina
http://web.csd.sc.edu/bgla/index.html

The Bisexual, Gay, and Lesbian Association of the University of South Carolina posts information about its meetings, officers, services, and events online, in addition to pointers to community resources in the Columbia area.

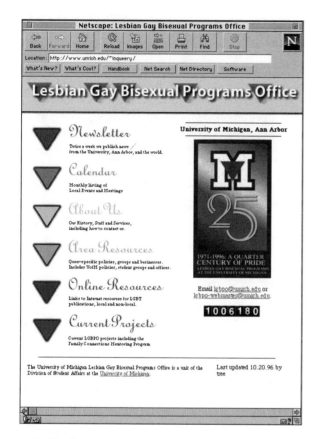

Figure 9.23
University of Michigan

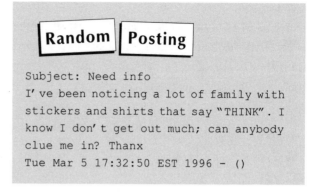

Washington University
http://pear.wustl.edu/~lambda/

Lambda Online is the Web home for the Gay, Lesbian, and Bisexual community at Washington University in St. Louis. Learn about the groups on campus, upcoming events, and link to other resources in the St. Louis area.

Yale
http://www.yale.edu/lgb/

"Yale is a wonderful place to be lesbian, gay, bisexual or transgendered," the Lesbian, Gay, Bisexual, Transgendered Cooperative at Yale informs. The organization's wonderful Web space includes discussion groups for men (GAYalies) and women (YaLesbians), news and current events, and an e-mail directory of "out" Yalies and Alumni.

University of Texas-Austin
http://www.utexas.edu/ftp/student/lbgsa

The Lesbian Bisexual Gay Student Association at the University of Texas at Austin provides online information about regular activities and Austin organizations, as well as "links to the outside world."

University of Virginia
http://scs.student.virginia.edu/~lambda1/

The Lesbian, Gay and Bisexual Union at the University of Virginia includes students, alumni and faculty, as well as "townies" from the Charlottesville gay and lesbian community. It is the largest organization of its kind at the university, and Charlottesville's oldest.

SILENCE DOES NOT EQUAL DEAF

The deaf queer community has made great strides over the past several years. Most major cities are homes to deaf queer social organizations; there are national conferences, national archives, a Deaf Lesbian and Gay Awareness Week (each May)—even deaf leather organizations. The Deaf Queer Resources Center (http://www.deafqueer.org/) is the community's hub in the virtual realm. Dragonsani Renteria, the Center's developer and maintainer (see

Q&A sidebar), refers to the Net as "a great equalizer" in terms of communication. Her request of fellow Webmistresses and -masters: "that the queer community will consider it an absolute must to ensure their sites are accessible to all aspects of our diverse queer community.

"And we, in turn, will caption our sign video sites on the Web for you."

CTN Magazine
http://www.geocities.com/WestHollywood/ 1309/

CTN (which stands for "Coming Together Newsletter") is the world's first magazine for, by, and about deaf gays, lesbians, and bisexuals. It started as a newsletter in 1992 and evolved into magazine status shortly thereafter. For now, the CTN home page offers subscription and advertising information, but promises online articles and "pix of hot deaf lesbigays" in the near future. Stay tuned.

Deaf Gay and Lesbian Center
http://www.hooked.net/users/dqrc/dglc.html

This San Francisco-based social service agency was the first in the country to focus exclusively on the needs of the deaf gay, lesbian, and bisexual communities. Its Web presence covers agency basics.

Deaf Queer Resource Center
http://www.deafqueer.org/

Former Deaf Gay and Lesbian Center director Dragonsani Renteria developed and maintains this online information center (Figure 9.24) for the deaf queer community. And what an information center it is, alive with such networkers as bulletin boards for pen-pals, and a "Point of View Cafe," where discussion boards range from "Deaf Lesbigay Parents" to "Thoughts on the Word Queer." The site's people directory—accented by a rotating photo collage—includes a directory of e-mail and home page addresses. And big plans are in the works (an on-site library promises articles, research papers, and newsletters by and about the deaf queer community).

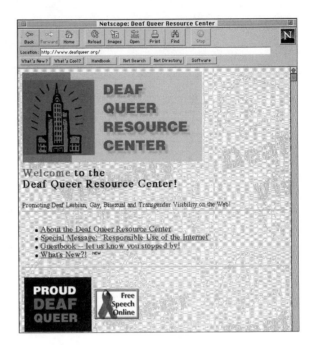

Figure 9.24
Deaf Queer Resource Center

Even when it's under construction, though, the center packs a hard-hitting punch. Or, as one deaf queer acquaintance puts it: "This site kicks ass."

Rainbow Deaf Society
http://members.aol.com/sfrds1/index.html

The Rainbow Deaf Society is a "proudly gay" San Francisco-based social and support group. General news and events are available on site.

San Jose Lambda Society of the Deaf
http://home.earthlink.net/~wer/SJLSD/ sjlsd.htm

This San Jose-based society is 10 years strong in furthering the well-being and development of the deaf and hard-of-hearing gay and lesbian community. Nice Web site, too.

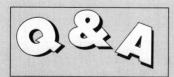

DRAGONSANI RENTERIA, DEVELOPER AND MAINTAINER OF THE DEAF QUEER RESOURCE CENTER

For a 28-year-old, Dragonsani Renteria (Figure 9.25) has had quite a career. To date, she has served the gay, lesbian, and bisexual deaf community in the real world (as director of the Deaf Gay and Lesbian Center in San Francisco), in paper publishing (as publisher and editor of *CTN* magazine), and in the virtual realm (as developer and maintainer of the Deaf Queer Resources Center). "The growth of our community has been remarkable," she says. "Yet, we still have a way to go in terms of unity and political clout." Renteria took some time out of her holiday schedule last December to answer a few questions about her community and the online information network she continues to develop for it.

Q: What kind of role is the Net playing in the deaf community?

A: The Internet has become a great equalizer in terms of communication and information distribution for deaf people. Because of the way information has traditionally been distributed, usually by radio and TV (news programs have only recently been closed captioned), deaf people have often been the last to have access to late-breaking news. The Internet has changed that and this has been truly exciting to see and experience. I fear, however, that this honeymoon may prove to be short lived as new audio-focused technology, such as voice e-mail and all-audio Web sites, catch on and become commonplace. If this happens, it will undoubtedly feel as if the deaf community has been thrown back into the information dark ages. It's important for the deaf community to keep abreast of new technology and work to ensure that this incredible new medium remains accessible to us.

![Netscape browser window showing deafqueer.org profile page](Netscape: Dragonsani Renteria)

CTN Magazine-style profile

■ **Name**: Dragonsani Renteria ("Drago" for short)
■ **Age**: 28
■ **Sign**: Virgo
■ **Birthplace**: El Paso, TX
■ **Current residence**: San Francisco, CA (recently relocated temporarily to the East Coast)
■ **Family**: "I'm half Chicana, half Italiana. I grew up speaking both Spanish and Italian fluently. I'm also a second generation queer. My mom is a lesbian and one of my two brothers is gay. My other brother, who is straight, is referred to playfully as 'the black sheep of the family.'"
■ **Education**: B.A. in Women's Studies from the University of California at Berkeley. Did part of my undergraduate work at Gallaudet University in Washington, DC.
■ **Current occupation**: CTN Magazine Publisher & Editor, Internet/Web Publishing Consultant, queer activist
■ **Past occupation**: Director, DCARA's Deaf Gay & Lesbian Center (3

Figure 9.25
Dragonsani Renteria

Q: What inspired you to develop the Deaf Queer Resource Center?

A: Information is a very powerful tool, one that not everyone always has access to. As a journalist and activist, I wanted to provide a place on the Web where the deaf queer community could go to find information and resources by, for and about our community. And at the same time, I also wanted to offer a way for the community to celebrate our diversity, network, feel empowered, and be visible on the Web.

Q: What kinds of special needs for the deaf queer community are you trying to address with the site?

A: Special needs? I don't think that there are necessarily special needs being met. As I mentioned, I see the Net as an equalizer. Deaf queers can finally communicate in the same way that hearing queers do.

Q: What has the response been like so far?

A: The response to DQRC has been incredible! We receive letters of thanks on a daily basis from people all over the world who have just discovered for the first time that such a thing as a "deaf queer community" exists. This is especially important to me because I believe so much in the power of visibility. I think it's imperative for the deaf queer community to be out, proud, and visible.

PFLAG IN THE USA

Parents, Familes and Friends of Lesbians and Gays
http://www.pflag.org

PFLAG Talk and TGS PFLAG
http://www.critpath.org/pflag-talk/

They're here, they're not queer, and they're fighting for your rights. They're the Parents, Families, and Friends of Lesbians and Gays (Figure 9.26), and chapters are (mom and) popping up all over the place—including cyberspace, where PFLAGers celebrate the Hawaii Marriage Decision and zap messages to Capitol Hill along with the best of the gay and lesbian keyboard activists. Visit the National site for the PFLAG story, or to locate (or start) a local chapter. The PFLAG Talk and TGS PFLAG site gives details on the PFLAG Talk and TGS PFLAG mailing lists. And check out the list below of local PFLAG chapters which have graced the Web with their own sites.

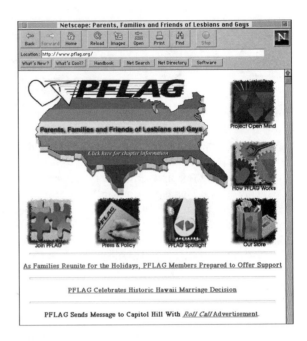

Figure 9.26
PFLAG

Boulder County (Colorado)
http://www.tde.com/~pflagbldr/

Brooklyn (New York)
http://www.panix.com/~pflag/

Columbia/Howard County (Maryland)
http://members.aol.com/MDLambda/pflag/index.htm

Houston
http://vellocet.insync.net/~pflagwww/index.html

Las Vegas
http://www.geocities.com/WestHollywood/1082/

Northern New Jersey
http://www.qrd.org/QRD/www/usa/nj/PFLAG/

Olympia (Washington)
http://members.tripod.com/~claytoly/PFLAG-Olympia

Portland (Maine)
http://www.qrd.org/QRD/www/usa/maine/pflag.html

Queens (New York)
http://www.dorsai.org/~pflag/

San Francisco
http://www.backdoor.com/pflagsf/

Chapter 10

PRIDEWORLDWIDE

Like the chapter which precedes it, this one takes a different approach from the rest of the book's tendency to put a monocled eye on specific subjects. Rather, it stands back, cranks up the browser and spins the globe, attempting the impossible (laughable?) feat of covering the expanse of gay and lesbian World Wide Webness.

Yes, it's impossible. Sites wither on the line almost as frequently as they blossom. That's just the way of the Web, so get used to it. Language barriers for this stateside surfer don't help matters much either. That said, consider PrideWorldWide to be just a hint of what's out there in the way of International resources. The sites included here appear to have staying power and are (or at least were) being updated regularly. Their worldly Webmasters are sure to keep the rest of us informed about how up-to-date (or archaic) the gay situation is in their respective dots on the globe.

We begin with sites that affect us all—those from organizations such as the International Gay and Lesbian Human Rights Commission, which is busy filling the gap between the international human rights movement and the gay rights movement as we speak; and the International Association of Lesbian/Gay Pride Coordinators, instrumental in making sure those annual Pride throw-downs get bigger, bolder, and better each year. From there, check out the collection of major sites from around the world, arranged geographically, from Asia (which has a few) to the Middle East (which could use a few more). Along the way, you'll find side items on queer immigration, and WestHollywood, the global gay ghetto. As the French might say at this point: Bon voyage.

WORLDWIDE

Famous Queers, Queens and Dykes
http://www.efn.org/~mastrait/
famousqueers.html

This alphabetical list of modern day and historical famous "queers, queens, and dykes" includes links to more detailed sites on its subjects, and sometimes even a photograph. It may be one of the only lists on which British pop musician Marc Almond is sandwiched between Horatio Alger and Greek poet Anacreon. It also takes a while to download, which, in the case of this "partial list," is not such a bad thing.

International Association of Lesbian/ Gay Pride Coordinators
http://www.tde.com/~ialgpc/

This nonprofit org is made up of organizers in more than 60 cities around the world that produce gay and lesbian pride events. Each year, IAL/GPC holds an international conference and five regional conferences to conduct corporate business, and to discuss future plans, merchandising, political concerns, and so on. "Equality through visibility" is the motto.

International Gay & Lesbian Human Rights Commission
http://www.iglhrc.org/

Based in San Francisco, the International Gay and Lesbian Human Rights Commission (Figure 10.1) attempts to fill the gap between the international human rights movement and the gay rights movement—"neither of which fully addressed human rights violations against sexual minorities," the organization explains with its Web presence. On the long list of abuses IGLHRC has recorded to date: murder as "social cleansing"; electroshock "therapy"; forced psychiatric "treatment"; and torture. The site contains press releases ("Historic South African Bill of Rights Includes Sexual Orientation"), action alerts, a newsletter, and information on how to get involved.

Figure 10.1
International Gay & Lesbian Human Rights Commission

International Lesbian and Gay Association
http://www.seta.fi/inat/ilga.html

Based in Brussels, the International Lesbian and Gay Association is a world-wide federation of national and local groups working for human rights for gays and lesbians. The group's more than 400 members range from individuals to small collectives to national networks and entire cities. Check the ILGA home page for the latest information on its history and campaigns, the bi-yearly conference, and bi-monthly bulletin, "an indispensable source of information.

The Lavender Pages World Search
http://www.lavenderpages.com/world.html

The Lavender Pages is a comprehensive printed business and professional directory by and for the San Francisco Bay Area gay, lesbian, and bisexual community. In addition to the Bay Area, its Web site also features an excellent business and resources search for cities around the world. Most of the searchable cities are located in the U.S., but Amsterdam, London, Mexico City, and a handful of other international cities, are in the mix.

ONE Institute International Gay & Lesbian Archives
http://www.usc.edu/Library/oneigla/

International Gay & Lesbian Review
http://www.usc.edu/Library/oneigla/onepress/index.html

ONE Institute (Figure 10.2)—an independent educational institution affiliated with the University of Southern California—houses the world's largest research library on gay, lesbian, bisexual, and transgendered heritage and concerns. Its West Hollywood stacks are for research visits in the flesh (not electronic), though the Web site offers plenty of fascinating information about the organization (formed in 1952, it's the oldest ongoing gay/lesbian org in the Western Hemisphere) and its wide range of

Figure 10.2
ONE Institute

volunteer and contributor opportunities. It also points to its in-house publication, "a new kind of interactive journal," the International Gay & Lesbian Review. The Review provides abstracts and reviews of books that relate to gay, lesbian, bisexual, and transgender studies, along with selected unpublished Ph.D. dissertations and Master's theses. It was in development on our visit, but appeared to be shaping up nicely.

ASIA

Barazoku
http://freedom.gavie.or.jp/jp/barazoku/index.html

Barazoku is an online gay magazine, in Japanese only.

Gay Hong Kong
http://sqzm14.ust.hk/hkgay.html

The Gay Hong Kong pages cover everything from hot karaoke and publications, to saunas and fitness centers.

Kakasarian: the Filipino Queer Directory
http://www.tribo.org/bakla/bakla.html

"Philippines is relatively relaxed in its attitude (about homosexuality), though ambitious gay politicians may not get very far," explains this massive Filipino Queer Directory with attitude. Visitors will find listings for gay studies, groups, and "cruising spots," along with a handy glossary of "swardspeak," the language of the Filipino gay community.

Keanoo's Gay Asian Links
http://www.geocities.com/Tokyo/4550/gay.htm

It has absolutely nothing to do with Mr. Reeves. Rather, Keanoo's page (the Toronto-based Webmaster is actually named Duc Nguyen) was designed as "a simple way to find all available Asian Internet sites of interest to gay Asians and their friends." Check out Keanoo's many hot finds, or, if you've got a site that should be listed, submit the URL and a quick description.

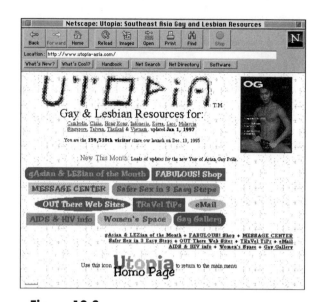

Figure 10.3
Utopia: Southeast Asia Gay and Lesbian Resources

Outrageous Tokyo

http://shrine.cyber.ad.jp/~darrell/outr/home/
outr-home.html

Anthony Fox, editor of this, "Japan's first free English-language gay magazine," wanted to see a publication that "would not only bring all the information needed to fully participate in gay life in Tokyo, but also to offer an outlet to express opinions, meet other people, and develop a sense of community that will expand our minds and enrich our lives." Outrageous Tokyo is available in print in Tokyo bars, and online for the rest of the world. By the end of last year, however, it was in desperate need of a new issue. Even in its moldy state, it serves as a decent source of information on local clubs, bars, and venues of interest to gays and lesbians; from Kusuo, a karaoke bar "frequented by muscular men with short hair," to the tanning salon Sun Muscle ("not gay, but the scenery is good").

Utopia: Southeast Asia Gay and Lesbian Resources

http://www.utopia-asia.com/

This colorful, up-to-date site covers a lot of territory, with individual sections for Cambodia, China, Hong Kong, Indonesia, Korea, Laos, Malaysia, Singapore, Taiwan, Thailand, and Vietnam (Figure 10.3). It also includes feature sections such as "gAsian & LEZian of the Month," "Women's Space," and a message center.

VN-GBLF

http://www.viet.net/Gallery/vietgal/vn-gblf/

VN-GBLF is a mailing list for Vietnamese Gays, Bisexuals, Lesbians, and Friends, providing information to promote better understanding and compassion for the experience of Viet GBLFs. Based on VietGate, the "gateway to the online Vietnamese community," the Web page offers subscription information and topical links.

AUSTRALIA AND NEW ZEALAND

Aotearoa New Zealand

http://nz.com/NZ/Queer/

This section of the larger Akiko International site contains information on the New Zealand queer community, with lists and links in politics, history, events, and special sections for such issues as "queer marriage."

The Australian Queer Resources Directory

http://www.queer.org.au/QRD/

The AusQRD (Figure 10.4) is a white pages style directory (by region) of material of interest to Australian gays, lesbians, bisexuals, and "trannies." It's a service of the Sexuality Project of the Australian Student Christian Movement, of all things. Directory sections include News, Community Groups, Spirituality, Humor, and a Tranny Guide.

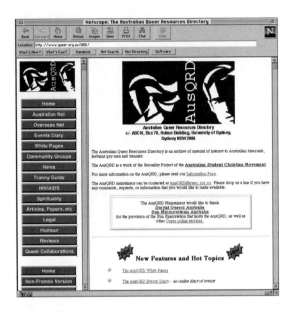

Figure 10.4
The Australian Queer Resources Directory

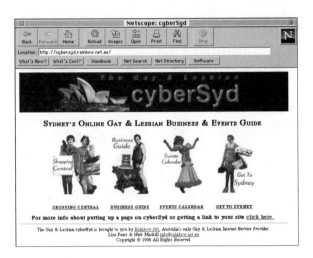

Figure 10.5
CyberSyd

Capital Q

http://www.bigblock.com/capitalq/index.htm

Sydney's weekly gay and lesbian online magazine features news, "night grooves," travel information, and "live gay chat for all of us."

CUPIE: Queer Perth

http://www.iinet.net.au/~lezderin/

News, organizations, businesses, and pride photos make up this colorful guide to "all that is happening in Queer Perth today."

Cyberqueer Australia

http://cyberqueer.rainbow.net.au/

Cyberqueer Australia seeks to initiate and promote outreach, support, unity, and queer information exchange (all virtual, of course). The site includes news, chat, an e-mail directory, and "sleaze photographs" from an authority, the "Sydney Star Observer."

CyberSyd

http://cybersyd.rainbow.net.au/

Sydney's artfully designed online gay and lesbian guide (Figure 10.5) features sections for shopping, business,

events, and travel (you know, for getting to Sydney in the first place).

Out in Sydney

http://www.outinsydney.com.au/home.html

This site wants to give you more than taste of gay and lesbian Sydney; rather a "firm meaty bite" of the great Australian city. From "boys, clothes, and accessories" to "adult concepts" and accommodations for travelers, if it's out in Sydney, you'll find it here.

The Pink Board

http://www.pinkboard.com.au/

"A place for gay men and lesbians and our friends," the Darlinghurst-based Pinkboard is Larry Singer's (he's also known as the Panther; get it?) hot sheet to gayness Down Under. Sections are on site for community groups, businesses, festivals, and personals. Also, learn more about Singer and Pinkboard, which has grown from a service provider in 1986 to Australia's "first gay Internet node" in 1995.

Queensland Queers

http://www.powerup.com.au/~qldq/
qldqhp.html

"Not all queers live in Sydney or Melbourne," this site exclaims. And actually, seems like more would live—or

Subject: New Zealand babes!!!
Hello! This is for all of those
beautiful women of New Zealand! I have
just returned back to Dallas from a
business trip to Auckland and
Wellington and there were so many
lovely ladies to look upon. Next year,
I shall return to Wellington, so as
they say here, "pull up the truck and
let the gate down! It's party time."
See you there!!
Thu Dec 12 12:14:38 EST 1996 - ()

at least want to live—in a state with a name like Queensland. At any rate, the home page of Queensland Queers does an excellent job doing what it sets out to do—increase the visibility of gay, lesbian, transgender, and bisexual people in this part of Australia. Visitors to the site will find sections on gay music, gay newspapers, gay businesses, and community groups.

Riverina Gay and Lesbian Support Group, Inc.

http://www.wagga.net.au/~rglsg/

This Wagga Wagga community organization provides a contact point and follow-up social welfare and support services for gays, lesbians, and their supporters in the area. It also provides education regarding homosexuality to the general public. Contact information, details on upcoming events and "South West," the monthly newsletter, are available online.

Sydney Gay and Lesbian Mardi Gras, Ltd.

http://www.geko.com.au:80/~mardigras/index.html

Here's the virtual hub of "the world's premier gay and lesbian festival," the Sydney Gay and Lesbian Mardi Gras (Figure 10.6). Each year in June, the festival uses celebra-

Figure 10.6
Sydney Gay and Lesbian Mardi Gras, Ltd.

tion and the arts to promote community, political, and social objectives. The organizational site provides the most up-to-date information on development, along with details on the parade, the party, and the festival (including photo galleries for each). Visitors will also find plenty of history—from 1978, when the first Mardi Gras was held as the finale to International Gay Solidarity Day, to modern times, where the outdoor parade is recognized as the largest in the world.

10% Plus Business Association of Western Australia

http://tenplus.ednet.com.au/

10% Plus supports the gay and lesbian professional community of Western Australia. The small group hopes that through community support it will eventually be able to provide advisory groups, lobby groups, employment opportunities, financial assistance, and many other services currently unavailable to its constituency.

CANADA

Atlantic Canada PFLAG
http://www.unb.ca/web/P-FLAG/

Parents, Families, and Friends of Lesbians and Gays affiliates are located in more than 340 communities across the U.S., and in 11 other countries—including Canada, where the Fredericton, N.B.-based Atlantic Canada chapter is online with organizational information, brochures, and links of interest.

Canadian Gay, Lesbian and Bisexual Resource Directory
http://www.cglbrd.com/

The Canadian Gay, Lesbian, and Bisexual Resource Directory, a.k.a. Gaycanada (Figure 10.7), claims to be the world's largest and most comprehensive source for the information and resources of gay Canada. Even from just glancing at the site, you probably wouldn't argue the fact. Search by category or location for Canadian events, services, publications, and classifieds. The site's excellent Business Directory provides free listings for gay and gay-friendly businesses throughout the country, and its alphabetical index lists entries by category, province, and city.

Canadian Lesbian and Gay Archives
http://www.web.net/archives/

The Canadian Lesbian and Gay Archives—which claims to be the world's largest lesbian and gay archives—collects and maintains information and materials relating to the gay and lesbian movement in Canada and elsewhere, and it makes the holding available for research and education to the public. The Web site provides an overview of what's inside the Toronto facility.

Equality for Gays and Lesbians Everywhere (EGALE)
http://www.islandnet.com/~egale/

Lobbying for equality, fighting for justice in the courts, and building a communications and action network across Canada, EGALE is a national organization (based in Ottawa, Ontario) committed to advancing equality and justice

Figure 10.7
Canadian Gay, Lesbian and Bisexual Resource Directory

for gays, lesbians, and bisexuals at the federal level. The group's Web site includes sections for politics, legal issues, and archives. It also features action alerts and press releases.

Fredericton Lesbians and Gays
http://www.unb.ca/web/gala/

The home page of Fredericton (N.B.) Lesbians and Gays features resources of relevance to the local gay community and links to the "gay Web" at large.

Gay and Lesbian Community Centre of Edmonton
http://freenet.edmonton.ab.ca/glcce/

The Gay and Lesbian Community Centre of Edmonton serves its population of gays, lesbians, bisexuals, and transgendered people with a reference library, peer counseling, professional referrals and more. Its Web site includes contact information and a bulletin board for announcements and upcoming events.

Gay and Lesbian Center of Montreal

http://www.gaibec.com/ccglm/index.html

Montreal's gay and lesbian center serves its community with a place for reflection, business, and research. More information is available on site, in English and French.

Gay Toronto

http://www.gaytoronto.com/

This "ever changing window" on gay Toronto is set up as an interactive magazine. Fashion spreads, celebrity interviews, and regular columns are rolled in with such extras as a chat zone and an interactive soapbox ("rant 'n rave, bitch & complain ..."). The site also serves as a "village guide" to restaurants, bars, and various gay and gay-friendly establishments and orgs. So whether you're living in the city or just planning a visit, Gay Toronto turns out to be an invaluable resource.

Gay Vancouver Online

http://users.uniserve.com/~mrobins/
guide.html

This guide to gay Vancouver (Figure 10.8) is directed at LesBiGay travelers. Its pages include listings for supportive gay and gay-friendly restaurants, shops, and lodgings. Those who live in Vancouver will find listings for social groups, computer services, Net resources, and more.

Lambda Institute of Gay and Lesbian Studies

http://gpu.srv.ualberta.ca/~cbidwell/cmb/
lambda.htm

The mission statement reads: "The Foundation promotes research into gay and lesbian issues and lifestyles for the purpose of public education" (FYI, the founding members arrived at this "over many cups of coffee" and after a brainstorming session that lasted "until their heads ached"). Find out about the University of Alberta-based organization's many strides since then on this informative home page, which covers services (life skills training, peer support, libraries, and archives ...), membership information, and links to other community resources.

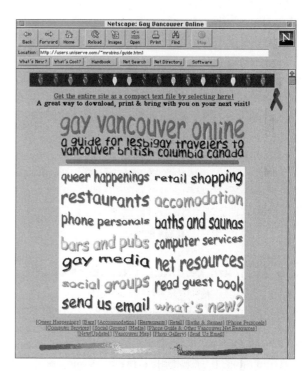

Figure 10.8
Gay Vancouver

Lesbian, Bisexual, Gay and Transgender Students of McGill University (Montreal)

http://www.vub.mcgill.ca/clubs/lbgtm/

The Lesbian, Bisexual, Gay, and Transgender student organization at Montreal's McGill University posts such items as a recent study on gay youth and suicide, and photos from the group's fall hiking trip. It also includes first-rate sections on coming out, and a student's perspective on the Montreal queer scene.

Newfoundland Gays and Lesbians for Equality

http://www.geocities.com/WestHollywood/
4291/

NGALE is a community-based, nonprofit volunteer organization dedicated to providing support, education, and advocacy to and for gays, lesbians, bisexuals, and other sexual minorities in the province of Newfoundland and Labrador. Its Web site includes meeting times, and links to other local resources.

Victoria Pride Society
http://www.islandnet.com/~ila/vicpride.htm

The Victoria, B.C., Pride Society uses the Web to list upcoming events and committee meetings. It also points to other pride organizations around the world, and includes a photo album covering the previous year's celebrations.

EUROPE

Austria

The Austrian Lesbian, Gay, Bisexual and Transgender Home Page
http://www.oeh.uni-linz.ac.at:8001/homo/

From Dornbirn to Innsbruck to Vienna, this Austrian Page covers the best in local resources, tourist information, and more. English and German versions were promised to be coming soon.

Belgium

Gay and Lesbian Groups at Limburg
http://www.tornado.be/~lach/

"At about 6 million ordinary (?) Flemisch people there are about 300,000 boys who like boys and girls who like girls," this site from the Dutch-speaking province in Belgium explains. In both Dutch and English, it highlights some of the activism, social activities, and gay community services available in Limburg, including workshops for parents of gays and lesbians, and for married and divorced gays and lesbians.

Croatia

Croatian LesBiGays on Internet
http://www.geocities.com/WestHollywood/1824/

Despite the fact that there are no direct laws prohibiting consensual relations between men or women, Croatian LesBiGays on Internet explains that "societal and cultural constraints have forced many Croatian LesBiGays to remain closeted and hidden." The site points to some general information on Croatia, but mainly serves as a jumping-off point to other queer sites in Europe and the U.S.

Czech Republic

SOHO Czech Republic
http://www.infima.cz/soho/

The Association of Homosexual Citizens' Organizations (Czech abbreviation SOHO) is some 20 organizations which make an effort to be "useful for gays and lesbians" throughout the Czech Republic. Information about the SOHO organizations and activities is available on site.

Denmark

Copenhagen Gay Homepage
http://www.cgh.dk/gayhome.htm

Claiming to be the number-one gay site in Denmark, the Copenhagen Gay Homepage is the personal creation of two guys who live there. Site offerings include the city gay guide, a "male gallery," and international personal ads. Available in Danish and English.

Finland

The LBG Student Association of Helsinki University
http://www.helsinki.fi/jarj/oho/engindex.html

Online antics from the "biggest, queerest, and gayest bunch of sexually non-normative students at the Helsinki University." The group provides details of its weekly meetings, women's group, and activities, which include "plenty of tea, high-spirited debate, culture, excursions, parties, and other leisure."

Suomen Sapfo
http://www.helsinki.fi/~eisaksso/sapfo.html

It's the Finnish Sappho, and this page will hook you up to the Finnish language, women-only list for—you guessed it—sapphic discussion.

QUEER IMMIGRATION

The issues surrounding immigration are sticky enough for straight folks. When you throw words like queer, gay, and lesbian into the mix, depending on where you live, immigration often becomes impossible. In the United States, it's a basic right of heterosexual Americans to live with their loved ones—the Immigration and Nationality Act allows for the immigration of a foreign spouse. If you're gay and involved with a foreigner, however, you have no such right. Also in the U.S., individuals with HIV are not allowed to immigrate, though HIV exclusion can be waived for heterosexual spouses. This isn't the case everywhere in the world. Australia, Canada, Denmark, New Zealand, Norway, and Sweden at least allow for immigration of same-sex partners (though stipulations may not exactly make the process as carefree as a drive-thru wedding).

The Web is a natural medium for relaying information on the details which can keep international partners apart—or those which can allow for them to be together.

The Lesbian/Gay Immigration Rights Task Force, headquartered in New York City with chapters across the U.S., is advocating the reform of discriminatory immigration laws in the U.S. as we speak. It's just one of the Queer Immigration resources available on the Queer Immigration Home Page of the Queer Resources Directory. The page lists contact information for queer immigration groups around the world. It also provides information on asylum cases, legal rulings, and current immigration law, along with links to other useful information sources on the subject.

Sites dealing with queer immigration in the U.K., Australia, and the Netherlands have also taken root. Expect many more as the gay rights movement builds momentum around the world.

Queer Immigration Home Page
http://qrd.tcp.com/qrd/www/world/immigration/

Frequently Asked Questions on Gay and Lesbian Rights in the Netherlands
http://www.xs4all.nl/~heinv/dqrd/dqrdfaq.html

The Gay and Lesbian Immigration Task Force—Australia
http://www.glitf.org.au/

The Stonewall Immigration Group (U.K.)
http://www.tyger.co.uk/sig/

Lesbian/Gay Immigration Rights Task Force (U.S.)
http://qrd.tcp.com/qrd/www/world/immigration/lgirtf.html

AN INTERVIEW WITH THE QUEER RESOURCE DIRECTORY'S RON BUCKMIRE

He may live in the U.S., but thanks to this thing we call the Net, Ron Buckmire has—perhaps somewhat unwittingly—affected the worldwide queer community with his tireless keyboard activism. A Netizen since 1990 (check out his home on the Web, http://abacus.oxy.edu/~ron), Buckmire recalls being one of the first people doing "queer stuff" on the Net. His accomplishments to date include wiring and maintaining the legendary Queer Resources Directory; creating the official Web site for the National Freedom to Marry Coalition; heading up a variety of queer Internet mailing lists (including Queer-Planet, QueerLaw, and Queer-Politics); and serving on the board of directors for the recent start-up PlanetOut. "Oh yeah," he adds, almost as an aside. "The QRD is an appellant in the Reno v. ACLU case before the U.S. Supreme Court which challenges the constitutionality of the 1996 Communications Decency Act."

For reasons personal and logical, two of the issues Buckmire is most passionate about are queer immigration and same-sex marriage. He took some time out of his schedule to answer a few questions about his work in those specific areas—and about being perhaps the Net's most well-known queer activist.

Q: Through your work with Queer Resources Directory and other Net-based projects, what kind of effect do you think you've had on the worldwide queer community?

A: Well, that is a hard question. I'm sure that my actions have had *some* kind of effect on the worldwide community by facilitating the flow of information about international queer events to *other* international queer activists. Just finding out that there are other activists facing the same problems that they are and that there exists a worldwide community of people working toward

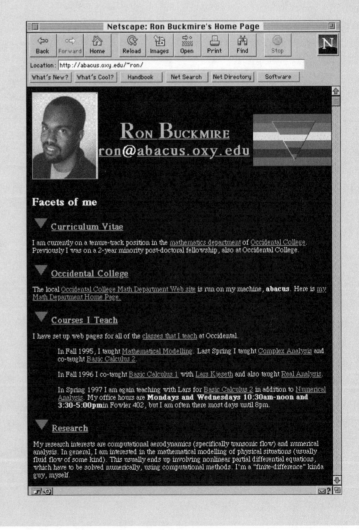

the same goal—the eradication of sexual orientation discrimination—is enough to energize many activists toiling in awful situations around the world.

spouse to immigrate, but that long term same-sex couples are treated as absolute strangers by the U.S. government.

Besides, same-sex marriage is

rate information about the immigration rules of other countries is incredibly useful. Recently there was a story that in the U.S. Embassy in Moscow the State De-

> **"Finding out that there are other activists facing the same problems...is enough to energize many activists toiling in awful situations around the world."**

Q: In which areas do you think your activism has had the most impact?

A: Raising the profile of the international queer rights movement. Also, I think I have facilitated the flow of queer legal information from the elite few to the interested masses. I'm confident that by providing technical support to Paula Stockholm's Maine GayNet our side was able to defeat the 1995 anti-gay statewide ballot measure known as Proposition 1.

Q: What inspired you to take on the issues of queer immigration and same-sex marriage in particular?

A: Initially because I'm in a binational relationship and one of the most obvious solutions to such couples is that they be allowed to get married and then petition the INS to allow the foreign partner to immigrate. It is incredibly galling to couples who have been together for *years* that some heterosexual can meet someone on a week's vacation in a foreign country, get married, and immediately sponsor the foreign

such an *obvious* thing. There *is* no logical argument against it. The opponent's best argument is, "We think Marriage should be one man-one woman because we think that is the way it has always been." Completely ignoring the fact that marriage has changed drastically over the years and that same-sex couples, either sanctioned by the state or not, have existed throughout all times and cultures also.

As a math professor the sheer illogic of the other side really annoys me. I am convinced that our side will win, because eventually everyone will get enough unbiased factual information about homosexuality which will make the right thing to do immensely obvious to *everyone*.

Q: What kind of role does the Net play in your efforts there?

A: The Internet has been incredibly useful in assisting with organizing the fight to end marriage discrimination against same-sex couples. Especially the mailing lists I run. In terms of queer immigration, having a Web site where people can get accu-

partment was handing out flyers which say that any known homosexual is prevented from even visiting the U.S. as a tourist. Before 1990, that was true, but it has been six years since that provision was repealed!

Q: Based on what's happening with regards to same-sex marriage and queer immigration in the U.S., are there any other countries which are particularly progressive in those areas?

A: Yes. Check out the Lesbian and Gay Immigration Rights Task Force site (http://www.lgirtf.org/). Basically there are seven countries in the world where a citizen can petition to have their same-sex partner immigrate to join them, based on the same-sex relationship. For example, Australia and Canada (which do not have any form of gay marriage or registered partnership) allow this, together with the typically progressive countries of Norway, Denmark, Sweden, the Netherlands, and New Zealand. I believe Iceland has it in its new registered partnership law as well.

SETA

http://www.seta.fi/english.html

SETA is the Finnish organization of sexual equality. Its main purpose is to serve the Finnish queer community, though it provides pages in English and Swedish.

France

Etudes et Ressources Homosexuelles

http://www.swarthmore.edu/Humanities/ clicnet/etudes.homosexuelles.html

In French only, this page leads the way to various special-interest sites throughout gay France.

Europride '97 - Paris

http://www.casti.com/FQRD/events/97/ paris97/paris97-en.html

This year, Paris will be the center of gay and lesbian Europe as host of the annual Europride celebration. Visit this page, filed in the France Queer Resources Directory, for details on the Europride Parade, EuroSalon (a forum for lesbian and gay associations and enterprises from all over Europe), and the fifth EuroGames. Information is provided in French, English, German, Spanish, and Italian.

La France Gaie et Lesbienne (France Queer Resources Directory)

http://www.casti.com/FQRD/fglb.html

France's Queer Resources Directory promises everything you always wanted to know (but were afraid to ask) about gay and lesbian life in France. Visitors will find the France directory, along with extras such as pride celebration photos, personal advertising, and a map of the country.

Germany

Gay Berlin

http://www.informatik.hu-berlin.de:80/~holz/ privat/

The Webmaster behind this guide to gay Berlin informs us that the city has more than 150 gay bars, cafes, and

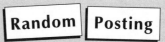

dance floors, and goes on to recommend some favorites. Other lists on the site include local organizations, publications, and art galleries.

LesPress

http://www.cologne.de/~macman/man/ groups/lespress/index.html

LesPress is "Germany's first nationwide newspaper for lesbians and forward thinking women." Issues of the monthly publication are available online, in German.

FliederNet Nurnberg

http://members.aol.com/fliederlic/ welcome.html

FliederNet is Nuremberg's nonprofit gay and lesbian organization. Its Web page is loaded with information; most of it in German only.

Homo Homepage Cologne

http://www.macman.org/

Known alternately as MacMan and the Homo Homepage, this site is loaded with info on gay groups and other resources in Cologne, "the gay centre west." In German, with some English.

Hungary

Masok

http://www.datanet.hu/masok/

Masok is a monthly gay Hungarian magazine. The current issue and back issues are available online in Hungarian only.

Italy

Babilonia
http://sexcity.it/babilon/homepage.htm

Babilonia (Figure 10.9) is Italy's gay and lesbian magazine. Content from the current issue is available online, in Italian.

Gaytalia
http://www.vol.it/itf/gaytalia/

This gay Italian site includes listings, feature sections, and links to personal home pages. In Italian.

Latvia

Latvian Queer Resources Directory
http://dspace.dial.pipex.com/town/parade/gf96/

The Latvian Queer Resources Directory (Figure 10.10) includes a gay guide and special sections for lesbians and "Latvian Boys of the Month."

Lithuania

Lithuanian Gay and Lesbian Home Page
http://cs.ektaco.ee/~forter/

The Lithuanian Gay and Lesbian site maintains pages for local organizations (the Lithuanian Gay League, Lithuanian Movement for Sexual Equality), and lists information on bars and discos. It also includes a "penpal connection."

Netherlands

COC the Netherlands
http://www.xs4all.nl/~heinv/dqrd/index.html

The Dutch Organization for Integration of Homosexuality, called COC, is a nationwide group focusing on gay and lesbian rights. It works with politicians and the community at large to gain equal rights and further acceptance of homosexuality in society. Its Web site contains a wealth of topical information and links, mostly in Dutch.

Figure 10.9
Babilonia

Figure 10.10
Latvian Queer Resources Directory

De GAY Krant

http://www.gayworld.nl/gaykrant/nederlands/
gkn-nederlands.html

De GAY Krant features daily gay news, classifieds, and a photo magazine. Available in Dutch and English.

Dutch Queer Resources

http://www.xs4all.nl/~heinv/dqrd/index.html

Dutch Queer Resources lists legal and political info, along with recreation, health, media, and "HomoStudies" links.

Norway

Blikk magazine

http://www.glnetwork.no/BLIKK/

Blikk (Figure 10.11), Norway's gay magazine, is online and in Norwegian only.

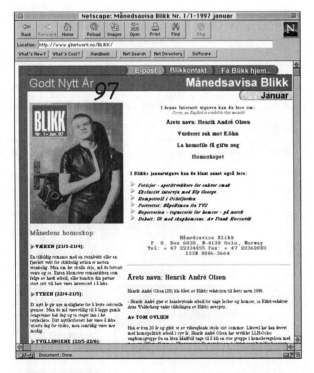

Figure 10.11
Blikk magazine

The Norwegian Association for Lesbian and Gay Liberation

http://www.stud.unit.no/studorg/llh/llh/
english/llh.html

The Norwegian Association for Lesbian and Gay Liberation is the only national Norwegian gay rights organization. Get details on local chapters and Norwegian legislation and gay rights on site.

Poland

PolGay

http://qrd.tcp.com/qrd/www/world/europe/
poland/

Housed by the U.S. Queer Resources Directory, PolGay is "the first attempt to construct a Web page that could be a beginning of service for gay people" in Poland. Places to go, organizations, and the gay press are covered. In English and Polish.

Portugal

ILGA Portugal

http://www.ilga-portugal.org/

From the ILGA Portugal manifesto: "We won't live in ghettos. We won't run away from reality. We won't be kept in hiding. We will respect and wish to be respected. We will be ourselves, without masks." The organization's Web site (Figure 10.12) outlines goals and actions, provides electronic brochures, and features special sections such as "Being Gay in Portugal" and "Portugal Gay Guide." In Portuguese and English.

Portugal Gay

http://www.ip.pt/~ip001704/

Portugal Gay is not intended for people who don't speak Portuguese, but the site's Roteiro Portugal Gay section (gay guide) uses universal symbols so that the site may be of interest to foreign surfers.

Figure 10.12
ILGA Portugal

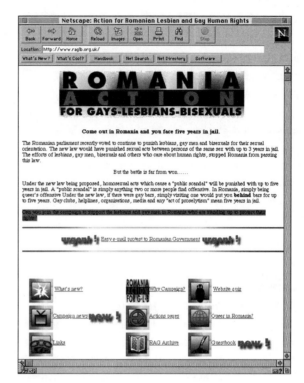

Figure 10.13
Romania Action for Gays-Lesbians-Bisexuals

Romania

Romania Action for Gays-Lesbians-Bisexuals

http://www.raglb.org.uk/

Under a new law being proposed in Romania, homosexual acts that cause a "public scandal" (a "public scandal" is defined as anything two or more people find offensive) may get you up to five years in jail. The U.K.-based Romania Action for Gays-Lesbians-Bisexuals site (Figure 10.13) gives visitors the chance to protest by zapping e-mail to the Romanian Government. The site also includes concise information on how gays are treated by the institutions and government of Romania, from the churches to the media to the courts. That, and current reports from the front line of the campaign.

Romanian LesBiGays on Internet

http://www.geocities.com/WestHollywood/ 1811/

Romanian LesBiGays on Internet features news reports and pointers to Web resources of interest to gay Romanians.

Russia

Russian Gay Life Pages

http://www.vmt.com/gayrussia/

Most of the information to be found on these pages of Russian gay life deal with Moscow and St. Petersburg—"the main centers of half-legal gay community," as the site explains. Visitors will find listings for gay organizations, entertainment, and culture and art. The site also hosts a Gay Russia bulletin board.

Slovenia

Slovene Queer Resources Directory
http://www.kud-fp.si/~siqrd/index.html

The Slovene Queer Resources Directory (Figure 10.14) offers a to-the-point guide for what to do and where to go when in the cities of Ljubljana, Marior, Celje, and Piran; from the hottest nightclubs and beaches to the steamiest saunas. The site also gives a history of the country's gay and lesbian movement and links to organizations and events of interest throughout Slovenia.

Spain

Coordinadora Gai-Lesbiana
http://www.pangea.org/org/cgl/

The Barcelona-based Coordinadora Gai-Lesbiana comprises a well-rounded assortment of five associations. Stop Sida is committed to the fight against AIDS. Gais Positius offers a supportive environment in which gays with HIV/AIDS can meet. Grup Lesbos works to increase visibility and acceptance of lesbians. Grup Jove promotes self-acceptance among gay youth. And Associacio Cristiana de Gais i Lesbianes promotes acceptance of homosexuality within the church and educates about the presence of Christianity within the gay community. The Web site provides much more information on each association and Coordinadora Gai-Lesbiana's many community services.

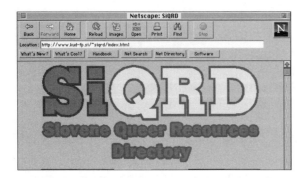

Figure 10.14
Slovene Queer Resources Directory

Sweden

Stockholm Europride '98
http://www.astro.su.se/~robert/Europride/index_en.html

Looking forward to being the 1998 host of Europe's annual summer celebration for gays, lesbians, and bisexuals, the Stockholm Europride (Figure 10.15) committee maintains this page "to tell you how the construction's going." Contact information is also available.

Swedish Federation for Gay and Lesbian Rights
http://www.rfsl.se/

This massive site—which includes a magazine, a news section, a bulletin board, chat, and much more—is presented mainly in Swedish. Two gay guides, however, are presented in English—the Complete Swedish Gayguide, and the Stockholm Gay Guide. Use a clickable map or menus to locate resources by region, province, or town.

Figure 10.15
Stockholm Europride '98

U.K. and Ireland

Brighton Pride Home Page
http://freedom.co.uk/Brightonpride/
HOME.HTML

The home page of the annual Brighton Pride Festival and Carnival. Information on merchandise, the "membership scheme," and a look back on previous years' festivities are included.

Freedom.co.uk
http://freedom.co.uk/

GAYtoZ Internet Directory
http://freedom.co.uk/gaytoz/

The U.K.-based search engine for gay, lesbian, bisexual, and transgendered sites around the world allows visitors to search by title or "description," and by country. It also points to a selection of "way cool sites" and houses the GAYtoZ Internet Directory, described as "the U.K.'s Gay Phonebook."

Gay Business Association
http://www.gba.org.uk/

The GBA was formed by U.K. businessmen and women to improve standards of and promote gay business. It's also a networking group for sharing information and experiences with professional peers. Membership information and the organizational newsletter are available online.

Glasgow Gay & Lesbian Centre
http://www.dircon.co.uk/gglc/

Glasgow's center for the gay, lesbian, and bisexual community strives to become the natural focus for the city's gay population. Along with information services and meeting rooms, the center houses a cafe, a mortgage and assurance business, and a gift shop. Find out about its history, organization, and upcoming events on the Web site.

GETTING IN TOUCH WITH THE WORLD: OUT.COM'S GLOBAL FORUM

Sleepless in Slovenia? Feeling deserted on Prince Edward Island? Looking to meet new friends in Tunisia? Out.com's Global Forum may be just the ticket. Visit the home page at http://www.out.com and click on "Community." You'll be whisked directly to "Global Forum" options for Africa, Asia, Australia & Oceania, Canada, Europe, and Latin America. The "Regional Forum" next door covers the sections of the United States (Northeast, the South, Midwest, etc.). Relish the comments, wishes, and musings from your geographic (or would-be geographic) peers, and post your own words and responses for all the world to see. Be anonymous if you like. Just don't be shy.

Ireland's Pink Pages
http://abacus.oxy.edu/qrd/www/world/
europe/ireland/

"Homosexuality in the Republic of Ireland is considerably more liberal than in the U.K. or many U.S. states," Ireland's Pink Pages explains. "So come on over and check us out!" A virtual visit is made easy with this by-city listings guide, which covers gay and gay-friendly organizations and services (even local orientation) from Belfast to Wexford.

Figure 10.16
ScotsGay Magazine

Lesbian Archive and Information Centre (Glasgow)
http://www.quine.org.uk/resources/glasgow_womens_library/lesbian_archive.html

This U.K. national collection of material relating to lesbians is housed in Scotland and maintained by the Glasgow Women's Library.

ScotsGay Magazine
http://www.scotsgay.co.uk/

ScotsGay (Figure 10.16) is the magazine from Scotland for gays, lesbians, and bisexuals, "wherever they may be." It strives to reflect the diversity of the gay experience in Scotland without putting too much weight on "the scene" or "the arts field." The magazine—and its supplemental guide to the cities, "Inside Out"—is available in paper to Scots, and online for the rest of us.

U.K. Gay
http://www.demon.co.uk/world/ukgay/index.html

This online gay guide to the U.K. takes a magazine approach, with news and columns, along with listings for pubs and clubs.

U.K. National Union of Students Lesbian, Gay and Bisexual Campaign
http://www.bath.ac.uk/~su4lgbs/NUS/home.html

It's a bird, it's a plane, it's ... it's ... the unofficial NUS LGB WWW pages. "If you think you can cope with that set of initials then carry on reading," the site advises. If you do, you'll find full details on the Bath University-based organization for gay student groups and its Lesbian, Gay, and Bisexual Liberation campaign. That, and a full page of links to LGB societies around the U.K., from Birmingham University to the University of York.

LATIN AMERICA

Arenal
http://www.indiana.edu/~arenal/Homepage.html

Arenal is "the Spanish-speaking lesbigay home page." It's based in Indiana, but contains a wealth of information about the laws in Latin America and Spain ("places to go and places to avoid"). Special sections include "famous lesbian writers in Latin America," "News from the Front," and "Society and the Law Country by Country." Most of the material is available in English, too.

Buenos Aires Gay Guide
http://giga.com.ar/bagay/bagay.htm

The Buenos Aires Gay Guide leads the way to the city's choice bars, restaurants, and organizations. In Spanish.

Community Organizations in Puerto Rico
http://www-lib.usc.edu/~calimano/organizations.html

This chart runs down gay Puerto Rico's organizational offerings and includes contact information. It also links to accommodation, club, and restaurant recommendations.

THE GLOBAL GAY GHETTO
GEOCITIES' WESTHOLLYWOOD COMMUNITY

Anyone who says Cyberspace is cold and impersonal hasn't been to GeoCities. And any gay person who senses a lack of community on the Web hasn't been to WestHollywood.

Begin your pilgrimage to the global gay ghetto at GeoCities (http://www.geocities.com), the leader in "Net homesteading and segmented communities." Click on "neighborhoods," and scroll down almost to the bottom of the list of options. In between WallStreet, "where GeoCitizens do business," and Yosemite, "the venue for outdoor recreation enthusiasts," you'll discover WestHollywood, "a community with a culture based on gay and lesbian identity" (http://www.geocities.com/WestHollywood/). And what a community it is. Just think about all of the sites you've seen (in this book and out on the surf) whose URLs include the words "geocities" and "WestHollywood." Here's why:

GeoCities is a Web company dedicated to offering "rich and dynamic content" (how's that for a concept?). The strategy is in providing free personal home pages and a free e-mail account to those who join one of the dozens of themed communities. In other words, if you've got Web access, creative energy and time, GeoCities has a pad for you, rent free.

If you decide WestHollywood is the right 'hood for your site, register and claim your street address. You may be the next door neighbor of a gay man who "tells his story"; just down the way from

"a proud mother's tribute to her gay son"; or within earshot of the San Francisco Gay Men's Chorus. At the very least, you can tell people you live in West Hollywood.

Special neighborhood facilities include forums ("meet & greet," "coming out stories"), chat, a resident birthdays section, and a virtual office for the WestHollywood community leaders, "homesteaders who have volunteered to watch over your community and help their neighbors set up home pages, answer questions, and generally keep everything running smoothly."

So what are you waiting for?

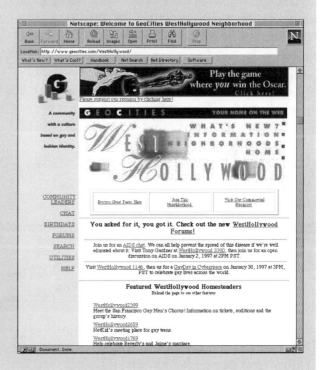

MIDDLE EAST

Boolboolnet
http://boolboolnet.co.il/

Boolboolnet (Figure 10.17) is the Israeli Gay Magazine online. In Hebrew.

Figure 10.17
Boolboolnet

Gay and Lesbian Arab Society
http://leb.net/glas/

Based in New York City, the Gay and Lesbian Arab Society serves as a networking organization—with chapters all around the world—for gays and lesbians of Arab descent and those living in Arab countries. On the home page, learn how to subscribe to the Queerarabs mailing list, or check out the organizational newsletter, *Ahbab*, online.

Lambda Istanbul
http://qrd.tcp.com/qrd/www/world/europe/turkey/lambda.html

Lambda Istanbul is a liberation group for gay, lesbian, bisexual, and transgender people in Turkey. Its Web site features headline news from the country ("Lesbian and Gay Festival Banned"), bi-monthly bulletins, and a gay guide to Turkey. The guide includes listings for friendly lodging, food and entertainment, along with phone codes and organization contacts for the gay community.

IT'S YOUR BUSINESS

Chapter 11

OUT@WORK (OR NOT)

According to a 1996 *Newsweek* magazine poll, 84 percent of Americans who voted in the previous year support equal workplace rights for gays and lesbians. Major corporations seem to be warming up to the idea, as well. The fact that more than half of the Fortune 500 companies have non-discrimination policies inclusive of sexual orientation is testament to that. What's more, Human Rights Campaign documentation shows that more than 300 employers have adopted same-sex domestic partner benefits, and more than 100 companies have support groups in place for their gay and lesbian employees. Obviously, there is plenty of room for improvement in those numbers, but the equitable workplace is a trend that seems to be catching on—even without help from the pending Employment Non-Discrimination Act (ENDA).

Many business-oriented Web sites reflect the interest of gays and lesbians in making the workplace a safe and healthy place for all employees. The Human Rights Campaign and the American Civil Liberties Union both provide excellent online tool kits and resources for getting the job done (with close attention to activity surrounding ENDA). Elsewhere, gay and lesbian employee resource groups use the Web to network with and inspire the international business community.

For occupations in which ground rules aren't necessarily created to aid in capitalist endeavors (notably in religion, education, and the military), the struggle is apparent, and the efforts are more strained. It is exciting, however, to see organizations such as the Servicemembers Legal Defense Network, the Gay, Lesbian & Straight Teachers Network, and the Interfaith Working Group, all making bold and dexterous use of the medium. They know there is plenty of work to do, but these pros are doing the best job possible.

HUMAN RIGHTS CAMPAIGN'S WORKNET: A GOLD MINE FOR GAY WORKPLACE ISSUES

Figure 11.1
Human Rights Campaign WorkNet

Human Rights Campaign WorkNet
http://www.hrcusa.org/issues/workplac/index.html

Simply put, the goal here is fairness in the workplace. But The Human Rights Campaign (HRC) doesn't do things simply; it works overtime with this texty collection of documents and connections for gay employees, their employers, and leaders in business (Figure 11.1). Section by section, page by page, HRC's Workplace Project—whose objective is to persuade a majority of Congress to endorse the aims of the Employment Non-Discrimination Act and to work for its passage—delivers legal documents, statistics on the state of the workplace for gays and lesbians, and tools for individual activism and improvement. An "ENDA Fact Sheet" gives the down and dirty on the Act, and a section on the 1996 hearing on ENDA by the Government Programs Subcommittee of the House Small Business Committee includes transcripts of testimonies from members of the Business, Discrimination, and Expert panels. Lists of Fortune 500 companies whose equal employment policies do (and do not) include sexual orientation are on site, along with a rundown of states, cities, and counties which prohibit discrimination based on sexual orientation. Liz Winfield, author of *Straight Talk About Gays in the Workplace*, contributes an extensive article on domestic partnership, working from "the whys and what-fors" of such benefits through sexual orientation education. A bite of reality,

the site also documents discrimination with detailed accounts from various states, broken down geographically; from a media specialist who was denied a New York P.R. job because of homophobia to a Tampa bartender who was replaced because she is *not* gay. If you have experienced job discrimination based on sexual orientation, WorkNet provides a form you can fill out and return to the HRC headquarters in Washington.

ENDA Fact-Sheet
http://www.hrcusa.org/issues/workplac/enda/enda.html

Job discrimination is widespread and legal, and the Human Rights Campaign has documentation of cases to prove it. Get the facts here on how the Employment Non-Discrimination Act would provide basic protection for gays and lesbians in the workplace, why the need is so great, and who is in support of it.

The State of the Workplace for Gay and Lesbian Americans
http://www.hrcusa.org/issues/workplac/enda/endarept.html

The special (and lengthy) report on "Why Congress Should Pass the Employment Non-Discrimination Act" covers the state of the gay workplace, and issues such as domestic partner benefits and employee support groups. It also lists corporations and organizations which endorse ENDA.

Out.com News—Employment and Housing Issues
http://www.out.com

For historical and of-the-moment perspectives on gay workplace issues, visit Out.com's "News" section and click on "Employment and Housing Issues" (Figure 11.2). Articles range from "Gay Vets Sue American Legion in California" to "Disney's Largest Union Says Gay Benefits Unfair."

Figure 11.2
Out.com News—Employment and Housing Issues

Domestic Partnership Article
http://www.hrcusa.org/issues/workplac/articles.html

Liz Winfield, author of *Straight Talk About Gays in the Workplace*, contributes this extensive article on domestic partnership. She covers "the whys and what-fors" of DP benefits, the "cost of equity," and successful sexual orientation education.

WorkNet Workplace Tools

Non-Discrimination in the Workplace
http://www.hrcusa.org/issues/workplac/tools/ndpol.html

Employee Support Groups and Workplace Diversity Programs
http://www.hrcusa.org/issues/workplac/tools/empgrps.html

Gay and Lesbian Workplace Issues: A Bibliography
http://www.hrcusa.org/issues/workplac/tools/biblio2.html

Part of the HRC Workplace Project's focus is on creating and distributing gay and lesbian employment information. To that end, it posts a series of text tools which succinctly cover such issues as non-discrimination policies, the role of ENDA, and several "models" of workplace policies and employee resource groups that have been adopted by some of the nation's major employers. After providing background and a solid argument, the tools instruct viewers on how to go about establishing a non-discrimination policy at work, or how to go about forming a new employee resource group. Finally, a bibliography page lists the books that are available on gay and lesbian workplace issues.

GAY BUSINESS GROUPS AND RESOURCES

Transgendered airline employees, lesbian health-science librarians, custom cabinetmakers in Chicago, innkeepers in Key West, career women in San Diego, attorneys in Helms country, pride coordinators, postal employees, copyeditors, plant taxonomists, teachers, techies, judges, shrinks, docs, cops, preachers, firefighters, more cops ....

What do all of these working folks have in common? For one thing, they're all represented in a gay-specific business organization that is with-it enough to have a presence on the Web. Yep, looks like we're everywhere.

AGOG
http://glyphic.com/agog/

Synonyms for this word range from "agitated" to "aflame," but in San Francisco, AGOG means "a group of groups," or a federation of local lesbian, gay, transsexual, and transgender employee associations, companies, and friends. AGOG's Web presence provides all the details, along with links to some possible job opportunities.

American Airlines
http://www.americanair.com/aa_home.htm

Diversity at American Airlines
http://www.americanair.com/aa_home/aa_hr/diversity.html

AMR OnBoard
http://www.amrcorp.com/

Gay, Lesbian, Bisexual and Transgendered Employees at AMR
http://users.why.net/gleam/index.htm

Hop on board with Texas-based American Airlines, which prides itself in giving full consideration to "how all our people—who have many diverse racial, cultural and social backgrounds—can positively impact the quality of the decisions we make about our business." Elsewhere, check out the Web site for AMR Corporation's—American Airlines's parent company—gay, lesbian, bisexual, and transgendered employees.

American Civil Liberties Union
http://www.aclu.org/

ACLU Lesbian and Gay Rights
http://www.aclu.org/issues/gay/hmgl.html

ACLU Workplace Rights
http://www.aclu.org/issues/worker/hmwr.html

The mammoth ACLU site combines a user-friendly magazine format with reference library functionality. Individual sections are set up for more than a dozen areas of interest, including "HIV/AIDS," "Lesbian and Gay Rights," and "Racial Equality"—each equipped with its own news, indices, and summaries. The "Lesbian and Gay Rights" section features top-rate materials about the Employment Non-Discrimination Act, and explains what you can do to ensure its success. The site's "Workplace Rights" section (Figure 11.3) explores such areas as lifestyle discrimination, drug testing, and artistic freedom in the workplace. Each section also features a topical rundown of what's happening in the courts.

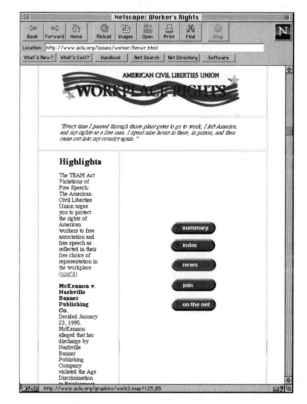

Figure 11.3
American Civil Liberties Union Workers' Rights

The Association of Gay and Lesbian Psychiatrists
http://members.aol.com/aglpnat/
homepage.html

If the thought of a large group of psychiatrists and psychiatry residents semi-creeps you out, take comfort in the fact that all of the ones in this organization serve as a voice for the concerns of gays and lesbians in the profession. The Association is also committed to fostering a more accurate understanding of homosexuality, opposing discriminatory practices against gays and lesbians, and promoting supportive, well-informed psychiatric care for lesbian and gay patients. Nothing creepy about all that. Get the group's history, newsletter, and list of upcoming events on the Web site.

Chicago Area Gay and Lesbian Chamber of Commerce
http://www.glchamber.org/

Chicago's gay and lesbian business community shows that it has its act together with its own private Chamber of Commerce. The Chamber strengthens the gay business community and the city alike through networking, promotions, marketing, and tourist attractions. The group's Web site provides membership information and a directory of supportive area businesses.

Chicagoland Gay and Lesbian Building and Trade Professionals Directory
http://www.suba.com/~glbtp/

Conceived to bring gay and lesbian building-industry professionals in and around Chicago together for referrals, the Chicagoland Gay and Lesbian Building and Trade Professionals Directory provides loads of contacts (including many by direct e-mail) for gay carpentry contractors, custom cabinetmakers, plumbers, and more. Yes, we are everywhere.

Digital Queers
http://www.dq.org/dq

Digital Queers in D.C.
http://www.dc.dq.org

Figure 11.4
Digital Queers

Digital Queers New England
http://www.actwin.com/DQ/index.html

The legendary Digital Queers (Figure 11.4), a good-time group of queer computer professionals and technology aficionados, arrived on the scene in 1992 with a vision of equipping gay rights groups with the "silicon horsepower" necessary to organize and communicate more effectively, or digitally. Look around; obviously the DQs were on to something. The volunteer organization has performed its trademark "computer beauty makeovers" on such worthy recipients as NGLTF, GLAAD, P-FLAG, and the Lambda Legal Defense. The founders have more recently gone big time with PlanetOut, but individual city chapters (notably Digital Queers in New England and D.C.) rage on.

GALAXe: Gays and Lesbians at Xerox
http://www.servtech.com/public/racer/galaxe/

Enter the great big galaxy created for the gay and lesbian people who work for the great big document company. GALAXe (which stands for Gays and Lesbians at Xerox) is a corporate-recognized caucus group for promotion of the welfare of and support of gay and lesbian employees at Xerox. The organization's site for U.S. members features Xerox articles that mention the group, links to other professional groups, and company policy as it pertains to gays, lesbians, and people with AIDS.

GAP: The Business & Professionals Association (Wellington, New Zealand)
http://shell.ihug.co.nz/~markr/gap.htm

The GAP of Wellington, New Zealand, is not a trendy clothing store; nor is it "dominated by a crippling sense of oppression." Rather, it is an environment "where thinking, feeling men and women can share their thoughts, energy, and desire for professional companionship with like-minded individuals." Check out the organization's newsletter and upcoming events online.

Gay and Lesbian Postal Employees Network

http://www.eden.com/~kaos/

The vision: to eliminate homophobia and discrimination against sexual orientation minorities. The mission: to serve as an advocate and resource for sexual orientation minority employees and advance their recognition and legitimacy within the United States Postal Service. The network was formed in 1992. Get the history online, along with a "who's who," "what's new," and, of course, a stamp collection.

Gays and Lesbians Working for Cultural Diversity at NYNEX

http://soho.ios.com/~msmigels/glcd/glcd.html

"Who are we and what are we doing here?" That is the question posed by the gay employees of NYNEX Corp. As this organizational site illustrates, they're doing quite a bit for gays in corporate America. Get the history of GLCD, find out about its mentoring program with gay and lesbian youth at the Harvey Milk School, and check out a summary of the benefits that NYNEX now extends to same-sex domestic partners.

Gay, Lesbian & Straight Teachers Network

http://www.glstn.org/freedom/

"Teaching respect for all" is top curriculum for the Gay, Lesbian & Straight Teachers Network (Figure 11.5), a coalition of parents, teachers, students, and concerned citizens working to create schools where everyone is valued. The group's impressive Web site lists directions for organizing a regional GLSTN chapter, sample letter excerpts for a school letter-writing campaign, and professional tools for educators and community leaders. The site's vast array of files includes pieces on "Understanding the experience of openly gay and lesbian educators," "Ideas for educators addressing homophobia in schools," and "Breaking the Silence: a Resource Guide for Independent Schools." It's a real learning experience.

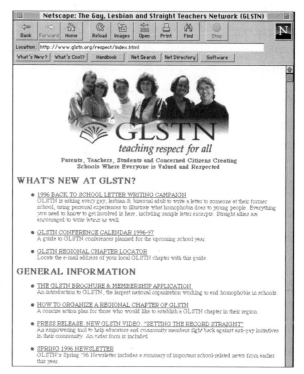

Figure 11.5

Gay, Lesbian & Straight Teachers Network

Gay Workplace Issues Home Page

http://www.nyu.edu/pages/sls/gaywork/

"Webmeister" Sharon Silverstein directs her many talents towards making the workplace a better place for gays and lesbians. And she works at it diligently. With her Gay Workplace Issues Home Page (Figure 11.6), she provides contact information for various professional organizations, listings of employer policies at major companies, and a link to information on the book she co-authored, *Straight Jobs, Gay Lives*.

GOAL New York

http://users.aol.com/goalnys/index.htm

GOAL stands for Gay Officers Action League, and it is an international organization serving lesbian, gay, bisexual, and transgender criminal justice professionals. Founded in 1982, GOAL has grown to include numerous affiliated chapters worldwide, but New York is the one that's online, where a membership application and photo album are available to visitors.

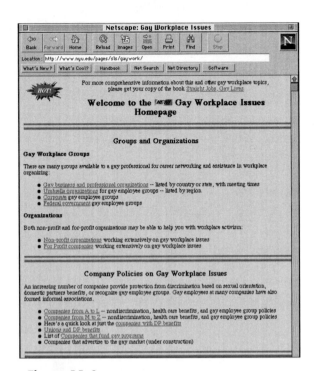

Figure 11.6
Gay Workplace Issues Home Page

Golden State Peace Officers Association
http://www.geocities.com/WestHollywood/3780/

The Golden State Peace Officers support the fire fighters and law enforcement officers of Southern California. Get the history, membership information, and details on upcoming events.

Greater Atlanta Business Coalition
http://www.gaypride.com/gabc/

The Greater Atlanta Business Coalition is a nonprofit org dedicated to the development and growth of businesses that support the gay and lesbian community. Specific purposes include education and training to empower gays and lesbians to start and expand their own businesses. Get information here on GABC officers, members, and news.

High Tech Gays
http://www.htg.org/

High tech gays in San Jose? Who would have guessed. The high-tech activist group's home page is surprisingly low-tech, though the premise—to assist gays and lesbians in job searches and become active in the gay rights movement—is clearly laid out. Where do they meet? When do they meet? Get the details here, along with back issues of the "High Tech Gazette" newsletter.

Hollywood Supports
http://www.hsupports.org/hsupports/

Not everyone in Hollywood is in the closet, as is proven by this entertainment-industry workplace education and support project. Launched in the fall of 1991 by "leading entertainment industry figures," Hollywood Supports works to stamp out discrimination based on HIV status and sexual orientation. The org is perhaps best known for spearheading the annual "Day of Compassion," on which television programming highlights compassion and support for people affected by HIV and AIDS. Get details on Hollywood Supports and the various workshops it offers here.

Human Rights Campaign's Gay/Lesbian/Bisexual Employee Groups
http://www.hrcusa.org/issues/workplac/empgrp.html

Human Rights Campaign's Gay Professional Organizations
http://www.hrcusa.org/issues/workplac/gayprof.html

A segment of its exemplary WorkNet site, the Human Rights Campaign provides contact information for organizations and/or individuals who have been officially and/or unofficially recognized by their companies as working towards a better understanding of gay, lesbian, and bisexual issues. Contact information is provided—mostly addresses and phone numbers—for gay professional organizations across the country.

IBM EAGLE
http://www.mindspring.com/~morpheus/eagle/

If you thought "Eagle" was the name reserved for all seedy neighborhood bars, think again. Here, it stands for Employee Alliance for Gay and Lesbian Equality at IBM. The organization works for equal benefits for gay and lesbian IBMers and fosters an "open and safe" work environment. Not officially recognized by IBM (though recognition is allegedly on the way), the group's independent Web site outlines goals and objectives, provides internal contacts, and spreads good news about IBM—like the fact that the company now extends benefits to the domestic partners of employees.

Intel Gay, Lesbian or Bisexual Employees
http://www.glyphic.com/iglobe/

Intel's gay and lesbian employees' group, IGLOBE (Figure 11.7), affirms the company's commitment to equality and diversity. Its home page provides newsflashes about Intel's progress, and lays out the organization's goals. The site FAQ even answers some questions that non-gays may have ("Why do people want to be openly gay at work?" and "What's it like living in the closet?"). E-mail contacts to gay employees representing all major domestic sites are also included.

The Interfaith Working Group
http://www.libertynet.org/~iwg/

The Interfaith Working Group (Figure 11.8) believes that the characterization of religion as inherently conservative—and the portrayal of social debates as disagreements between the religious and the nonreligious—undermines faith and "the ideal of religious diversity." The group expresses the diversity of religious opinion on social issues where it is not widely recognized, mainly by providing a voice and a forum for religious organizations that favor gay rights, reproductive freedom, and separation of church and state. Its activities include writing letters of support for gay teachers, protesting censorship, upholding marriage for same-sex couples, and argument

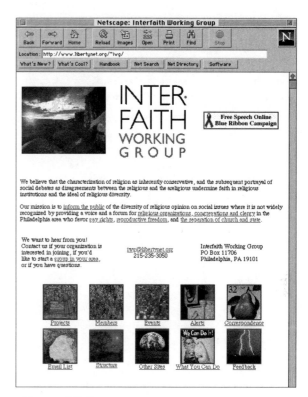

Figure 11.8
The Interfaith Working Group

against the policies of the "Radical Religious Right." Though Interfaith is based in and predominately serves Philadelphia, its Web site enables visitors from all around to search for a local religious organization whose policies are compatible with their own beliefs.

International Association of Lesbian & Gay Judges
http://pages.prodigy.com/ialgj/

Short but sweet, the home page for the International Association of Lesbian & Gay Judges gives its history ("In April 1993, 25 lesbian and gay judges and judicial officers met in suburban Washington, D.C. ..."), objectives ("to increase the visibility of lesbian and gay judicial officers..."), and links to association contacts.

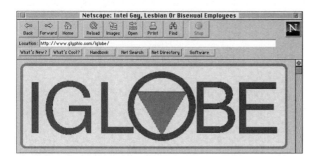

Figure 11.7
Intel Gay, Lesbian or Bisexual Employees

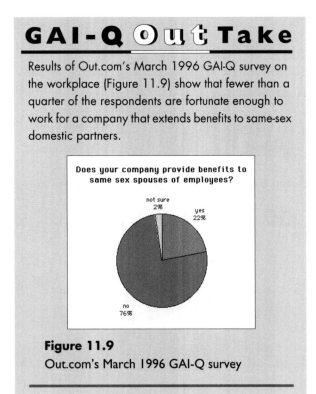

GAI-Q Out Take

Results of Out.com's March 1996 GAI-Q survey on the workplace (Figure 11.9) show that fewer than a quarter of the respondents are fortunate enough to work for a company that extends benefits to same-sex domestic partners.

Does your company provide benefits to same sex spouses of employees?

not sure 2%
yes 22%
no 76%

Figure 11.9
Out.com's March 1996 GAI-Q survey

International Association of Lesbian/ Gay Pride Coordinators
http://www.tde.com/~ialgpc/

This nonprofit org is made up of organizers in more than 60 cities around the world that produce gay and lesbian pride events. Each year, IAL/GPC holds an international conference and five regional conferences to conduct corporate business, and to discuss future plans, merchandising, political concerns, and so on. "Equality through visibility" is the motto.

The Key West Business Guild
http://www.gaykeywestfl.com/kwbgpage.html

Since 1978, the Key West Business Guild has been promoting Florida's little jewel to domestic and international gay markets. Today, the guild is 400 members strong, and, obviously, doing a bang-up job.

LEGAL International
http://members.aol.com/legalint/index.html

LEGAL, which stands for Law Enforcement Gays and Lesbians, was organized in 1995—an outgrowth of the first International Lesbian-Gay Criminal Justice Conference. The International group's Web site provides information on how to join the LEGAL-LIST discussion group, along with a listing of all known gay and lesbian criminal justice groups and more. LEGAL of Minnesota, the chapter which hosted the 1996 International Conference, also makes a home on the Web featuring more localized information.

Lesbian, Gay and Bisexual Health Science Librarians
http://www.lib.uchicago.edu/~rfwhitco/ mlalgb/home.html

Queer health-science librarians who think they are the only ones need look no further—a whole bundle of people like you are lurking in the virtual stacks of this painstakingly organized organizational site. This special interest group of the Medical Library Association lists its current officers, posts a position statement, and leads the way to a variety of topical Web resources.

Lesbian & Gay Law Association of Greater New York
http://www.users.interport.net/~le-gal/

This first Web site by an association of lesbian and gay lawyers promotes the expertise and advancement of gay and lesbian legal professionals; educates the public on legal issues facing lesbians and gay men; and works with other gay and lesbian organizations to gain equal rights for all people, among other things. Organizational information is available here, as well as hot links to various international legal and political resources.

National Gay and Lesbian Business Alliance
http://www.nglba.com/

The people who produce the "Gay Expo" business extravaganza promote it online here. Little information is available on the National Gay and Lesbian Business Alliance itself, but visitors will discover plenty on the Expo and its major sponsors.

The National Journal of Sexual Orientation Law

http://sunsite.unc.edu/gaylaw/

The National Journal of Sexual Orientation Law spreads information and ideas about law and sexual orientation in a timely manner. Those researching gay issues in the workplace will find help in such articles as "Recognition of Domestic Partnerships by Governmental Entities and Private Employers" and "Coming Out and Stepping Up: Queer Legal Theory and Connectivity."

The National Lesbian and Gay Health Association

http://www.serve.com/nlgha/index.htm

Based in Washington, D.C., the National Lesbian and Gay Health Association serves as a single, comprehensive resource for physical and mental health-related issues, advocacy, education, and research. (It was the result of a merger between the National Alliance of Lesbian and Gay Health Clinics and the National Lesbian and Gay Health Foundation in 1994.) With several major gay and lesbian community health centers and tens of thousands of gay and lesbian health-care providers on board, it also lends a powerful voice for educating public health officials of our often unique health needs. The organization's Web presence provides details on NLGHA's activities and its annual National Health Conference. It also lists contact information and descriptions of member clinics across the country. At press time, NLGHA promised a resource library and clearinghouse on health services provided to the gay, lesbian, bisexual, and transgender communities. Stay tuned.

National Lesbian & Gay Journalists Association

http://www.journalism.sfsu.edu/nlgja.html

NLGA-Tampa Bay/Central Florida Chapter

http://members.aol.com/anglesfla/angles.html

The National Lesbian & Gay Journalists Association works to ensure equal benefits and workplace conditions for gay employees in news organizations. It also works within the industry for fair, accurate, and comprehensive coverage of gay issues. History of the organization and membership information is online at the official Web site. Nationally,

there are more than 1,200 members and 17 chapters, one of which, in Central Florida, has its own hub online.

National Lesbian and Gay Law Association

http://www.nlgla.org/

The National Lesbian and Gay Law Association consists of lawyers, judges, students, and lesbian and gay legal orgs. It has been an affiliated organization of the American Bar Association since 1992 and exists to promote "justice in and through the legal profession for lesbians and gay men in all our diversity." Membership and contact information is available on site, along with details of upcoming conferences.

National Organization of Gay and Lesbian Scientists and Technical Professionals

http://www.pride.net/noglstp/

Doesn't exactly roll off your tongue, but then, techie types just adore those long titles and NOGLSTPesque abbreviations. This Pasadena-based group serves its various professionals (physics teachers, tropical biologists, plant taxonomists, and more), first, by demonstrating the presence of gay colleagues in scientific fields—something it has been doing since the early eighties. Find out more about the group's history, demographics, and goals at its well-organized site.

Northampton Area Lesbian & Gay Business Guild

http://www.westmass.com/nalgbg/

"Businesses and professionals who actively maintain and encourage a business climate open to diversity and committed to support of the lesbian and gay community" of Northampton, MA.

North Carolina Gay and Lesbian Attorneys

http://members.aol.com/ncgala/index.htm

North Carolina Gay and Lesbian Attorneys is a voluntary, non-profit and non-partisan organization providing visibility and advocacy for the state's lesbian, gay, and bisexual communities. The site features a "Legal Guide for

Lesbians & Gay Men in North Carolina" (much needed in Helms country), and a referral directory of NC attorneys. Membership information is also available.

New South Wales Police Gay & Lesbian Liaison
http://www.eagles.bbs.net.au/~gllos/ index.html

This site is slow as molasses, but if you're a gay or lesbian cop in Australia, it's probably well worth the wait. Find information on everything from "beat policy" and "gay hate" to "Star Trek." Still have questions? Another section enables visitors to "ask a cop" via e-mail.

NYPD Pride Alliance
http://members.aol.com/nypdpride/index.html

NYPD Pride represents the interests of lesbian and gay uniformed members of the New York City Police Department. Site features include the group's mission statement, preamble, and by-laws, and links to other gay and lesbian criminal justice groups on the Web—even one to the official NYPD Home Page.

Out at Work (or Not)
http://www.qrd.org/qrd/www/usa/illinois/oaw/

Out at Work (or Not) is a Chicago-based organization which brings together gay employees from various companies to provide networking, resources, and support around gay issues in the workplace. The group's "homo" page is loaded with lists (of companies with gay-inclusive non-discrimination policies) and articles ("Out on a Job Interview?") and includes a stealthy collection of pointers to online resources related to gay issues in the workplace. Hey, this site doesn't even discriminate against browsers or low-speed lines.

PROGRESS
http://www.bayscenes.com/np/progress/ home.htm

PROGRESS formed in 1995 as a two-day forum for gay, lesbian, bisexual, and transgender employee resource groups. Since then, the organization has come to provide information and resources to employee resource groups, employers, and anyone concerned about safe and equitable workplaces. The mission is simply to "help make the

American workplace safe and equitable for all lesbian, gay, transgender, and bisexual people." PROGRESS maintains communications with more than 100 employee resource groups across the U.S. Its Web site (Figure 11.10) files the bi-monthly newsletter, and a Resources Library contains bibliographies for subjects such as "HIV/AIDS Workplace Issues," "Career Development/Planning," and "Domestic Partner Benefits."

San Diego Career Women
http://www.sdcw.org/

The social and business group of—you guessed it—promotes professional networking, educational, recreational, social, and cultural events for all gay women. The goal: "to provide a safe and confidential environment for quality opportunities within the community." Find out about the group's monthly dance mixers, or learn how to join one of its special interest groups (Coffee House, Golden Girls, Traveling Dinner Club).

Servicemembers Legal Defense Network
http://www.sldn.org/

Servicemembers Survival Guide
http://www.sldn.org/scripts/ menu.ixe?pagetype=Survival+Guide

The Servicemembers Legal Defense Network (Figure 11.11) is the sole national legal aid and watchdog organization that assists those targeted by the military's policy on homosexuals. With a nationwide network of more than 200 attorneys, SLDN offers the legal advice and assistance that servicemembers need to effectively respond to investigations. The organization's excellent Web site points out

Figure 11.10
PROGRESS

Figure 11.11
Servicemembers Legal Defense Network

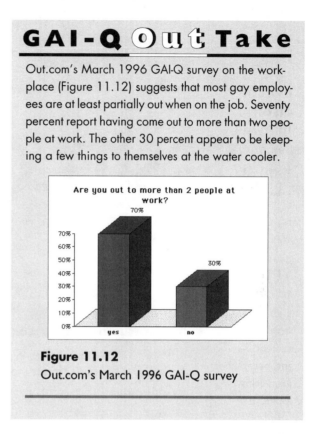

GAI-Q Out Take

Out.com's March 1996 GAI-Q survey on the workplace (Figure 11.12) suggests that most gay employees are at least partially out when on the job. Seventy percent report having come out to more than two people at work. The other 30 percent appear to be keeping a few things to themselves at the water cooler.

Figure 11.12
Out.com's March 1996 GAI-Q survey

that, despite the Clinton administration's "Don't Ask, Don't Tell, Don't Pursue" policy, military commanders and investigators continue to question recruits and servicemembers about their sexual orientation; and that suspect servicemembers still face harassment, physical violence, jail, and an untimely end to their careers. In other words, not much has changed. Visitors to this site will find an "Alerts" section which archives topical news flashes ("Update on Dornan Military HIV Exclusion Policy"), a history of "Don't Ask, Don't Tell, Don't Pursue," and a direct link for those currently under investigation. Most impressive is the online "Survival Guide," which reviews the major provisions of the policy as well as trends in its implementation, working in essential "survival tips" and covering the practical aspects of military culture along the way. Items covered range from "asking" (some commanders have used "creative" phrasing, such as "Do you find other men attractive?") to attending pride parades (may attend, but only in civilian clothes) to a definition of the "Corporal Klinger Provision." It's an essential resource for gay servicemembers, and a fascinating read for the rest of us.

10% Plus Business Association of Western Australia
http://tenplus.ednet.com.au/

10% Plus supports the gay and lesbian professional community of Western Australia. The small group hopes that through community support it will eventually be able to

provide advisory groups, lobby groups, employment opportunities, financial assistance, and many other services currently unavailable to its constituency.

Town Meeting, Inc.
http://www.townmtg.com/

Based in Houston, Texas, Town Meeting, Inc. is a nonprofit org dedicated to improving the lives of gays and lesbians through the growth and understanding of business, entertainment, and social issues. Various methods include a business and art expo, a speakers program, and a "LeTs Bi Gay Mall."

The Valley Business Alliance of Gay & Lesbian Professionals
http://ourworld.compuserve.com/homepages/
charles_barrett/vba.htm

Totally gay. Totally business. Totally San Fernando Valley.

Chapter 12

DIVERSITY.COM

As the Human Rights Campaign points out, philosophically the workplace policy espoused by the Employment Non-Discrimination Act mirrors business trends that are already occurring across the country and around the world. Even without the nudge that ENDA would provide, business leaders from many of the Fortune 1000 companies have already adopted principles of non-discrimination based on sexual orientation—and many have gone the extra mile to extend benefits to same-sex partners of employees. Following the lead of the leaders of world business, companies large and small are being added to the list each week.

This section takes a look at a handful of the corporate home pages of those Fortune 500 companies leading the way to ensuring safe and equitable workplaces for all. It's only a handful because, frankly, the list of all companies and conglomerates considered to be mindful of and "friendly" towards their gay and lesbian employees could make for a hefty book all its own.

For a more complete list, and a better example of the scope of the trend, check out HRC's WorkNet, which does an excellent job of keeping track of the states, cities, counties, companies, and organizations which have extended benefits to same-sex partners of employees and/or have included "sexual orientation" in the language of their non-discrimination policies. Seeing how Ben and Jerry are not the only good guys in Corporate America is encouraging, and even a little inspiring.

HRC WorkNet—Employers with Domestic Partnership Policies
http://www.hrcusa.org/issues/workplac/statedp.html

HRC Non-Discrimination List
http://www.hrcusa.org/issues/workplac/statec.html

HRC Corporations Endorsing ENDA List
http://www.hrcusa.org/issues/workplac/enda/endacorp.html

HRC Employers with Domestic Partnership Policies List
http://www.hrcusa.org/issues/workplac/statedp.html

HRC List of States, Cities and Counties which Prohibit Discrimination Based on Sexual Orientation List
http://www.hrcusa.org/issues/workplac/statues.html

CORPORATE CULTURE WARMS UP TO DOMESTIC PARTNERSHIPS

A simple matter of cash and equality, domestic partner benefits have become a litmus test for the degree to which corporations are inclusive of all employees. In her HRC article on domestic partnership, Liz Winfield (author of *Straight Talk About Gays in the Workplace*) notes that, for gay employees, extension of benefits to same-sex domestic partners is a simple matter of equal pay for equal work. "The extension of DP benefits will not cost the organization more than 1 to 2 percent over what it is already paying for spousal/dependent benefits," Winfield writes. "Domestic partner benefits are, simply, a low cost, low maintenance, high return-on-investment way to attract and retain highly sought after competent labor."

Many major corporations see the common sense in all of this. From Ben and Jerry's Homemade to Charles Schwabb; from Starbucks to Kaiser-Permanente; from the City of Berkeley to the City of Madison, the trend—or, rather, the attempt to retain highly sought after competent labor—is catching. But where does it stop?

In November of last year, an independent arbitrator sided with the Walt Disney Company in ruling the corporation did not have to extend the same domestic partner benefits to non-gays as it does to gay employees and their partners. Disney's desire to not extend benefits to the domestic partners of heterosexual employees—and the arbitrator's agreement that this is just—makes a not-so-indirect statement in favor of same-sex marriage. Domestic partnerships can be tricky; with marriage, it's either legal or it's not. But, oddly, that's another issue altogether.

For now, here's a look at some of the Fortune 500 companies that have domestic partnership policies in place. Links to online employment opportunities with these companies have been provided whenever possible, so be sure to keep these URLs in mind the next time you get ready to make your competent, laborious self available.

Advanced Micro Devices
http://www.amd.com/

Employment
http://www.amd.com/html/employment/employment.html

Advanced Micro Devices is a California-based supplier of integrated circuits for personal and networked computer markets. Plenty of product and corporate information here, along with a section for job and college opportunities with AMD, where "teamwork is promoted by an egalitarian atmosphere and accessibility of the top management."

Apple Computer
http://www.apple.com/

Apple Employment Information and Opportunities
http://www2.apple.com/employment/default.html

Gays and gay orgs just can't seem to get enough of their Macs. Maybe it's a style thing. Maybe it's an underdog thing. The rainbow that streaks across Apple's apple? The fact that Digital Queers is decidedly Maccentric? Perhaps it's just the cool Apple attitude: "Others can talk about boundaries. We don't believe they exist. Others can talk about risk-taking. We won't stand and wait. At Apple, we're already moving toward the next frontier. And there's no chance we'll turn back" (Figure 12.1).

Figure 12.1
Apple Employment Information and Opportunities

BankAmerica Corporation
http://www.bankamerica.com/

Career Opportunities
http://www.bankamerica.com/batoday/career.html

Online Career Center
http://www.occ.com/boa

Based in San Francisco, BankAmerica employs more than 90,000 employees worldwide in occupations ranging from retail to investment banking to information technology. "Our employees come from all walks of life, reflecting and representing our diverse customer base and bringing with them many different lifestyles, perspectives, and ideas," the site explains. The Career Opportunities section contains job listings for the Bay Area, and provides access to BankAmerica's Online Career Center.

Borland International
http://www.borland.com/

Borland Job Opportunities
http://www.borland.com/about/hr/jobindex.htm

The California-based provider of solutions for software developers extends domestic partnership benefits to employees. The Borland corporate site (Figure 12.2) tells you everything you could possibly want to know about the company, and provides a section with details on job opportunities.

Capital Cities/ABCM
http://www.abctelevision.com/

Capital Cities pitches a TV break to the online world with the ABC Television Network; for better or for worse, the site is devoid of corporate information. Instead it opts for trivia gaming in the CyberCity section and, of course, plenty of details on favorite prime-timers like "Rosanne," "Ellen," and "Spin City." The ESPNET Sportszone, Disney.com, and PoliticsNow are all conveniently attached at the hip.

Figure 12.2
Borland Job Opportunities

Chase Manhattan Bank
http://www.chase.com

Chase Career Opportunities
http://www.chase.com/noframes/careers/
index2.html

Learn all about the largest banking institution in the U.S. On its career opportunities page, Chase adds "affectional preference" to "sexual orientation" for the non-discrimination policy language.

Eastman Kodak
http://www.kodak.com/

Employment Opportunities
http://www.kodak.com/cgi-bin/hr/
webJobPost.pl

The Rochester, N.Y.-based company promises "one of the most remarkably advanced technical environments you will ever experience." Besides the corporate line, Eastman Kodak also serves up resources for photographers.

Federal National Mortgage Company
http://www.fanniemae.com./

Fannie Mae, at once the world's largest diversified financial company, the nation's largest source of home mortgage funds, and the most adorable moniker in the corporate world, packs its site with history and information for home buyers and investors.

Gannett
http://www.gannett.com/

Gannett Job Opportunities
http://www.gannett.com/newswatch/
jobop.htm

Gannett is one of the largest diversified news and information companies in the U.S. Its no-nonsense Web site provides a corporate profile, job listings, and links to on-line Gannett newspapers like "The Detroit News" and "USA Today."

Hewlett Packard
http://www.hp.com

Worldwide Employment Opportunities
http://wwwjobs.external.hp.com:80/

The Palo Alto, CA-based electronics and computer peripherals manufacturer lists employment opportunities in Canada, Europe, and the U.S.

IBM
http://www.ibm.com

Diversity@IBM
http://www.empl.ibm.com/diverse/
divhome.htm

IBM goes the extra mile to highlight its rainbowesque employee base on this exemplary corporate page (Figure 12.3). Visitors are treated to rotating snapshots of women, racial minorities, people with disabilities, and some white guys who must be gay. "We come from diverse origins, different lifestyles, and pursue our own dreams," says the intro, which goes on to highlight the "Open Culture@IBM" with quotes from real live employees ("No fear. No rules. No limits. Just like a day at the office"). The people section showcases the IBM faces with photos

Figure 12.3
Diversity@IBM

of a handful of gay and lesbian execs and employees. One lesbian is shown with her D-partner and their two children. Where do we apply?

Levi-Strauss
http://www.levi.com/

Levi-Strauss has fun with its online presence, which boasts "the most outrageous walk-in closet in cyberspace." Mostly its a big clothing promotion with clever gimmicks such as a "denim dictionary" and a "jacket search." You can also check out the company history, or it's "faded jean-eology," which dates back to 1853.

Microsoft
http://www.microsoft.com/

Microsoft Employment Opportunities
http://www.microsoft.com/jobs/

Diversity
http://www.microsoft.com/jobs/guide/
diversity.htm

Diversity & Social Groups
http://www.microsoft.com/jobs/guide/
divgroup.htm

Where do you want to go today? If the answer is, "to work for an equitable company," you may want to check Microsoft's home page (Figure 12.4). The company that put Redmond, Wash., on the map may be a monolith among monoliths, but according to this site, anyway, Microsoft has a heart of gold. The site's employment opportunities section lists the week's "hot jobs" and allows visitors to build their own resume, to be filed away in the Microsoft database (which they really use). The Diversity section profiles some of the employee clubs and groups, including Gay, Lesbian, and Bisexual Employees at Microsoft. And, of course, you'll find plenty of company facts and history, along with "speeches, columns, and information" from Mr. Microsoft himself.

Northern States Power
http://www.nspco.com/

The Minnesota-based power company posts company news, weather reports, and safety tips to keep your home safe and warm.

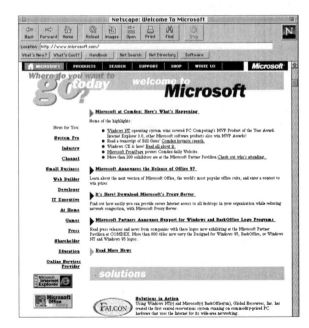

Figure 12.4
Microsoft

NYNEX

http://www.nynex.com

NYNEX says it's more than just "the phone company" for New York and New England. Find out exactly what it is at the corporate site.

New York Times

http://www.nytimes.com/

Always good to have the paper of record on your side (Figure 12.5). You'll have to register to view "all the news that's fit to print" with your Web browser, but it's free and the process is virtually painless.

Pacific Enterprises

http://www.pacent.com/

Employment Opportunities

http://www.pacent.com/class/careers/ emplops.html

Pacific Enterprises is a California-based utility holding company. Its subsidiary Southern California Gas Company is the nation's largest natural gas distribution utility, with more than 4.7 million customers and an annual gas throughput of one trillion cubic feet.

Pacific Gas and Electric

http://www.pge.com/

Silicon Graphics

http://www.sgi.com

Staffing Online

http://www.sgi.com/Misc/Jobs/

From low-end desktop workstations to servers and high-end supercomputers, Silicon Graphics specializes in high-performance interactive systems. The corporate site features loads of corporate information, contacts, and an online search for jobs.

Sprint

http://www.sprint.com/

News, Info & Jobs

http://www.sprint.com/sprint/

Sprint's world of communications seems like a good place to be if you're a gay or lesbian employee (Figure

Figure 12.5
New York Times

12.6). The Kansas-based company's corporate site includes links to "some Very Cool career opportunities."

St. Paul Companies

http://www.stpaul.com/

Employment

http://www.stpaul.com/employment/index.htm

Minnesota's St. Paul is a group of companies providing property-liability insurance, reinsurance, and insurance brokerage products and services around the world.

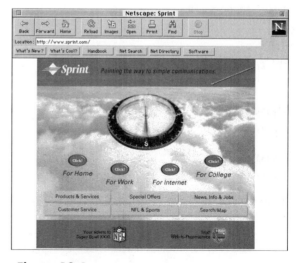

Figure 12.6
Sprint

Sun Microsystems
http://www.sun.com/

California-based Sun Microsystems serves up "the freshest, hottest jobs brought to you in real-time." (Plenty of fresh, hot Java computing reports, too.) The corporate culture is explored in its employment section. Commitment to diversity is described as a "subtle aspect of our teamwork ... By working together, Sun has created a vibrant and very diverse workforce that's truly reflective of the global markets we serve."

Time Warner
http://pathfinder.com/
@@TmlSWQYAikrdC0TL/Corp/

Social Responsibility Report
http://pathfinder.com/
@@TmlSWQYAikrdC0TL/Corp/responsibility/
srcover1.html

Never mind Time Warner's Pathfinder. Meet Factfinder, where you'll find the company line from "the world's leader in media and entertainment." The site features a "Social Responsibility" report in which it prides itself on being one of the first U.S. corporations to expand its health-care coverage to include same-sex spousal equivalents. It also notes that the Los Angeles Gay and Lesbian Community Services Center, and the National Gay and Lesbian Task Force, are among the organizations Time Warner supports. Right on.

Viacom
http://www.viacom.com/

Jobs at Viacom
http://www.viacom.com/x/jobs_main.html

"Exceptional content. Global reach." That's Viacom in a nutshell, and its intention statement is almost as modest: "to collaborate throughout the corporation and flourish in every medium, every language, in every region of the planet." What are you watching? What are you reading? Chances are good that Viacom has something to do with it (this book included). The corporate site showcases the many businesses (MTV, Paramount, Blockbuster), and its job opportunities section is exceptional, featuring a search option which helps visitors locate jobs by entering keywords.

SAME-SEX BENEFITS IN CANADA

Canadian Gay, Lesbian & Bisexual Resource Directory
http://www.gaycanada.com/

The Canadian Gay, Lesbian & Bisexual Resource Directory (Figure 12.7) provides a comprehensive listing of major Canadian businesses which offer same-sex benefits to employees. From the main menu, click on "Same Sex Benefits."

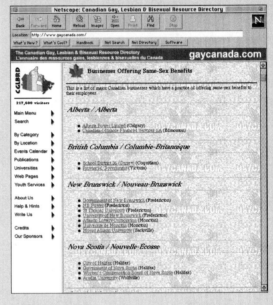

Figure 12.7
Canadian Gay, Lesbian & Bisexual Resource Directory

Walt Disney
http://www.disney.com/

The Walt Disney Company has turned out to be a virtual lightning rod when it comes to gay issues in the workplace. Yes, the world's premier entertainment company includes "sexual orientation" in its non-discrimination policy and, yes, it extends benefits to same-sex domestic partners. But corporate information is like a footnote on Disney.com. Instead, the site focuses on one of the many things Disney does so well: creative promotion. Hunchbacks, Dalmatians, beauties, and beasts are what this site is made of.

Wells Fargo & Company
http://www.wellsfargo.com

Employment Opportunities
http://wellsfargo.com/jobs/

Well, well, well. If it isn't the company that made the first electronic transaction (by telegraph in 1864). Today, Wells Fargo & Co. continues to provide personal, responsive service by connecting customers to essential financial services 24/7—these days, by ATM, phone, or PC. Naturally, the company which got its start delivering mail and cash across the American West plays up the history, with photographs and paintings. The employment section, with openings that range from tellers to telemarketing experts; from personal bankers to system programmers, may just make you want to go west.

Xerox
http://www.xerox.com/

Xerox informs us documents are "the single most important communications vehicle that people work with on a daily basis," which is very convenient for an organization which calls itself "the document company." The site is so document driven that it offers an online documentary about documents. Little documentation is provided on Xerox's progressive employee policies, but at least we know they're documented somewhere. Doc on.

CORPORATIONS SAY NO TO SEXUAL-ORIENTATION DISCRIMINATION

The following section takes a look at the corporate home pages of many Fortune 500 companies which haven't necessarily made the leap to offering same-sex domestic partnership benefits, but which have at least voluntarily taken the first step by making "sexual orientation" a non-issue in the workplace by making it, officially, a corporate issue. The HRC reports that new companies, large and small, are added to this list each week. May they prosper, and may they keep on stepping in the right direction.

Abbott Laboratories
http://www.abbott.com/

Abbott Careers Page
http://www.abbott.com/career/generalinfo.htm#

A pioneer developer of HIV drugs, Illinois-based Abbott Laboratories offers corporate information and career opportunities.

AFLAC
http://aflac.com/

AFLAC is a world leader in health insurance, based in Georgia.

Air Products and Chemicals
http://www.airproducts.com/

Air Products and Chemicals is a worldwide supplier of industrial gasses and equipment, specialty and intermediate chemicals, and environmental and energy systems. Based in Allentown, PA.

American Express
http://www.americanexpress.com/

All the poop on American Express financial services and philanthropic endeavors, which strive to be "inclusive and respectful of the diversity in communities where we operate" (Figure 12.8).

Ameritech Library Services
http://www.notis.com/

Online home of the Illinois-based library services provider.

Amoco
http://www.amoco.com/

Amoco's online magazine features news releases, daily industry briefs, stock prices, and job openings. The site

Figure 12.8
American Express

also offers a bird's eye view of Amoco operations as they dot the globe.

Aon
http://www.aon.com/

Illinois-based Aon is a family of insurance brokerage, consulting and consumer insurance companies. The corporate site offers a no-frills look at the business.

Armstrong World Industries
http://www.armstrong.com/

Pennsylvania's Armstrong World Industries is responsible for home and commercial products such as vinyl flooring, ceilings, insulation, and ceramic tiles. Company vitals are accompanied by information for the commercial and residential markets.

AT&T
http://www.att.com/

Business Opportunites
http://www.att.com/hr/employment/
overview.html

The New Jersey-based telecommunications giant highlights its service options, daily news, and employment opportunities.

Baltimore Gas and Electric
http://www.bge.com/

Banc One
http://www.bankone.com/

A "career navigator" is your virtual guide to employment opportunities with the Ohio-based corporation. The site also features a Small Business Center.

Bank of Boston
http://www.bkb.com/

Bankers Trust New York
http://www.bankerstrust.com/

The Bankers Trust New York site includes corporate news, information on markets and services, and career opportunities.

Baxter International
http://www.baxter.com/

Baxter's vision is to be recognized around the world as a leading provider of innovative health-care technologies, products, and services to improve lives. Its Web site touches on biotechnology, cardiovascular medicine, and IV systems. Employment opportunities, too.

Bell Atlantic Corp.
http://www.bell-atl.com/

Bristol-Meyers Squibb
http://www.bms.com/

The New York-based health- and personal-care products company invites you to explore its world, which includes a help-wanted page.

Campbell Soup
http://www.campbellsoup.com/
!!rsxo91wEmrsxo91wEm/Welcome1.html

Recipes, menu planning, and "Campbell's Treasures." Because soup is good food.

Central & Southwest
http://www.csw.com/

"The Powers That Be" is an electrifying online presence from the Dallas-based provider of electric service and communications-based energy solutions to customers in Texas, Oklahoma, Louisiana, Arkansas, "and beyond."

Chevron

http://www.chevron.com

"Drill" the site map for details on the San Francisco-based corporation.

Chubb

http://www.chubb.com/

Chubb's insurance subsidiaries have been leading providers of insurance protection and services for more than 100 years. And what a great name!

CIGNA

http://www.cigna.com/

CIGNA is ... 45,000 people dedicated to caring by helping 10 million people stay healthy, 5 million people save for retirement, and 23,000 companies provide valuable benefits for their employees. The corporate page also includes a special section on Breast Cancer Awareness.

Citicorp

http://www.citicorp.com/

This Citi never sleeps. Check out the latest Citibank news, investor bulletins, and career opportunities.

Coca-Cola

http://www.cocacola.com

Have a Coke and a smile, virtually, with the Atlanta-based soft drink giant.

Colgate-Palmolive

http://www.colgate.com/

Smile, it's a global company serving billions of people around the world with products that make their lives "healthier, cleaner, and more pleasant" (Figure 12.9).

Comdisco

http://www.comdisco.com/

Comdisco's services range from health care to electronics to disaster recovery, and have absolutely nothing to do with mirror balls and wailing divas.

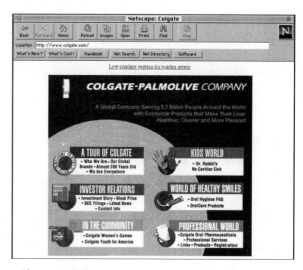

Figure 12.9
Colgate-Palmolive

Consolidated Natural Gas

http://www.cng.com/

Located in Pittsburgh, CNG operates one of the nation's largest natural gas systems and markets natural gas and electricity throughout North America.

Cray Research

http://www.cray.com/

Purveyor of hardware, software, and networking tools and services to solve "the most challenging problems."

Dell Computer

http://www.dell.com/

Find the right system, configure it, price it, and order it ("Buy a Dell. Click here").

Digital Equipment

http://www.digital.com/

Digital Equipment is a leading worldwide supplier of networked computer systems, software, and services. It also claims to lead the industry in interactive, distributed, and multivendor computing.

Dole Foods

http://www.dole5aday.com/

The Dole "5 A Day Homepage" features "fun stuff," a nutrition center and corporate information on the world's largest grower and supplier of fresh and packaged fruits, juices, vegetables, and nuts.

Dow Chemical

http://www.dow.com

Press releases and a corporate overview of the Michigan-based company. Information about employment opportunities greet those with chemistry degrees and open minds.

Dun & Bradstreet

http://www.dnb.com

Corporate information on the New York-based provider of information solutions and more.

E.I. du Pont de Nemours and Company

http://www.dupont.com/

With science and technology as a foundation, the Delaware-based company develops products that make a difference in everyday life, including chemicals, fibers, petroleum, and plastics. Find out about the company, the products, and some of the people who make them.

Exxon

http://www.exxon.com

A corporate overview and current Exxon news is accompanied by an environmental health and safety report.

Federal Home Loan Mortgage

http://www.freddiemac.com/

Over the years, Freddie Mac (Fannie Mae's brother) has helped finance one in six American homes by supplying lenders with the money to make mortgages, and packaging the mortgages into marketable securities. Corporate financial disclosures, homes for sale, and employment opportunities are online.

Federated Department Stores

http://www.federated-fds.com/

Macy's, Bloomingdales ... can we imagine life without these folks? Besides the corporate line from Ohio, Federated incorporates irresistible extras, like "Macy's West Barbie Collectibles" and "Beauty Focus." Other sections give details on Federated's "major diversity initiative" and its status as a corporate trailblazer in the fight against AIDS (Figure 12.10).

First Bank System

http://www.fbs.com/home.html

The First Bank System human resources department is now online. As is "the Business Page," a "one-stop resource for entrepreneurs seeking sound financial advice."

First Chicago NBD Corporation

http://www.fcnbd.com/

First Chicago gives details on its personal, corporate, and small-business financial services.

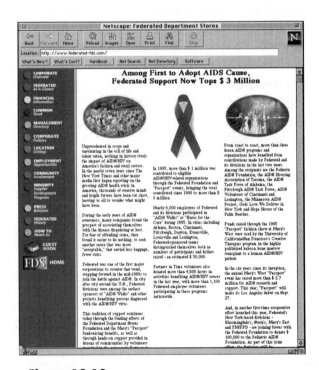

Figure 12.10
Federated Department Stores

First Union

http://www.firstunion.com/

North Carolina-based First Union's goal is to be the indispensable source of financial services for its customers. Apply online.

Fred Meyer

http://www.fredmeyer.com/

What's on your list today? Fred Meyer wants to help you find it at one of his stores. But if you can't make it out, sit back and enjoy a folksy history of his company.

Gateway 2000

http://www.gw2k.com/

Learn how a business started by a 22-year-old in a farm house on the outskirts of Sioux City, Iowa now sells more PC-compatible systems through direct marketing than any other vendor in the United States.

General Mills Recruiting

http://jobs.genmills.com/index.htm

The Minnesota-based packaged food giant (aka "the company of champions") spares visitors any kind of interactive Cheerios adventure and dives straight into the General Mills world of recruiting.

Greyhound Lines

http://www.greyhound.com/

Whether you're leaving from Aberdeen or Zanesville, you can look up fares and schedules here. Get on the bus.

Hannaford Brothers

http://www.hannaford.com/shop/

The Maine-based supermarket and superstore chain offers an interactive meal planner, a store locator, and details on products and services.

Harley-Davidson

http://www.harley-davidson.com/

Rather convincingly, the site encourages visitors to get off the InfoSuperHighway and get on the real one (Figure 12.11). "Overexposure to the Net may cause severe

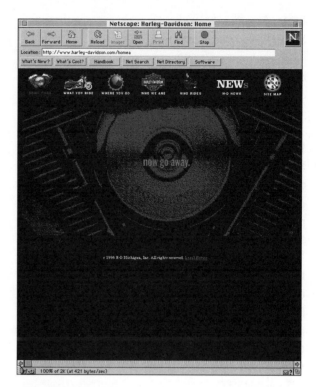

Figure 12.11
Harley-Davidson

cabin fever. In such cases, shut off your computer, pack a small bag, and see the world on a Harley-Davidson."

H.F. Ahmanson & Company

http://www.investquest.com/InvestQuest/a/ahm/

H.F. Ahmanson & Company is the parent company of Home Savings of America, which operates financial service centers in four states and mortgage lending offices in nine. Check out the corporate profile, or download the "entire company presentation."

Home Depot

http://www.homedepot.com/

Nuts and bolts information on the world's largest supplier of home improvement products. Use the locator to find the store nearest you, or flip through "Environmental Greenprint" to learn ways to minimize the effects our homes have on the environment.

Homestake Mining
http://www.homestake.com

Homestake is an international gold mining company with major mines in the U.S., Canada, and Australia. Read the company's annual report, or view a global map of Homestake locations.

Honeywell
http://www.honeywell.com/

The Minnesota-based company explains how its control technology saves energy, protects the environment, promotes peace, and, of course, creates value for shareholders.

Inland Steel Industries
http://www.inland.com/

Inland Steel Industries is a materials management, logistics, and technical services company with operating units that make and market steel; fabricate, market, and distribute industrial materials; and distribute and trade industrial materials.

Intel
http://www.intel.com

Get inside Intel, the world's largest chip maker, via product and company information, including "hot job" opportunities (Figure 12.12). The site also includes a customized news service, and technology tips and trends for home and business computing.

International Paper
http://www.ipaper.com

The premier paper and forest products company offers two ways to find out about it on site: "the corporate way" or "the challenge." (Neither will require you to use a forest product.)

ITT
http://www.itt.com/

New York's ITT is one of the world's leading hotel, gaming, entertainment, and information service companies.

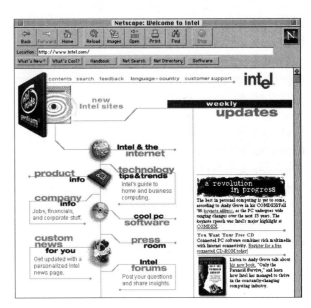

Figure 12.12
Intel

Johnson Controls
http://www.jci.com/

Milwaukee-based Johnson Controls is a market leader in automotive seating and interiors, facility management and control systems, plastic packaging, and batteries. It employs more than 70,000 people in some 900 locations around the world.

Johnson & Johnson
http://www.jnj.com

The company credo states: "Everyone must be considered as an individual. We must respect their dignity and recognize their merit. They must have a sense of security in their jobs." Find out on site about career opportunities around the world with J&J.

J.P. Morgan & Company
http://www.jpmorgan.com/

The global financial services firm provides corporate information along with market data, and details on its recruiting efforts.

Kellogg
http://www.kelloggs.com/

Welcome to "Cereal City, a vitamin-fortified Web site, complete with your daily dose of essential links, hot Java games, and tasty snacks for the famished cybersnacker." In other words, bring some kids.

Lincoln National
http://www.lnc.com/

Lincoln National owns and operates financial services businesses that provide annuities, insurance, mutual funds, and investment management services.

LSI Logic
http://www.lsilogic.com/

The "system on a chip" company explains how they do it, and provides a section for employment opportunities.

Marrriott International
http://www.marriott.com/

The world's leading hospitality company (which claims to go through 320,000 bars of soap each day) operates Marriott hotels, Fairfield Inns, Residence Inns, and the Courtyard chain. The corporate site leads to a "worldwide lodging traveler's companion."

McGraw-Hill
http://www.mcgraw-hill.com/

The New York-based publisher covers the ABCs of aviation, broadcasting, and construction, among many other things, with its titles and productions. Corporate news and information is on site.

MCI Communications
http://www.mci.com

The Washington, D.C.-based long-distance company includes "sexual orientation" in its non-discrimination policy, but gay and lesbian employees are still on hold for D-partner benefits and a "(sister)friends & (we are) family" promotion.

McKesson
http://www.mckesson.com/

News, the annual report, and employment opportunities from the California-based company providing pharmaceutical management solutions.

Medtronic
http://www.medtronic.com

Medtronic, a world leader in medical technology, specializes in implantable and invasive therapies. Sound intriguing? Check out about the company's history, philanthropy, and employment opportunities here.

Mellon
http://www.mellon.com/

This major financial services company is headquartered in Pittsburgh, PA., and engages in banking and investment services. The family includes Mellon Bank, Dreyfus Corporation, and the Boston Company.

Merck
http://www.merck.com

This leader in research-driven pharmaceutical products and services (Figure 12.13) provides a corporate overview and product information along with a "Disease Infopark." The Infopark houses a "building" for HIV/AIDS.

Merisel
http://www.merisel.com/

The computer products distributor offers Web ordering capabilities. Become a customer, place an order, and read all about the company.

Metropolitan Life
http://www.metlife.com/

Life insurance info online. And a "Peanuts" gallery, to boot.

Minnesota Mining and Manufacturing (3M)
http://www.3m.com

Three markets, three technologies, and three Values equal more than 50,000 products.

Figure 12.13
Merck

Mobil Corporation
http://www.mobil.com

Global Diversity and Inclusion
http://www.mobil.com/diversity/vision.html

Based in Virginia, Mobil has oil, gas, and petrochemical operations in more than 100 countries. Its non-greasy Web site includes a section on "Global Diversity and Inclusion."

Motorola
http://www.mot.com/

Employment Opportunities
http://www.mot.com/Index/jobindex.html

Motorola is a major manufacturer of semiconductors, electronics, and wireless communications products.

New England Electric Systems
http://www.nees.com/

Niagra Mohawk Power
http://www.nimo.com

The Syracuse, N.Y.-based, investor-owned energy services company provides electricity to more than 1.5 million customers and natural gas to more than 500,000.

Northern Trust
http://www.ntrs.com/

Corporate and career information is available on the Chicago-based multi-bank holding company.

Norwest
http://www.norwest.com

The financial services company covers commercial and consumer information to the Nth degree.

Northwest Mutual Life Insurance
http://www.northwesternmutual.com/

The Wisconsin-based life insurance company's site features novelties such as an "insurance-speak" glossary and an "inflation quiz" along with a corporate profile and tips for personal planning and small businesses.

Occidental Petroleum
http://www.oxychem.com/

"OxyChem" is one of the world's largest producers of chemicals, including petrochemicals, polymers, and plastics. The corporate site includes sections on safety and environment, and educational resources.

Paccar
http://www.kenworth.com/

History, financials, and job opportunities from the world's leading truck manufacturer.

Pacificorp
http://upl.com

This energy utility and telecommunications company in Oregon has its own planet online.

Pacific Telesis Group
http://www.pactel.com/

Corporate and financial information about one of the country's top communications providers.

PECO Energy
http://www.libertynet.org:80/peco/

Philadelphia's investor-owned electric and gas utility is also "your source for energy information."

Pfizer
http://www.pfizer.com

Find out how Pfizer is "leading the way to better health care through research and innovation." The site features special sections on career opportunities, animal health, and Zoloft.

Pharmacia
http://www.pharmacia.se/

Link out to individual Pharmacia & Upjohn sites for information leukemia, cataracts, and impotency.

Polaroid
http://www.polaroid.com

The site instructions are simple: Just push a button. Watch. Wait. And see what develops. Naturally, it's something very pretty (Figure 12.14).

Perkin-Elmer
http://www.perkin-elmer.com/

Connecticut's Perkin-Elmer is the leading worldwide supplier of analytical, bioresearch, environmental, and process analytical systems for research, analysis, and quality assurance.

Pitney Bowes
http://www.pitneybowes.com

The company that enables customers to manage the exchange and distribution of messages and packages serves up a treasure trove of information regarding its products, services, and software solutions.

Figure 12.14
Polaroid

Price/Costco
http://www.pricecostco.com

PriceCostco operates hundreds of members-only warehouse stores in North America, Britain, and South Korea. Find a store locator, membership information, and the company line at its home page. Also includes a "small business zone" for live chat, resources, and breaking news (Figure 12.15).

Procter & Gamble
http://www.pg.com/

From Crisco to Ivory, the world of Procter & Gamble is thoroughly examined online.

Prudential Insurance
http://www.prudential.com/

Whether you're looking for your first home, or trying to decide which life insurance to go with, this site strives to

Figure 12.15
Price/Costco

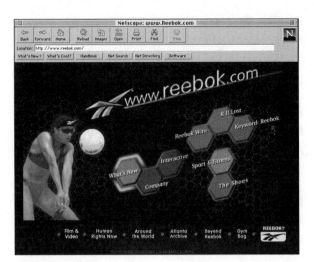

Figure 12.16
Human Rights Now

help you make an educated choice. "Just ask the virtual customers here."

Quaker Oats
http://www.quakeroats.com/

A brief history, shareholder information, and product-specific 800 numbers make up the Quaker Oats home page.

Reebok International
http://www.reebok.com

Human Rights Now
http://www.reebok.com/humanrights/index.html

The international footwear giant's colorful Web presence (Figure 12.16) delivers corporate information and press releases, and devotes a special section to "Human Rights Now." (Reebok's commitment to human rights began in 1986 when it stopped doing business in South Africa in support of the movement to end apartheid.) On the "What are Human Rights?" page, Reebok quotes the U.N.'s Declaration: "Everyone is entitled to freedom without any distinction based on race, color, sex, language, religion, national origin, or birth." Though the words "sexual orientation" are absent from the U.N.'s statement, they are not missing from Reebok's own non-discrimination policy.

Revco Drug Stores
http://www.revco.com

You've got "a friend for life" and a friend online in Revco. The drug store company provides financial information, details on its managed care services, and employment opportunities.

RJR Nabisco
http://www.triadonline.com/rjrt/

News and information about the tobacco company takes a back seat to a variety of activism site sections. From a youth non-smoking program (and screen saver) to details on the "Smokers' Rights" movement.

Ryder System
http://www.ryder.inter.net/

Hop on the Ryder System online. The world's largest provider of logistics and transportation solutions covers corporate news and financials, capabilities, and employment information.

SAFECO
http://www.safeco.com

The Washington-based "safe agent" introduces a virtual family (the Johnstons) and offers details on its insurance programs and array of other financial services.

Sears, Roebuck and Company
http://www.sears.com/

The flashy Sears site features much more than a cart full of product information for enthusiastic shoppers. Search for more than 2000 tools in the "Ultimate Craftsman Workshop." Or, if you want to get up close and personal with the Chicago-based retailer, search online for the Sears store nearest you. The site also includes a career section, with details on opportunities and employee benefits.

ServiceMaster
http://www.svm.com

Once known for yellow trucks and heavy cleaning, ServiceMaster is "more than you know," the site assures us, and goes on to tell all about its diverse array of "market-leading brand names" for products and services that assist with lawns, bugs, grime, hospitals, and long-term care patients. So perhaps it will even end up to be "more than you wanted to know."

Spiegel
http://spiegel.com/spiegel/

Of course they're online. With "the most extraordinary catalog on the Web," no less (Figure 12.17).

Storage Technology
http://www.stortek.com/

Get all the latest information about StorageTek hardware, software, network, partners, and open systems product solutions for global information storage. And lots more where all that came from.

Tandy
http://www.tandy.com

The Texas-based consumer electronics giant provides product information, press releases, and corporate financial updates.

Times Mirror
http://www.latimes.com/

The Times Mirror company drops you directly at its prize paper, the *Los Angeles Times*.

Figure 12.17
Spiegel

Toys "R" Us
http://www.tru.com

You have three choices: Geoffrey the giraffe's picks, the corporate "Info Zone," or the "Fun Zone." Decisions, decisions.

Transamerica
http://www.transamerica.com/

Learn all about the California-based company's life insurance, consumer, and commercial lending, leasing, real estate services and investments. A corporate overview is accompanied by the latest news about products and services.

Unisys

http://www.unisys.com

The information management company provides corporate information and details on career opportunities. Elsewhere, stroll through the online software store.

United Airlines

http://www.ual.com/

Fly United's (gay-) friendly skies. The airline's home page features a flight search (by airport code or city), online reservations, a flight-status check, airport maps, and much more.

United Technologies

http://www.utc.com/

United Technologies provides a broad range of high-technology products and support services to customers in the aerospace, building, and automotive industries around the world. UTC's best-known products include aircraft engines, escalators, and helicopters.

USAir

http://www.usair.com

Get details, facts, and figures on Virginia-based USAir, along with flight schedules and a "consumer forum."

U.S. Bancorp

http://www.usbank.com/

If you're looking for answers to money questions—"the short concise variety or the kind that require worksheets, a little thought, and some creativity"—the U.S. Bank page will be right up your alley.

Walgreen

http://www.walgreens.com/

A lot has changed since Charles Walgreen opened his first pharmacy on Chicago's South Side in 1901. Walgreens is now the nation's leading pharmacy, and has set up a friendly neighborhood location in cyberspace. Who knew? Sorry, you won't find online drug ordering. Yet. For now, use the online directory to find the actual location nearest you. And don't forget to check out the "Opportunity Knocks" section. Walgreens is ever in pursuit of top-Q candidates to be part of its future.

Warner-Lambert

http://www.warner-lambert.com/

The New Jersey-based marketer of prescription drugs and personal health products (cough syrup, gum, antacids, and so on) features an online encyclopedia of brand-name items along with the corporate goodies.

Washington Post

http://www.washingtonpost.com

The *Washington Post* delivers a good read along with some interactive extras (Figure 12.18). Besides thorough coverage of top news in D.C., the 50 states, and around the world, it features a regular influx of extras (an "interactive citizenship test," for example, based on the actual INS test). Elsewhere, build a customized portfolio for checking stock quotes, or work through a week's worth of online crossword puzzles. It's all free, and you don't even have to register.

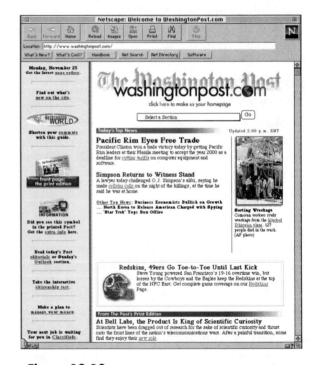

Figure 12.18
Washington Post

W.W. Grainger

http://www.grainger.com/

Grainger is a leading business-to-business distributor of equipment, components, and supplies to more than a million commercial industrial, contractor, and institutional customers around the world. The site features an online catalog and ordering, a store locator, and a company overview.

Zenith

http://www.zenith.com/

Zenith.com will be a hit with Web surfers and channel surfers alike (you navigate the site with a big, fat remote control). Read all about the electronics technology pioneer and its products. Investor info and employment listings are also on site.

GAI-Q Out Take

A July 1996 GAI-Q survey asked Out.com viewers how they would respond if presented with a common heterosexist comment from coworkers (Figures 12.19 and 12.20).

Men: If a coworker were to point to a woman walking past the office window and say to you, "Hey, look at her, she's cute, don't you think?," what would be your response?

- 39 percent would think fast and say "She's not my type."
- 30 percent would smile and agree.
- 25 percent would agree that she's cute, but confess that they're actually attracted to men.
- And then there's the bold 6 percent who would turn beet-red and accuse the coworker of fanning the flames of sexism and heterocentrism that is tearing apart our common humanity.

Women: If a coworker were to point to a man walking past the office window and say to you, "Hey, look at him, he's cute, don't you think?," what would be your response?

- 36 percent would think fast and say, "He's not my type."
- 35 percent would smile and agree.
- 26 percent would agree that he's cute, but confess that they're actually attracted to women.
- Only 3 percent would fly off the handle and accuse the coworker of fanning the flames of sexism, etc.

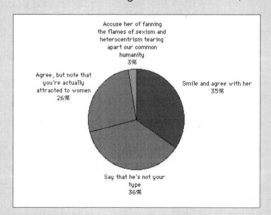

Figure 12.20
July 1996 GAI-Q survey—women's responses

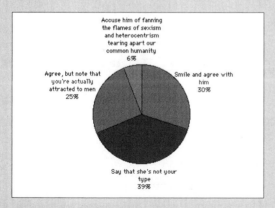

Figure 12.19
July 1996 GAI-Q survey—mens' responses

Chapter 13

OUR BUSINESS

In a fact sheet published a few years back, the National Gay and Lesbian Task Force reported that results from 21 different local discrimination surveys conducted throughout the 1980s showed between 16 and 44 percent of respondents faced some form of work-related discrimination due to sexual orientation. Discrimination included being fired, not being hired, not being promoted, on-the-job harassment, and fear of reprisals.

But that was the eighties. In the middle of the nineties, as the previous chapter explored, corporate America appears to be taking the lead in establishment of equitable workplaces for all. Sure, without laws, incidents such as the Cracker Barrel restaurant chain's notorious policy requiring the termination of employees "whose sexual preferences fail to demonstrate normal heterosexual values" will rudely exist. But we don't have to spend gay money at the Cracker Barrel, now, do we?

As was also hinted at in the last chapter, it's no longer difficult to support a corporation which is working—usually ahead of the government—to ensure equality for gay and lesbian employees. From moving services to long-distance phone companies, from airlines to video stores, from toy stores to restaurant chains; most of the time, you now have a choice to go with a gay-friendly corporate competitor.

Increasingly, you also have a choice to support businesses that are gay-owned or operated. In large urban areas, gay restaurants, bookstores, music stores, and more have been springing up and thriving for years. With the advent of the Web, gay businesses discovered a cheap and easy way to open their doors with style to the global gay community.

This chapter takes a look at the Web homes of many of those businesses that proudly employ and cater to gays and lesbians around the world. Check out their virtual storefronts. And do drop in in person if you happen to be out and about in their actual neighborhoods. Build the community and make it stronger by keeping gay money in the loop.

LOCALIZED GAYBIZ GUIDES

The Austin (Texas) Gay-Friendly Directory
http://www.webcom.com/austin/welcome.html

Central Texas's only comprehensive guide for gay and lesbian consumers. Browse the massive services and retail index. Other features include a detailed list of organizations, bar and club listings, and an entertainment section. Makes you want to get lost in Austin.

BGL Advertising (Gay Boston)
http://www.bgladco.com/

Blowing in to Boston and need a limousine? A place to stay? A hair salon? BGL Advertising's guide to gay Boston businesses and services seems to be the place to start.

The Canadian Gay, Lesbian and Bisexual Business Directory
http://www.cglbrd.com/categories/

The CGLBRD Business Directory provides free listings for gay and gay-friendly businesses throughout Canada. The on-site index lists entries by category, province, and city. It also provides individual city listings.

Dallas-Fort Worth Lambda Pages
http://www.lambdapages.com/lambdapages/home.html

Gay Yellow Pages-type business directory for the Dallas-Fort Worth area lists its advertisers by category and

provides a nice breakdown of the city's bars and some gay-friendly restaurants.

Gay.Guide New York
http://www.gayguidenewyork.com/main.html

"Gay.Guide New York (see Figure 13.1) is not an online magazine and will not become one," asserts the editor of this useful site. Rather, it's an information source regarding products, service providers, and entertainment options relevant to the big, gay apple. Beyond the hot links and classifieds, the Gay.Guide also throws out some pointed star-rating reviews on places like Barney's ("the only cool department store in the city") and The Gap ("every other block").

GayLA
http://www.GayLA.net/

With business listings for health & fitness, hotels & travel, and food & drink, this site is totally L.A. and totally gay. Special features include a map of West Hollywood, and "Starwalk," your guide to the Hollywood stars.

Gay & Lesbian Business Directory of Greater Vancouver
http://www.glba.org/

Body piercing, embroidery, tiling, you name it. The Web site of the Gay and Lesbian Business Association of Greater Vancouver proudly serves up "the most

Figure 13.1
Gay.Guide New York

comprehensive and up-to-date" information resource for British Columbia's gay community.

Gay and Lesbian Indianapolis
http://www.gayindy.org/

Get all the details here on supportive local businesses, bars and restaurants, youth groups, and general gay Indy pride.

Gay Los Angeles Guide
http://www.gayla.com/

Consider it a "safe and discreet way" to learn about the myriad gay-friendly businesses in the City of Angels. Free personal-ad placement and live chat, too.

The Lavender Pages (San Francisco)
http://www.lavenderpages.com/

Updated and printed twice yearly, the Lavender Pages is a comprehensive business and professional directory by and for the San Francisco Bay Area gay, lesbian, and bi-sexual community. Order a copy of the printed version, search the Lavender Pages database for resources in other cities, or link out to an "absolutely fabulous" Bay Area guide to fine dining, love and laughs, accommodations, and more.

Out in Sydney
http://www.outinsydney.com.au/home.html

This site (see Figure 13.2) wants to give you more than a taste of gay and lesbian Sydney; rather a "firm meaty bite" of the great Australian city. From "boys, clothes, and ac-cessories" to an "adult concepts" and accommodations for travelers, if it's out in Sydney, you'll find it here.

Out! Resource Guide (Chicago)
http://www.suba.com/~outlines/adverts.html

Whether it's florists, futons, or financial services you seek in the Windy City, let Out! Resources be your guide to gay supportive businesses, professionals, and organiza-tions. It's a service of Outlines, the online voice of the gay and lesbian community in Chicago.

Figure 13.2
Out in Sydney

The Pink Web (Boston)
http://www.pinkweb.com/

Surrender to the Pink, a regularly updated guide to gay- and lesbian-owned and gay-friendly businesses in the Boston area (see Figure 13.3). The site includes a travel section to assist you in vacation travel, free online refer-rals to any place in the world, and thousands of business listings.

Pride NorthWest (British Columbia, Washington and Oregon)
http://pridenw.vservers.com/pridenw.htm

With individual sections for Oregon, Seattle, and Van-couver, Pride NorthWest covers the essential area gay and lesbian restaurants, bars, and shops.

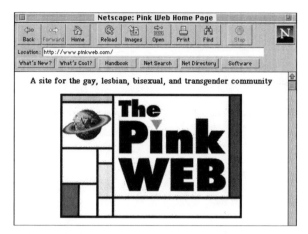

Figure 13.3
The Pink Web (Boston)

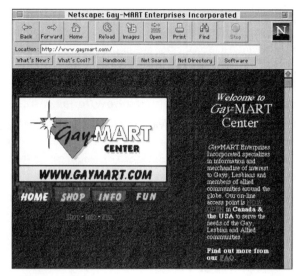

Figure 13.4
Gay Mart

WORLDWIDE GAYBIZ DIRECTORIES

Gay BizNet
http://www.gaybiznet.com/gbiz.html

Gay BizNet presents this online Yellow Pages-type directory of "everything from gAy to Z." With a definite SoCal bent, the site boasts "User-friendly gay professionals, services, bars, restaurants, and more" (we assume they mean the site is user-friendly; not the gay professionals). It's all a service of Gay WebWorld, which also hosts a queer zine, a shopping guide and a lounge for "dykes' eyes only."

Gay Mart
http://www.gaymart.com/

Gay Mart (See Figure 13.4) specializes in information and merchandise of interest to gays and lesbians around the globe. All products come from gay- or lesbian-owned operations (or those which are at least gay positive). Whether you're looking for calendars, books, CDs or "that right little thing at gift giving time," you should be able to find what you need. Headquartered in Vancouver,

Gay Mart is exclusively a mail-order catalog operation. Which pretty much rules out the thrill of a flashing-blue-light special.

GayWeb
http://www.gayweb.com/menu.html

"Your guide to gay and lesbian business" peddles clothing and popular CDs and videos, but seems to focus heavily on products "to enhance your sensual pleasure."

GLBNet
http://www.glbnet.com/

GLBNet creates and hosts promotional pages for gay and gay-friendly businesses based in Ohio, Kentucky, Indiana, Michigan, West Virginia, and Pennsylvania (for a small fee, of course). The site includes a business directory, classifieds, pricing information, and usage stats.

The Lavender Pages World Search
http://www.lavenderpages.com/world.html

The Lavender Pages is a comprehensive printed business and professional directory by and for the San Francisco Bay Area gay, lesbian, and bisexual community. In addition to the Bay Area, its Web site also features an excellent business and resources search for cities around the world. Most of the searchable cities are located in the U.S., but Amsterdam, London, Mexico City, and a handful of other international cities are in the mix.

The Rainbow Cafe
http://www.3wnet.com/rainbow/index.html

The virtual Rainbow Cafe features a palatable menu which includes snacks such as book and film reviews along with the main course—a business directory where gay-owned and gay-friendly businesses can advertise by service area. The gluttonous may want to check out the site's "After Hours" section, "for open exchange of words, images, and ideas of an erotic nature." Bon appétit!

The Rainbow World Directory
http://www.rnbow.com/rwd/

The Rainbow World Directory (see Figure 13.5) offers an index of pointers to gay and gay-friendly business. A service of Irvine, CA-based Rainbow Marketing, the directory provides a forum for display ads and allows businesses to list for free. Business categories are arranged in an A-to-Z index, most of the categories of which were pretty vacant on a recent visit. The category titles are a hoot, though: "Galleries to Gynecology," "Hair Replacement to Hypnotheraphy," "Karate to Koi Fish." More power to 'em.

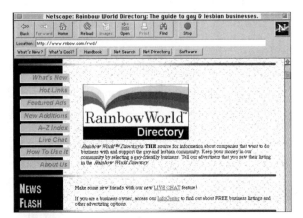

Figure 13.5
The Rainbow World Directory

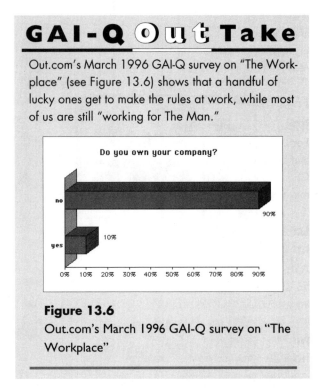
LEG-FREE SHOPPING SPREE

Whether you seek replication Scottish lace curtains or the Monarch butterfly's Mexican trail, it's becoming increasingly easier to ride your mouse to make most of the arrangements. Here's a look at some virtual storefronts set up by gay and lesbian merchants around the world. Let your finger do the walking.

Art and Photography

Alternative Creations
http://www.alternative-creations.com/

Alternative Creations is a lesbian-owned and -operated business for production and promotion of art for and by women. The goal is to design and distribute products that are "not only fun but are also needed in our society." Items are offered in a variety of categories, including jewelry, sculpture, cards, and videos. Pick up a matted and framed print of the hot Melissa Etheridge PETA poster, or check out the hip review column by *Claire of the Moon* author/director Nicole Conn.

Free Spirit Rainbow Art
http://www.gcrc.ufl.edu/~cchurch/fsra.html

For those who thought original uses for the rainbow flag had been exhausted. Check out Ocala, FL-based Charlie Church's hand-sculpted figurines, incense holders, and magnets in the flying colors.

Latent Images
http://www.io.com/~photoguy/

Austin, Texas-based photographer Mark Lynch presents his original works (tastefully done homoerotica) in an online gallery and gallery store.

Mirror Images
http://www.acmeweb.com/mi/index.html

Colorado Springs-based Sandra Marin founded this Internet gallery to "promote womyn artists and feminine culture." Her own pen 'n pencil show, "Impressions of a Graceful and Elegant Culture," is on display (and for sale), and she invites other artists to join her online.

Vintage Beefcake photos
http://members.aol.com/davidp111/
beefcake.html

Arizona's David Parker displays his finest classic vintage "male beefcake photographs" (from 1947 to 1958) for the discerning collector (see Figure 13.7). The beefy pages with samples of available photos take a long time to load—but they're well worth the wait if you're in to shiny classic vintage males flexing in their underwear.

Bookstores

Affinity Books
http://ns.cent.com/affinity/

Affinity may be located in beautiful downtown St. Petersburg, FL, but with this site, it becomes your local gay and lesbian bookstore, no matter how remote you are.

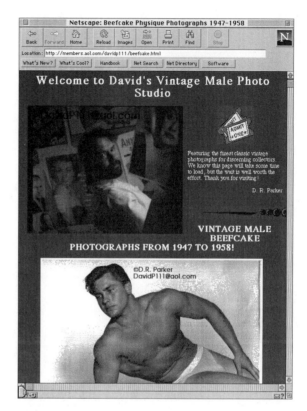

Figure 13.7
Vintage Beefcake photos

Afterwords Bookstore
http://www.afterwords.com/

Rainbow-tinged bookstore and espresso bar. You can't taste the espresso here, but you can buy books, videos, music, and gifts online.

Creative Visions Bookshop
http://www.hedda.com/creative-visions/

Creative Visions (see Figure 13.8) claims to be the largest gay-owned and -operated bookstore in Greenwich Village. Browse the Top 10 Book list or make an order online. It's an offering of Hedda Lettuce WorldWide.

Crossroads Market & Bookstore
http://www.crossmarket.com/welcome/

Browse through bestsellers and new releases in gay and lesbian literature. "Great flicks" in the video section, too. Place an order online.

Figure 13.8
Creative Visions Bookshop

A Different Light Bookstore
http://www.adlbooks.com/

With branches in New York, San Francisco, and West Hollywood, A Different Light is a touchstone for many. Its online bookstore is no exception. Localized information about signings and events is available for each of the branches. The "ADL Review" catalog is also on hand, along with its companion, online ordering capability. Across the way, the "Cafe" section hosts an open chat forum on queer literature, art, culture, and society. It's Java-based, natch.

Ex Libris
http://www.clo.com/~exlibris/

Toronto-based online book shop specializes in new and used gay and lesbian literature. Special services include a discount for prepaid orders, and a "loan programme" by

which you can make a deposit and pay a rental fee and take a book on loan.

Girlfriends Coffeehouse and Bookstore
http://www.bonzo.com/girlfriends/

The girls of Tucson await, with women's books, prints and music, metaphysical gifts, and "mouth watering treats to eat." Run, don't walk.

Glad Day Bookshop
http://www.tiac.net/users/gladday/

Boston's Glad Day Bookshop claims to be the second oldest gay bookstore in North America. More details at its Web site.

Gay Mart Entertainment Stop Books Library
http://www.gaymart.com/2catalog/
shopes.html

The Gay Mart Entertainment Stop Books Library peddles its wares in chatty, gossipy fashion. Take the bait on "find out the true gay story from your favorite gay personality when you sample this selection of autobiographical picks!" and you'll end up staring at product numbers for the Greg Louganis and Bob Paris & Rod Jackson books. When finished browsing for books, you can always visit one of Gay Mart's other action aisles. Alas, Jaqueline Smith was nowhere to be found.

Lambda Rising Bookstore
America Online
Keyword: lambda rising

For those of you still hanging out with America Online, the Lambda Rising Bookstore offers one of the finest shopping experiences you're likely to find there. Pick up the latest in queer literature and music without leaving the house. A major presence on the Web for Lambda Rising was forthcoming at press time, too.

Little Sister's Book & Art Emporium
http://www.lsisters.com/default.htm

Little Sister has been serving the community for nearly 20 years with gay and lesbian books, music, videos, magazines, cards, and adult toys. The site features product and ordering information, along with a special section on censorship.

Sapphisticate
http://www.sapphisticate.com/

The Sapphisticate ("for the dykescriminating reader") was created to provide access to lesbian literary work by those who "choose not to visit gay/lesbian bookstores or conduct credit card transactions with gay/lesbian identified sites" (see Figure 13.9). Billing goes through Amazon.com books (hello!), which "carries practically every book in print, and therefore specializes in nothing."

Sisterspirit Bookstore
http://www.elf.net/sisterspirit/

Located in San Jose, CA, Sisterspirit is a non-profit, all-volunteer org, designed to promote women's community and unity. The Web space features news, book reviews, and a reference section.

Figure 13.9
Sapphisticate

Thunder Road Book Club
http://ourworld.compuserve.com/homepages/
Thunder_Road_Book_Club/

Bruce Springsteen has absolutely nothing to do with this club, which deals in discounted mail-order lesbian books and videos. Catalogs and shipping only available in the U.S.

Clothing

Aussie Boys Australia
http://www.outinsydney.com.au/aussieboys/
index.html

Good thing Aussie Boys Australia survived "the abuse and bottle throwing of the early '80s," because the store has

ShopOut
http://www.out.com

Need that new RuPaul CD that's apparently outlawed in your neck of the woods? Out.com features ShopOut (see Figure 13.10), a safe and easy alternative to a trip to the record store. Shop your brains out online and use your credit card (and Out.com's secure server) to order what you need. A good fairy will deliver the booty to your doorstep within a couple of days. You better shop!

Figure 13.10
ShopOut

grown up to be, in their words, "the largest and most successful 'out' business in Australia ... perhaps the world."

Designing Men
http://www.designing-men.com

Shirts, caps, briefs, music, posters, and—wait for it—the Elton John collection. Step right up.

Mister B.
http://neturl.nl/mrb/index.html

Located in the heart of the Amsterdam leather scene, Mr. B claims to be "the finest asset of gay Amsterdam." If you're looking for leather, rubberwear, army clothing, or the like, you'll want to look him up.

Picky Women Sportswear and Accessories
http://www.pridewear.com/

Express your mood, attitude of lifestyle just like a picky woman would (see Figure 13.11). The mail-order and production company specializes in designs and products for the gay and lesbian community. Check out the goods (and order them) online.

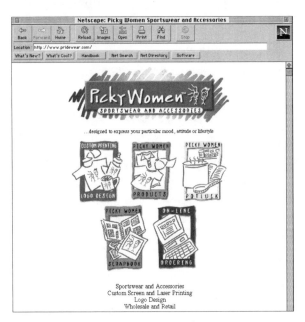

Figure 13.11
Picky Women Sportswear and Accessories

Shamrock Bodywear
http://199.172.47.106/shamrock/

Shamrock specializes in T-shirts specially designed to "wear with pride to special events, parades, marches," and more. The hot item is a five-leaf clover design.

GAY BARS ONLINE

Baltimore Eagle
http://www.smart.net/~leather/index.html

The Baltimore Eagle (aka the BEagle) caters to "those who appreciate the Leather/Levi lifestyle." So fly like a BEagle to the Web site for information on the club, local leather-circuit titleholders, and maps to Baltimore.

Bretz (Todedo, Ohio)
http://www.bretz.com/

Bretz of Toledo claims it has the best music, dance, lighting, and video entertainment between New York and Chicago—and the second best pizza in the Midwest. No doubt, the club's Web presence features more rotating GIFs than the home page for Reno, Nevada. Get Bretz history, a rundown of specialties, and directions from Ann Arbor and Detroit.

The Brownstone Cafe (Waterbury, CT)
http://www.corpcenter.com/bstone/

Directions, a bar menu, daily specials, and employment opportunities for Waterbury's only gay bar on the Net.

Buck's Southwest Lounge and Stockade (San Jose, CA.)
http://www.webaxxess.com/bucks/

If you know the way to San Jose, here's the 24-hour hot spot for cold drinks, darts, pinball, and pool. But you'll have to settle for soft-drinks between the hours of 2 and 6 A.M.

Club Escalando (Washington, D.C.)

http://207.96.122.68

Escalando is a nightclub *and* a festive Web site. Learn all about salsa classes, Thursday night erotica (much more entertaining than "Seinfeld," we're sure), and Hot Fudge Sunday. Mention you saw Escalando on the Web and pick up a free margarita.

Corner Pocket (New Orleans)

http://www.gayneworleans.com/The_Pocket/

New Orleans. Boys Dancin'. "Meat Night." Open 24/7. Pretty much says it all.

Daddy's (San Francisco)

http://www.wolfe.com/daddys/

The Castro's popular leather bar lets it all hang out online. Get facts about the bar, drop in on Daddy's Chat Room, or meet "Daddy's boys," aka the staff.

501 Tavern (Indianapolis)

http://www.501tavern.com/501/

It's Indy's only "real Levi leather bar," and supposedly you can "smell the difference." Still interested? Check out the upcoming events, or hop on the 501 Tavern mailing list.

The Heretic Atlanta

http://www.hereticatlanta.com

The Heretic claims to be Atlanta's "best place to meet men." Cheapest, too (there's never a cover). The club's Web site includes a calendar of events and a "Hanky Page" for demystification of that pesky code.

IBT's (Tucson)

http://bonzo.com/ibts

IBT's graces Tucson with a steady flow of "hot music, hot men, good times." Check the site for a weekly schedule.

La Cage Aux Follies (Washington, D.C.)

http://lacage.com/pages/welcome.htm

La Cage provides a safe and secure environment for people who like to watch male strippers over cocktails while in D.C. The site does a little striptease of its own to try and get you in the mood.

Lone Star Saloon (San Francisco)

http://www.slip.net/~lonestar/

Lone Star is the San Francisco connection for bears, bikers, and mayhem. The Web site features an extended events calendar with details on beer busts, baseball games, and Mah Jong Club meetings. The "Bear Grub" section even serves up a collection of "man-pleazin' old family recipes." Ursa Major-Alarm Chili, anyone?

The Lure (New York City)

http://www.thelure.com/

New York's premier leather bar uses its Web presence not so much to hook you as to shout out the dress code. FYI: codpieces, sanitation uniforms, and rope will get you in quickly. Disco wear, female drag, white sneakers, and Izod will get you nowhere in this place.

Picante (Cancun, Mexico)

http://www.cancun-hotbar.com/

The Picante Hot Bar adds some pepper to the Cancun gay scene. Get directions here, in English and Spanish, along with photos of what awaits you in Cancun.

The Ramrod (Boston)

http://www.ptown.com/boston/ramrod/

If time in New England gets to be too mundane, Boston's ever-so-subtle Ramrod club offers yet another leather and denim opportunity.

Sebastian Bar Cafe (Copenhagen, Denmark)

http://store.cybercity.dk/cgh/sebastian/sebhome.htm

The Sebastian Bar Cafe (see Figure 13.12) opened with the ambition of giving Copenhagen a hot spot that was "out, young, modern, and competed on the same criteria as the straight cafes." It's been a "booming success" since day one. Find out why at the promotional site.

Figure 13.12
Sebastian Bar Cafe (Copenhagen, Denmark)

GRAPHIC DESIGN AND PUBLISHING

Mediapolis
http://www.mediapolis.com/

Mediapolis is responsible for delivering some of the Web's most impressive gay and lesbian creations. Major clients include Out.com, HX (a weekly guide to gay and lesbian New York), GLAAD, and AIDS Project Los Angeles.

PhotoBytes
http://home.navisoft.com/photobytes/
index2.htm

Using your photographs, this New York-based company will design personalized calendars, albums, and online greeting cards. Take a bite of the site and check out the online gallery which features samples of work done for special events, businesses, and personals.

Quistory Publishing
http://www2.clever.net/quistory/

Quistory (see Figure 13.13) publishes educational and entertainment software for and about the gay, lesbian, and bisexual community. The company's Web site includes demos of several of the titles, including "Queers in History ... the most comprehensive list of historical gays, lesbians, and bisexuals," with more than 870 prominent people; and "Queeries," a computerized gay and lesbian trivia game. Learn more about the company, and order its products online.

Shadow Graphix
http://www.gaypride.com/shadowgrfx/

This Atlanta-based graphic design and printing company (founded by a gay couple in November 1995) offers "the answer to ad agency melodrama." Shadow Graphix specializes in small-business marketing, image consultation, banners, signs, and neon art. The company also calls itself the commitment ceremony experts. "We will assist you invitation styles, accessories like toasting glasses and matchbooks, as well as design and print a very special service program to forever commemorate the day you say your vows." Here, here.

Alternative Ventures
http://www.altventures.com

Based in South Boston, Alternative Ventures does Web page design and maintenance, Web site hosting, and computer consulting. It's also the developer of "Men on Disk," a "fun way to create and customize collections of images into a customized screen saver show with music and special effects." Download it here for free.

Figure 13.13
Quistory Publishing

HOME AND GARDEN

Forster & Lloyd Corporation
http://www.webcom.com/garden/

These Dallas-based gay green-thumbers promote and peddle their Gardener's Organizer book online. Find out about this "constant companion" for the nursery, the garden, the library, and other rooms, and order it electronically. The site also features a "plant of the month" section, seasonal gardening timetables, and the current Forster & Lloyd newsletter.

J.R. Burrows & Co.
http://www.burrows.com/

This gay-owned Massachusetts-based company specializes in decorative furnishings in the English tradition, including Arts and Crafts Movement wallpaper, furnishing fabric, and Scottish lace curtains. Find wallpaper and fabric designs online, and extras such as "A Brief History of English Carpets."

Steven-Thomas Antiques
http://www.steven-thomas.com/

If it's European antiques you seek, get to know Steven Shedd and Thomas Silk. Their grand furniture store in Santa Ana, CA is easily accessible online—in English, Farsi, French, German, Italian, and Spanish, no less. The 18,000 square-foot store contains a $1,000,000 inventory, while the Web site lists vitals on a sampling of their finest quality pieces.

TRAVEL

ADVance—Damron Vacations
http://www.advance-damron.com/

This gay-owned and -operated travel company offers exclusively gay vacation packages, including yacht cruises in Greece, Hotlanta River Expo, and gay ski weeks in Aspen and at Whistler. The company also offers everyday travel services such as airline ticketing and hotel reservations.

ADVance-Damron wants to be your one-stop travel consultant for business and vacation. And when you get a look at its dreamy site, you'll probably give the thought some serious consideration.

All Continents Travel
http://ptla.com/gaytravel/

All Continents Travel (see Figure 13.14) of Los Angeles reminds, "Now more than ever it is important to be able to count on a travel agent who can sort through the thicket of promotional hype surrounding the gay market." If you agree, you may want to check out this well-organized site of promotional hype, which contains tempting features on exotic locales ranging in feel from the "Garden of Eden" to "a walk on the wild side."

Alternative Holidays
http://www.bogo.co.uk/alternatives/

The U.K.-based Alternative Holidays specializes in luxury vacations exclusively for gay men—be it an "all-inclusive week in the fabulous French Alps" or European Gay Ski Week.

Alyson Adventures
http://www.channel1.com/alyson/

Alyson Adventures specializes in active vacations for gay men, lesbians, and friends. Typical Alyson adventures

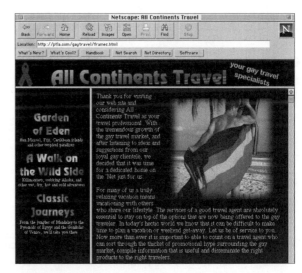

Figure 13.14
All Continents Travel

include exploration of Roman ruins, a medieval duchy, and a famous wine region; and discovering the five faces of Australia, including the world's biggest gay party. Pick up the trip schedule online, and get information on how to book a reservation.

Atlas Travel Service
http://www.tiac.net/vacation/atlas_travel/

Atlas Travel is based in Los Angeles and caters to the business and pleasure travel needs of the gay and lesbian community. Get information on the agency, and find out about current travel packages online.

Bob Wood's Travel Page
http://www.netcom.com/~bwood2/first.html

Bob has lived in Dallas for more than 30 years. After being laid off from his law firm job, he decided to follow his dreams and become a travel agent. Learn more about Bob and his business (and his cats) on the Travel Page, and follow his excellent collection of "links to the world," which include weekend airline fares, current travel specials, and a "great golf resort locator."

Bottom Line Travel
http://www.tops-n-travel.com/

This gay-owned and -operated travel service company claims to offer "the highest levels of service in the industry," from suppliers who have demonstrated that they are sensitive to the needs of the gay and lesbian community.

BreakOut Travel & Tours
http://breakout.com.au/

"We know Australia, it's our home," say the folks at BreakOut travel. Let Australia's leading gay and lesbian tour company be your guide to Sydney, Melbourne, Queensland, and more.

Colours Destinations International
http://www.travelbase.com/colours/

Colours came to life in Key West more than a decade ago with "An Inn for the Avant Garde" providing distinctive lodging for gay men and lesbians. These days, Colours operates three exotic lodging options (with digs in South Beach Miami and San Jose, Costa Rica), and its own reservation services, Colours Destinations International. Make a reservation online, and add some "colour" to your life.

Christopher Travel & Tours
http://www.icchi.com:2011/tourhi/

Christopher Travel & Tours (see Figure 13.15) is proud to be the first (and perhaps the only) gay-owned and -operated Hawaiian partnership specializing in travel and tours to the islands of Hawaii by "folks in 'our community.'" The company Web site features details on some favorite rental spots, and an electronic form in which visitors input ideas, dreams, past experiences, and hopes for an island holiday. Christopher does the rest.

Club Le Bon
http://www.provincetown.com/clublebon/

Club Le Bon books getaways in private resorts in some of the most beautiful places on earth for women who want to "get away from the tourist traps and enjoy a fabulous holiday among other women." Typical getaways include a Morocco Sahara Expedition, and the Monarch Butterfly's Trail in Central Mexico.

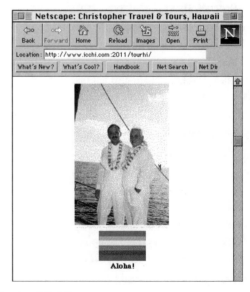

Figure 13.15
Christopher Travel & Tours

Deluxe Travel Professionals International
http://www.1travel.com/rainbow/

Deluxe Travel Professionals International does one thing: provides exclusive, all-gay vacation experiences at some of the finest resorts in the world. Get details on escapes to Club Med Turkoise, Sydney's Gay and Lesbian Mardi Gras, or Club Atlantis, on Mexico's Gold Coast. You'll also find information on RSVP cruises and resorts. An electronic form will help you to get quote online.

Dynamic Travel, Inc.
http://www.showmetravel.com/

Hard to resist a travel agency with promo lines like "Travel with Dorothy" and "Sydney Sleaze Ball." Learn all about Toto Tours ("in the same spirit as the first travelers to the 'Land of Oz'") and the current whereabouts of Jerry, Dynamic's very own "gay travel specialist," who sends virtual postcards from gay Meccas around the world. The St. Louis-based full-service agency has been serving the gay and lesbian community for more than 12 years.

Fantasy Tripping
http://www.festivetravel.com/fantinfo.htm

Gay-owned and -operated Fantasy Tripping has offices in the U.S. and Europe. The agency concentrates on destinations that appeal to "our style of travel."

Galah Tours, Western Australia
http://www.iap.net.au/~galah/

Galah is an acronym for Gay and Lesbian Adventure Holidays. It's a small company, eager to "help you enjoy your stay with people you know" and to help you with any "family"-related inquiries. On site—and in person on your next visit to Western Australia—hosts Ric and Steve usher you through some of their area's hot attractions; from motoring down an enchanted tree-lined country drive (with a stop or two at famous vineyards of the South West) to a gay-oriented tour of Perth, the capital city.

Hillside Campground
http://www.multicom.org/rcl/hillside.html

This members-only campground located in the Endless Mountains of Northeastern Pennsylvania includes some 165 secluded areas for setting up gay camp.

Kiwi Host
http://nz.com/webnz/kiwihost/

If you find yourself in Auckland, New Zealand, and are in desperate need of gay guidance, Kiwi Host has a deal for you. Let the hosts arrange for day tours, accommodations and onward bookings. Or, if you're the spontaneous type, have a host meet you at the airport to organize your stay on the spot.

Lizard Head Backcountry Tours
http://lizardhead.com/index.html

Lizard Head (see Figure 13.16) teaches outdoor sporting skills to gay men and women via instructional tours of some of North America's most magnificent backcountry. Explore the site for an extended tour calendar, with expeditions ranging from snowshoeing in the Colorado Rockies to desert foraging in Arizona's Superstition Mountains. Other site features include a photo gallery (organized by location and sport) and a gear guide with descriptions, prices, and recommendations on clothing and equipment.

Olivia Cruises and Resorts
http://www.oliviatravel.com

Set sail on an exotic lesbian adventure with Olivia, famous for exclusively chartered cruises for women only. Olivia's Web site makes a splash with details on Hawaiian, Mexican, and Tahitian cruises, among others. The company also specializes in resort vacations, for those who like to keep their feet on the ground. Get all the details online and learn how to book your reservation.

Figure 13.16
Lizard Head Backcountry Tours

Outside Sports

http://www.hooked.net/users/outsport/

Outside Sports is the first "adventure travel company" in the Bay Area specifically created for the gay and lesbian community. Active travel options for gays and lesbians have traditionally been "kind of like opening the closet and realizing you have only two outfits to choose from," the site explains. To fill the void for those who prefer to be active during their time off, Outside Sports has developed "tours packed with adventure and beautiful scenery." Packages are Northern California-specific and typically include biking and kayaking combos (topped off by a fresh cup of coffee or a glass of wine, of course). Read up on the next adventure online.

Pride InfoNet

http://www.pridetravel.com/

Pride InfoNet (see Figure 13.17) is 100 percent gay-owned and -operated and its gay travel site features a variety of planning options, including a databank of cities and gay hot spots in many states throughout the U.S. Also find details on gay tours and cruises, and a search feature for a gay or gay-friendly travel agency in your area.

Rainbow Destinations

http://cimarron.net/rd.html

Rainbow Destinations guides visitors to gay-owned and gay-friendly bed & breakfasts, country inns, guesthouses, resorts, and hotels around the world. Each accommodation is explored in colorful detail. It's brought to you by the same folks who publish the excellent general-interest resource, Bed and Breakfast Inns of North America <http://www.cimarron.net/>.

Rancho Mirage Travel

http://www.gay-travel.com/

Rancho Mirage (see Figure 13.18)—the gay and lesbian travel agency—claims to be the largest resource of the gay/lesbian traveler on the Net. The site is definitely action-packed, with special sections for Hot Lesbian Travel, Asia and Australia, and "of course," Palm Springs. Rancho Mirage is also the only Web agency to offer the opportunity to access Saabre—the Internet reservation system—on-site for reservations with professional backing and ticket delivery. "We'll double check your tickets, confirm with you and deliver them right to your doorstep making sure you really did book the flight you wanted at the lowest fare," they say.

Toto Tours

http://www.tototours.com/

Gay-owned and -operated Toto Tours takes "friends of Dorothy" to exotic settings somewhere over the

Figure 13.17
Pride InfoNet

Figure 13.18
Rancho Mirage Travel

rainbow. Get details on Toto packages like "Whales and Males in Maui" and "An Unorthodox Pilgrimage to the Holy Land." And you thought there was no place like home ...

The Travel House
http://www.thetravelhouse.com

The Travel House—"a travel company for the alternative lifestyle"—prides itself on its expertise and experience in understanding the needs of gay and lesbian travelers. The company site offers cost-effective vacation ideas and a "trip of the month" section. A portion of all profits goes to AIDS research and organizations.

Uranian Travel
http://www.uranian.com

Click here for the "Uranian experience," invites this U.K.-based gay tour operator with an ever-so-clever name. The site is loaded with ideas for "sun holidays," and "citybreaks" to places like Amsterdam, Paris, and Dublin. E-mail for a quote on a low-cost flight, or for an entire vacation package.

GAI-Q Out Take

From Out.com's October 1996 "Travel Bug" GAI-Q survey (See Figure 13.19), we learn that more viewers have left their hearts in San Francisco than they have in any other U.S. city. As for which country viewers find most entertaining: the U.S. takes it with a quarter. The Netherlands and Australia are the closest runners up.

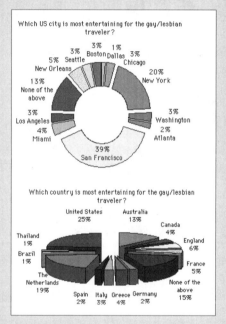

Figure 13.19
Out.com's October 1996 "Travel Bug" GAI-Q survey

Chapter 14

VESTED INTERESTS

POEM ON CLINTON'S SIGNING THE DEFENSE OF MARRIAGE ACT

Let Us Pray Psalm 1996

Bill Clinton is my shepherd, I shall not want.

He leadeth me beside the still marriage bureaus.

He restoreth my faith in the Libertarians.

He guideth me in the path of apartheid.

Yea, though I walk through the valley of the tax lines,

I shall not benefit.

Clinton has anointed my taxes with single returns;

My medical expenses runneth over.

Surely discrimination and hard living will follow me

all the days of my life.

The Democrats and I will live in separate houses forever.

— Jim Donovan, first published on the Internet.
("Living in sin for 21 years, I had hoped Clinton
would have made an 'honest woman' out of me at last.")

This politically charged creative burst—like so much amateur poetry these days—first found a home on the Net. It lyrically makes some observations that the Pollyanna in some of us may miss in a blurred rush to put faith in a fearless and "friendly" leader.

Early in his first term, plausibly friendly American leader Bill Clinton made "gays in the military" a household term—only to arrive at the abysmal "Don't Ask, Don't Tell, Don't Pursue" compromise shortly thereafter. As the Servicemembers Legal Defense Network (http://www.sldn.org/) points out, even with "Don't Ask, Don't Tell ..." in place, military commanders and investigators continue to question recruits and servicemembers about their sexual orientation; and suspect servicemembers still face harassment, physical violence, jail, and untimely ends to their careers. In other words, not much has changed; "asking," "telling," "pursuing" or not.

Then, in September of last year, Clinton made what the Human Rights Campaign called "a historical misjudgment," "cheap election-year politicking," and "a cynical strategy to scapegoat gay and lesbian Americans" by signing the Defense of Marriage Act. With that stroke, Clinton became the first president to intrude on states' jurisdiction over marriage, effectively excluding gays and lesbians from the federal benefits and responsibilities that come with marriage (if and when the option were ever made available to us in the first place). This means that gays and lesbians in long-term committed relationships will not be collecting each other's Social Security; they will not be allowed to file joint federal income tax returns; and they will be excluded from myriad other federal benefits that married heterosexuals by now take for granted—such as immigration, inheritance rights, access to family health coverage, and the ability to make medical decisions for an incapacitated spouse.

"In this world, nothing can be said to be certain except death and taxes." We often hear variations of this 200-year-old quote from Ben Franklin. For sure, we are no strangers to certain uncertainty; but even the mandatory obligations of death and taxes are made to be more intense, if you will, for gays and lesbians. Jobs. Partnerships. Homes. Estates. Taxes.

Death. Why does it all have to be so much more convoluted if you happen to be gay?

You won't find the answer to that question here. What you will find are professionals and organizations that are using the Web to specifically address the vested interests of gays and lesbians; be it through dexterous estate planning, specialized real estate services, or pointers on transferring the ownership rights of a life insurance policy.

Some even offer a direct link to the President (president@whitehouse.gov) (Figure 14.1). Vent at will.

GOING TO THE CHAPEL?

In May 1993, the Hawaii Supreme Court handed what legal experts called the biggest legal victory ever to the gay and lesbian community. The landmark *Baehr v. Lewin* case marked the first time an American court ruled in favor of the idea that it is discriminatory to deny gay men and lesbians the right to marry their partner of choice. Sending the case back to trial court, the Hawaii Supreme Court directed

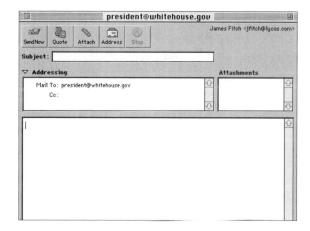

Figure 14.1
president@whitehouse.gov
Let the President know how you feel.

the state government to show a "compelling state in-terest" for discrimination. As of December 1996, it had failed to do so, and First Circuit Court Judge Kevin Chang declared the right of same-sex couples to marry as protected by the state constitution. His decision was an important step in the right to marry, but it's still only a step. Refer to the following sites and organizations for current news and views surrounding your right (or lack thereof) to get hitched.

The Case for Same-Sex Marriage
http://www.simonsays.com/titles/0684824043/index.html

This small promotional site for the book of the same name by William N. Eskridge, Jr. includes some excerpts which examine the historical precedents that support gay and lesbian marriages. It also takes a look at how the Web community has responded to the issue.

Equal Marriage Rights Home Page
http://nether.net/~rod/html/sub/marriage.html

The Web home to the marriage@abacus.oxy.edu mailing list features contact information for same-sex marriage lobby groups, news from around the U.S., and a collection of articles on the subject. Oh, and information on how to join the mailing list.

FORM Boston
http://www.calico-company.com/formboston/

Boston-based FORM (Forum on the Right to Marriage) is a national grassroots organization primarily engaged in education and outreach concerning the issues of same-sex marriage. The group provides resources and training to similar groups throughout the U.S., and, when feasible, works with gay and lesbian political groups to attain same-sex marriage rights. Site features include resources such as a "marriage primer" and a general letter for requesting inclusion of your wedding announcement in a local newspaper. It also provides information on starting a FORM chapter in your area.

Freedom to Marry
http://www.ftm.org/

Eastern Pennsylvania Freedom to Marry Coalition
http://www.libertynet.org/~pftmc/

Western Pennsylvania Freedom to Marry Coalition
http://www.cs.cmu.edu/afs/cs/user/scotts/ftp/wpaf2mc/

The Freedom to Marry Coalition (Figure 14.2) is a broad-based national group committed to organizing, educating, and advocating so that people in all U.S. states will be able to take advantage of civil marriage under Hawaii state law. The coalition has regional sub-committees around the country (the main Web site is maintained by members of the Los Angeles coalition steering committee). Evan Wolfson, director of Lambda Legal Defense and Education's Marriage Project, is the effective leader of the coalition, and he provides periodic updates on the state of the fight to this site. Besides lots of background information and legal texts, the site will also access "Info from Your State" via clickable map or pull-down menu. This leads to marriage legislation (if any exists), state news

Figure 14.2
Western Pennsylvania Freedom to Marry Coalition

briefs, and links to a local Freedom to Marry Chapter. Localized chapters for Eastern and Western Pennsylvania are already up on the Web in full effect; watch for many more to enter in the months ahead.

Human Rights Campaign Statement on DoMA
http://www.hrcusa.org/issues/marriage/index.html

An informative segment of its "Understanding Our Issues" section, the Human Rights Campaign gets busy with this interactive update on the "hot-button" issue. Beginning with HRC Executive Director Elizabeth Birch's response to President Clinton's signing the Defense of Marriage Act ("We regret that Clinton opted to sign this needless and mean-spirited bill"), the site-within-a-site features the actual text of the bill (!), a DOMA fact sheet, and some quick-and-easy options for taking action with Congress.

Hawaii Equal Rights Marriage Project (h.e.r.m.p.)
http://www.xq.com/hermp/

The Hawaii Equal Rights Marriage Project (Figure 14.3) was organized in 1993, in Honolulu, to help raise the funds necessary to pay for legal costs in *Baehr v. Miike*. (It is the sole support of Dan Foley, the attorney who makes all court appearances on behalf of the plaintiff couples.) Since then, "h.e.r.m.p." has become a volunteer public information source about the court case and about the civil rights issues involved in same-gender marriage, providing experts, resources, and articles on the subject. The organizational Web site includes a rundown of the benefits available to married couples in Hawaii, donation information, and regular updates—straight from the little state with the big case.

Lambda Legal Defense and Education Fund—The Marriage Project
http://www.gaysource.com/gs/ht/oct95/lambda.html#linkfive

The U.S.'s oldest and largest legal organization working to secure equal rights for gays and lesbians outlines its Marriage Project here. The project was initiated in 1994

to coordinate the legal and political groundwork for winning and keeping the right to marry. Background information, historical parallels, and the tasks ahead are covered.

National Gay and Lesbian Task Force: Talking Points on Hawaii Same-Gender Marriage Case
http://www.ngltf.org/press/talkhawi.html

In simple Q&A style, the National Gay and Lesbian Task Force answers some commonly asked questions on issues surrounding *Baehr v. Miike*. Questions addressed range from "What does the Hawaii trial court decision say?" to "Wouldn't same-gender marriages infringe upon the religious freedoms of some Americans?" (Answer to that last one is "absolutely not," btw.)

NOW Issue Report: Same-Sex Marriage
http://now.org/now/issues/lgbi/marr-rep.html

The National Organization for Women weighs in with a hefty source for people—particularly lesbians, whose rights the organization considers a priority issue—researching (or wanting to get active about) same-sex marriage. The "issue report" points out that a recent

Figure 14.3
Hawaii Equal Rights Marriage Project (h.e.r.m.p.)

study shows 71 percent of lesbians to be in committed relationships. From there, it launches into the key points ("Not long ago, marriage was traditionally limited to members of the same race and religion, and married women were virtually the legal property of their husbands") and outlines the plans NOW has, both current and future, to combat the government's refusal to recognize same-sex marriage, a.k.a. "discrimination masquerading as morality."

Out.com—Gay Marriage and Domestic Partnership

http://www.out.com

For historical and of-the-moment perspectives and reports on same-sex marriage, visit Out.com's "News" section and click on "Gay Marriage and Domestic Partnership" (Figure 14.4). Articles on file range from "Denver Extends Benefits to City Employees" to "Hawaii Judge Strikes Down Gay Marriage Ban."

Figure 14.4

Out.com—Gay Marriage and Domestic Partnership

| Random | Posting |

Subject: Marriage

The solution to the gay marriage trouble is as easy as it is equally difficult: Just get married! For now, it doesn't really matter how you do it. Big and fancy is nice, but plain and simple will do just as well. But do it. Go out and get rings, invite a few friends, make your vows before the crowd, put the rings on, and kiss the bride/groom! That's the easy part.

The hard part is sticking with it. Don't take the rings off. Don't hedge with people who ask. Simply say, "He's my husband." or "She's my wife." or "We're married." Don't be "in-your-face" about it (unless that's your style) but do be frank and adamant. People will say, "No you're not married." And that's when you respond: "Yes, I am. I may not have paperwork from the government, but that doesn't change the state of my heart and mind. I'm married and all I ask is that you respect that."

They may or may not, but the ice has been broken and the point has been made. And, if they're people you know, then most likely an attitude has been changed. And that's how we'll win our equality, you know. A person at a time who must realize that people they love are suffering.

Mon Dec 9 16:26:30 EST 1996 - ()
rgirdley@erols.com

Partners Task Force for Gay & Lesbian Couples
http://www.buddybuddy.com/toc.html

Legal Marriage Alliance of Washington
http://www.buddybuddy.com/lma.html

The Washington-based Partners Task Force for Gay & Lesbian Couples was founded back in 1986 by Steve Bryant and his partner of 13 years, Demian (who programs the Web site). The Task Force provides information, support, and advocacy for same-sex couples and those who serve them. Its excellent Web site loads viewers down with information on issues of concern to same-sex couples (legal data, ceremonial tips) and results of its national surveys of and about same-sex couples. The site also plays host to the Legal Marriage Alliance of Washington, made up of gay and lesbian couples and their supporters in Washington to prepare residents for the impact the Hawaii ruling will have in their state. "We will function as the local resource for information on same-sex marriages, and we will assist existing organizations by sharing information and coordinating strategies," the mission statement explains. The site includes a FAQ file on same-sex marriage, along with reports and images from community forums on the issue.

VIATICAL SETTLEMENTS

A viatical settlement occurs when someone with a terminal illness sells or transfers ownership rights of a life insurance policy to a person or company in return for a percentage of the policy face value. Because of the obvious AIDS connection, ads for such services are omnipresent in gay-oriented publications and points of interest (over urinal stalls in gay bars, for example). The following sites either attempt to demystify the practice by using layman's terms and guiding viewers through some of the legalese (The Viatical Settlement Page), or they simply want your business. Viatical companies like VSB

Corporation have set up shop on the Web to inform those with life-threatening illnesses of their financial options. Use these sites to become educated on the subject, but never make life decisions based on information you find on the World Wide Web. And as new treatment techniques render HIV infections less immediately life-threatening, watch for this industry to undergo some major changes.

Life Partners Inc.
http://www.lifepartnersinc.com

"Options abound. Simplify your life," encourages this Waco, Texas-based viatical settlement company, which claims to be a pioneer in the industry. Life Partners has served clients in the U.S., Canada, and the U.K. Its Web site explains the process and the benefits, and displays blurbed quotables from clients and the media. It also includes a "FasTrac" electronic application.

The Medical Escrow Society
http://www.med-escrow.com/

Founded by David Scott Reed and his partner, Cecil Ray DeLoach, as "an advocacy group to represent and assist terminally ill people in the negotiation and sale of their life insurance policies," the Medical Escrow society now claims to be recognized as "the original viatical settlement service organization." Since 1995, it has converted more than 85 million dollars of life insurance coverage into cash for clients. Find applications and answers to questions on this promotional Web presence.

Viatical Association of America
http://www.cais.net/viatical/

If you want the official line on viatical settlements, this professional association composed of brokers and funding companies provides a wealth of information. Site features include details about the viatical industry, the code of ethics and standards of business practice, and links to the various member companies.

The Viatical Settlement Page
http://www.global.org/viatical/

The Viatical Settlement Page (Figure 14.5)—not affiliated with a viatical settlement company, law firm, or broker—provides a plainspoken overview of the practice, along with viatical news reports, a listing of companies and groups that are involved in viatical settlements, and even a glossary to help visitors work around the legalese. Texan and systems architect Wynn Wagner III (see sidebar Q&A) started the site in 1995, simply because he couldn't find much good information on the subject. Wagner is very upfront about the fact that the material contained within was not written by a lawyer, or even by an expert on viatical statements, and that one should by no means make irreversible decisions based on information found here.

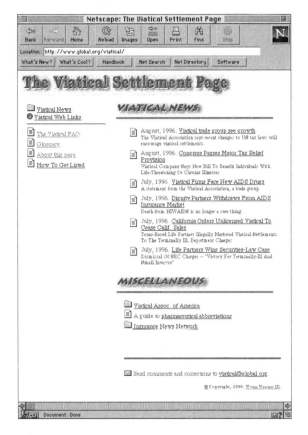

Figure 14.5
The Viatical Settlement Page

VSB Corporation
http://www.vrsc.com

VSB Corporation provides financial services to the seriously ill, including those living with HIV/AIDS. The Web site objectives include informing people living with life-threatening illnesses of this option, and educating medical professionals about this "important patient resource." The process is covered online—from qualifying to distribution of funds—along with frequently asked questions and links to HIV/AIDS, Cancer, and Cardiovascular resources on the Web.

REAL ESTATE AND HOUSING SERVICES

We'll safely assume that most gay and lesbian real estate agents aren't out declaring their sexuality on the Web. But from nationwide relocation services to queer roommate finders, there are a few individuals and businesses who have made it a point to target and serve gays and lesbians on the move.

Across America Real Estate Network
http://www.wilmington.net/businesses/rs/aaren/

North Carolina-based Mark Kasper offers this relocation referral service for gays and lesbians across the U.S. (Figure 14.6). Gay and on the move? Home or business to list? This is definitely the place to get started on the Web. The user-friendly site features include electronic forms for buyers, sellers, and agents, and e-mail access to Kasper, the friendly broker. Sorry, no rentals.

Gay Key West Real Estate
http://www.gaykeywestfl.com/real.html

Thinking of buying a B&B and escaping to island life? The Gay Key West site includes this page of contact information for gay and lesbian agents.

WYNN WAGNER, WEBMASTER, THE VIATICAL SETTLEMENT PAGE

Besides serving as chief systems architect for Computer Language Research, board member for Lesbian and Gay Democrats of Texas, and precinct chairman for the Democratic party, Wynn Wagner appears to find plenty of time to be creative on the Web—for fun (a Web page for his cat; one for his rose garden; one for his "seriously cute" boyfriend) and for business (DivaNet, his commercial Web server, which leads to the Gay Dallas Page, and the Dallas Gay/Lesbian Alliance). He also offers some invaluable information services, just to be helpful. The Viatical Settlement Page is one of those services. Why viaticals? "If you find a hole in what's available, I think you have a responsibility to fill it," he says.

Q: What prompted you to put up an info-site on viatical settlements?

A: I went out looking for information on viaticals and had a hard time finding anything. This was quite a while ago. There wasn't much available. As I found tidbits, I started collecting them and publishing them.

Q: Viatical settlements aren't inherently gay-oriented. Why, then, do you think it's beneficial to have viatical settlement information aimed at gay people—or at least written from a gay perspective?

A: I don't see gay-oriented viatical information as particularly beneficial. I mean, as a solid member of the gay community I always try to keep my dollars in the community.

Q: You're not selling anything, and the site is run "by some individuals who have a personal interest in the topic." So what do you hope to accomplish?

A: The Internet is a give and take kind of network. If you find a hole in

what's available, I think you have a responsibility to fill it. Imagine what the Internet would be like if nothing but sponges went surfing soaking up everything in sight. Boring. Somebody has to do content—and I really think it's every user's responsibility to give back something.

Q: Any examples of how your sites have helped viewers?

A: I've been helping the Sisters of St. Elizabeth of Hungary. Believe it or not, the largest HIV knowledgebase on the planet is run out of a convent in Southern California (http://www.AE-GIS.com). I did a piece called "Day One" for them. It's all about getting a positive HIV test. I've gotten several e-mail messages from folks on this. "You saved my life," et cetera, et cetera.

Q: What are some of the other ways in which you're using the Web?

A: My cat has a Web page—including his very own collection of cat jokes (http://www.global.org/stanley.) And my rose garden has a Web page. Somebody who is doing a photo CD on gardening bought a couple of my rose pictures (http://www.global.org/wynn/roses). Très cool—I'm a professional photographer now.

Last Halloween, my boyfriend took his digital camera to the big street party here in the Oak Lawn section of Dallas. The next day, we had a "Halloween In The Lawn" Web page full of pictures

(http://www.divanet.com/Halloween/). The Internet opens up the world of publishing to individuals. The Web is a big equalizer. My dinky little Halloween page can get in there and play in the same arena as Time-Life and CNN.

Q: Like you have done and continue to do, the global gay community is doing an excellent job of using the Web to "get the word out" on various topics. Are there any areas that you think could use some attention about now?

A: Prose, exposition, commentary. I don't see enough. We've got plenty of lists. We've got more than enough porn. Lots of folks are trying (e.g., *Out*). Some don't seem to know what to make of the Internet (e.g., *Advocate*). Others have really tried but haven't seemed to get it together (e.g., Project Inform).

I don't know what else we need right now. If I did, I'd probably be out there putting something together instead of talking with you in e-mail. ;-)

Figure 14.6
Across America Real Estate Network

LeTs Bi Gay Mall—Real Estate (Houston, Texas)
http://www.townmtg.com/mall/restate/restate.htm

A scant few businesses were listed within this Houston business directory on my visit, but there were a few gay Realtors, and a "cutting edge mortgage broker."

Pittsburgh Gay Travel and Real Estate Services
http://www.woodworks.com/pghlgb/travel.html

Strictly travel services on my visit, but poised and ready for real estate listings.

Provincetown Real Estate Page
http://www.provincetown-realty.com/

This comprehensive site for all your Provincetown real estate needs displays available properties for sale and for

rent, and includes current mortgage rates and a mortgage calculator.

Rainbow Roommates
http://nycnet.com/rainbowroommates/

In the New York City metro area and in need of a perfect roommate? Rainbow Roommates claims to be New York City's leader in gay apartment share and roommate referral services. "We understand what you need so that you can make the best decision about finding that perfect roommate," the home page explains. "And it is that insight that we hope you will come to value and continuously expect from us. Find out about the site's services, including apartment share listings (for lookers) and apartment share advertising (for owners). Register online.

The Winning Pair
http://www.glbnet.com/business/Oh/Col/WinPair/WinPair1.html-ssi

If you're Ohio-bound and need a home (or need to get rid of one), why not "call the lesbians" at King Thompson Realtors (Figure 14.7). Darla and Lorraine have 13 years of combined experience as licensed Realtors—and they've amassed some impressive achievement awards and honors. Learn all about "the winning pair" on their out and proud home page.

Figure 14.7
The Winning Pair

GAY LAW, FRIENDLY FIRMS

From up there in the Hollywood hills to down there in Auckland, New Zealand, gay lawyers and their friendly firms are definitely out there to help you through life's sticky situations. Thankfully, there are also plenty of public-service Web sites aimed at educating gays and lesbians about the fights for their rights that are happening around the world—and in cyberspace.

Bay Area Lawyers for Individual Freedom (California)
http://www.balif.org/

Bay Area Lawyers for Individual Freedom is a minority bar association, founded in 1980, with a membership of nearly 600 lesbians, gay men, bisexuals, and their supporters in the legal community. Among BALIF's many purposes: discussion and action on questions of law and justice affecting the gay community; coalition building with other legal organizations to combat discrimination; and promotion of appointment of lesbian, gay, and bisexual attorneys to the judiciary and public agencies commissions. Find out how to join, and check out job announcements on site.

Canadian HIV/AIDS Legal Network
http://www.microtec.net:8080/~jujube/

The Montreal-based Canadian HIV/AIDS Legal Network is the only national, community based, charitable organization in Canada that is working in the area of policy and legal issues raised by HIV/AIDS. It was formed in 1992 and remains "dedicated to promoting responses to HIV infection and AIDS that respect human rights." The org's site includes the Canadian HIV/AIDS Policy & Law Newsletter, along with various articles and reports on issues like "HIV/AIDS in Prisons," and "Prostitution Laws and Policies and HIV/AIDS."

GayLawNet
http://www.labyrinth.net.au/~dba/index.html

GayLawNews
http://www.labyrinth.net.au/~dba/news.html

Melbourne, Australia-based lawyer David Allan first hit the Net in November 1995. "My searches for legal information led me to thinking that the gay community could use a reference resource that addresses questions affecting the community," he explains. He's since done something about it. His Web-based GayLawNet (Figure 14.8) is dedicated to answering your questions and providing you with the simplest access to a gay lawyer—be it the Webmaster himself, or one of the many attorneys around the world listed on site. Allan also offers several excellent advice sections on interest areas from "Arrest by Police" to "Intellectual Property." Naturally, advice is delivered with an Aussie slant, but visitors will find much of the information to be of global interest. The site's GayLawNews section, for example, offers a monthly international digest of reports on changes in the law, and on possible future changes. The GayLawNews subject index includes "Censorship," "Military," "Taxation," and more.

George Allen DuFour (Tampa, FL)
http://www.interaccess.net/law/

Don't be nervous in this lawyer's office. "I have a very relaxed office atmosphere where you can feel comfortable making serious plans for the future," says Tampa's George DuFour. The lawyer, specializing in the preparation of wills for non-traditional couples, also has a big pink triangle on his informative home page.

Figure 14.8
GayLawNet

Duran, Loquvam & Robertson (West Hollywood, CA.)

http://home.earthlink.net/~dlrlaw/

From the heart of the Hollywood entertainment community, Duran, Loquvam & Robertson provides "vigorous and creative advocacy" in complex civil and criminal litigation. At the same time, it is "a firm with a social conscience." Check out sections on civil litigation, labor and employment law, estate planning, and more on site.

Fannon & Stomberg (Fresno, CA.)

http://www.cybergate.com/~stomberg/

Fresno's Michael J. Fannon and Nannete J. Stomberg open their law firm's promotional site—dubbed "Gay & Lesbian Rights: Legal Assistance for Unmarried Couples" (Figure 14.9)—with a chilling scenario: "You've spent the last 14 years living with the most caring, intelligent, sensitive, loving man you have ever known. ... In the moment when he needs you most, lying sick and disabled in a cold lonely hospital, his parents walk into the waiting room and tell you that they are going to have you excluded from his room." The scenario ends on a relatively upbeat note in that you "pull out your copy of their son's Durable Power of Attorney for Health Care appointing you as his attorney-in-fact, and carefully explain to them that if they don't behave, you will have 'them' excluded from 'your lover's' room." It drives home the need for special legal planning in an unmarried arrangement, and that's this firm's area of expertise. Get all the details online about how you can benefit from a non-marital relationship package. For customized information, use the site's interactive request form.

Figure 14.9
Fannon & Stomberg (Fresno, CA.)

Kilkenny, Donelson & Gambin (Denver, CO)

http://www.ecentral.com/KDG/

This Denver-based gay-friendly full-service firm "consists of talented lawyers with diverse backgrounds." Their site also provides business tips, free of charge.

Lambda Legal Defense and Education Fund

http://www.gaysource.com/gs/ht/oct95/lambda.html

Founded in 1973, Lambda is the U.S.'s oldest and largest legal organization working to secure equal rights for gays and lesbians. Lambda's work involves nearly every area of concern to gays, lesbians, and people living with HIV, including discrimination in employment, housing, and the military. The Web site is brief, outlining Lambda's current efforts. "The Marriage Project" gets the most substantial coverage here.

LEGAL: Lesbian & Gay Law Association of Greater New York

http://www.users.interport.net/~le-gal/

This first Web site by an association of lesbian and gay lawyers promotes the expertise and advancement of gay and lesbian legal professionals; educates the public on legal issues facing lesbians and gay men; and works with other gay and lesbian organizations to gain equal rights for all people, among other things. Organizational information is available here, as well as hot links to various international legal and political resources.

Lesbian and Gay Law Notes

http://qrd.rdrop.com/qrd/www/usa/legal/lgln/

Lesbian and Gay Law Notes is a publication of the Lesbian and Gay Law Association of Greater New York. Each month, Notes reports on legal developments related to gay rights and HIV/AIDS, tracking significant new legislation, and reporting on new court decisions, administrative rulings, and executive actions. It also serves as an information exchange about new job openings. The issues, stored within the Queer Resources Directory, are lengthy text documents. Typical headline: "Same-Sex Marriage Tops 1996 Lesbian/Gay Legal News as Hawaii Judge Orders

State to Issue Licenses." The focus here is primarily on U.S. law, but the publication does cover developments in other countries from time to time. Back issues are archived through January 1994.

Maurice Blackburn & Co. (Australia)
http://www.mblack.com.au/

With offices in Melbourne, Dandenong, Frankston, Ballarat, and Traralgon, Maurice Blackburn & Co. serves the gay and lesbian clients in a variety of specialty areas, including HIV/AIDS-related issues, anti-discrimination, and employment law.

Milne Ireland Walker (Auckland, New Zealand)
http://nz.com/webnz/miwsol/

Offering a full range of legal services, this Auckland-based law firm, established in 1987, claims to be "particularly sensitive" to the needs of the gay and lesbian community. Areas of expertise include real estate, litigation, family law, and immigration (New Zealand being one of the few countries to offer residency to same-sex partners of citizens).

North Carolina Gay and Lesbian Attorneys
http://members.aol.com/ncgala/index.htm

North Carolina Gay and Lesbian Attorneys (Figure 14.10) is a voluntary, non-profit, and non-partisan organization providing visibility and advocacy for the state's lesbian, gay, and bisexual communities. The site features a "Legal Guide for Lesbians & Gay Men in North Carolina" (much needed in Helms country), and a referral directory of N.C. attorneys. Membership information is also available.

Out.com—State Laws and Initiatives
Out.com—Internet Censorship
http://www.out.com

For archived reports on the growing list of state laws and initiatives affecting gays and lesbians, visit Out.com's "News" section and click on "State Laws and Initiatives." Articles on file range from "Alexandria Asks Virginia to Consider Gay Marriage" to "Utah High School Gay Club Protected by Fed Statute." For information on what's happening rules-wise in cyberspace, visit the "News" sec-

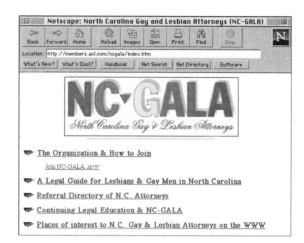

Figure 14.10
North Carolina Gay and Lesbian Attorneys

tion and click on "Internet Censorship," where you'll find such archival reports as "CompuServe Shuts Down German Gay Youth Page" and "Communications Decency Act Gets Day in Court."

Pat. Pending Company
http://www.rnbow.com/patpending/

With U.S. and U.K. offices, Pat. Pending has served the worldwide gay and lesbian community since 1991 with confidential advice and assistance in protecting, licensing, and utilizing copyrights, designs, ideas, inventions, trademarks, and your own confidential information.

James T. Perry, Attorney at Law (Wilmington, DE)
http://www.dol.net/~perrylaw/index.html

The two-attorney firm specializes in personal injury and worker's compensation claims, and also deals in domestic partnerships.

Queer Immigration
http://abacus.oxy.edu/qrd/www/world/immigration/

The Queer Resources Directory's immigration page lists contact information for queer immigration groups around the world. It also provides information on asylum cases, legal rulings, and current immigration law, along with links to other useful information sources on the subject.

QueerLaw
http://abacus.oxy.edu/~ron/queerlaw.html

QueerLaw is a mailing list devoted to discussion, analysis, and promulgation of queer legal theory and all other aspects of sexual orientation and the law. Find out how to subscribe here, or link out to the QueerLaw archives from here.

Queer Legal Resources
http://www.qrd.org/qrd/www/legal/

The Queer Resources Directory includes this hypertext page leading to legal documents, case listings, and other queer law resources. Sections include "U.S. Military Cases," "Statewide Gay Rights Laws," and "Queer Immigration Issues."

Queer Resources Directory— International Law
http://www.qrd.org/qrd/www/world/ legal.html

The Queer Resources Directory includes this hypertext page of legal documents and links related to gay legal issues around the world. Visitors will find text of gay marriage and domestic relations laws from other countries. AIDS, immigration, and sodomy laws are also covered.

Roper and Cain (Boston, MA)
http://www.tiac.net/users/davecain/ roper.html

The Boston-based Roper & Cain law firm claims to be a strong supporter of the gay and lesbian community. Its staff of gay and gay-friendly attorneys assist in drafting domestic partnership agreements and settling property disputes, and they contribute legal volunteers to the AIDS Action Committee of Boston.

Servicemembers Legal Defense Network
http://www.sldn.org/

Servicemembers Survival Guide
http://www.sldn.org/scripts/ menu.ixe?pagetype=Survival+Guide

The Servicemembers Legal Defense is the sole national legal aid and watchdog organization that assists those targeted by the military's policy on homosexuals. With a nationwide network of more than 200 attorneys, SLDN offers the legal advice and assistance that servicemembers need to effectively respond to investigations. The organization's excellent Web site points out that, despite the Clinton administration's "Don't Ask, Don't Tell, Don't Pursue" policy, military commanders and investigators continue to question recruits and servicemembers about their sexual orientation; and that suspect servicemembers still face harassment, physical violence, jail, and an untimely end to their careers. In other words, not much has changed. Visitors to this site will find an "Alerts" section which archives topical newsflashes ("Update on Dornan Military HIV Exclusion Policy"), a history of "Don't Ask, Don't Tell, Don't Pursue," and a direct link for those currently under investigation. Most impressive is the online "Survival Guide," which reviews the major provisions of the policy as well as trends in its implementation, working in essential "survival tips" and covering the practical aspects of military culture along the way. Items covered range from "asking" (some commanders have used "creative" phrasing, such as "Do you find other men attractive?") to attending pride parades (may attend, but only in civilian clothes) to a definition of the "Corporal Klinger Provision." It's an essential resource for gay servicemembers, and a fascinating read for the rest of us.

Weiss and Weissman (San Francisco, CA)
http://www.best.com/~marcw/

Weiss & Weissman, with offices in San Francisco, Foster City, and Berkeley) specializes in tax and real estate law, and assists gays and lesbians with estate planning.

Random Posting

Subject: To RGirdley

Darn tootin'! Actually, folks, here's a little story to brighten your day (I can't believe I'm telling inspirational stories, Next I'll be clipping teddy bears to my coat and preaching est in the subways...).

Anyway, when I came out to the Rush Supervisor of our chapter I thought, "Aaaaaah! This is going to be absolute Hell!" I mean, her whole family's been gung-ho Greek (frat/sorority) ever since they can remember, she's blonde, perky, and has an add-a-bead necklace... And she *works* for the *sorority's* *Executive Offices*. This isn't the kind of girl where you'd automatically think, "Oh! Gay-friendly!" When I did come out, though, she told me how her favorite aunt is gay, and how she wishes this aunt and her lover could get married, because the lover has a very serious medical problem, and the family of the lover (I think I'll say "wife") is trying to get the court to not let the aunt see her own wife... The supervisor is very much for gay rights, and she's very involved with P-FFLAG. So, this is just to let you guys know that, sure, you don't know who's your enemy on this issue, but, by the same token, we are everywhere; we are everyone's family, and you never know what kind of unexpected alliances there are out there... Smile, everyone!!!

Tue Dec 10 9:30:47 EST 1996 - ()

Appendix A

USING THE CD-ROM

The CD-ROM attached to the inside back cover of the book contains all the software you'll need to make it work. The disc contains a fully hyperlinked version of the printed book; the software enables you to link directly to sites of interest as you read.

In order to use the software, you'll need to install it on your computer's hard drive. It's a simple procedure and takes only a few minutes.

WHAT'S ON THE CD-ROM?

The CD-ROM includes the following content, and software that can be installed on your computer:

- A fully hyperlinked version of *Out's Gay and Lesbian Guide to the Web* for PC and Macintosh platforms. You can navigate it with a standard Web browser (included).

- Microsoft Internet Explorer Web browser for PC and Macintosh platforms.

- Earthlink Internet connection software for PC and Macintosh platforms.

VIEWING THE HYPERLINKED VERSION OF THE BOOK

The CD-ROM contains the fully hyperlinked text of *Out's Gay and Lesbian Guide to the Web*, including thousands of addresses to queer hot spots on the Web.

Used in conjunction with an Internet connection, every section of the disc allows you to instantly connect to the hyperlinked site being reviewed. But you don't have to be connected to the Net in order to use the CD-ROM and simply read the text.

USING THE CD-ROM

To read the hyperlinked version of the book, you will need to use a Web browser. Follow the steps below.

Running Most Web Browsers (Including Microsoft Internet Explorer and Netscape Navigator)

1 Place the CD-ROM in your CD-ROM drive.

2 Launch your Web browser.

3 Choose "Open File" from the File menu.

4 Select your CD-ROM drive. For PC users, this is usually drive D. Mac users should double-click on the CD-ROM icon.

5 Double-click on the file named "Welcome.htm."

Running Microsoft Internet Explorer

1 Place the CD-ROM in your CD-ROM drive.

2 Launch Internet Explorer

3 Choose "Open" from the File menu.

4 Click the "Browse" button.

5 Select your CD-ROM drive. For PC users, this is usually drive D. Mac users, double-click on the CD-ROM icon.

6 Double-click on the file named "Welcome.htm."

7 Click on "OK."

INSTALLING WEB BROWSER SOFTWARE

If you do not have a Web browser installed on your computer, you can find a copy of Microsoft's Internet Explorer on the CD-ROM. The steps for installing Internet Explorer are described below.

Recommended PC System

- 486 Processor (Pentium Processor preferred)
- Windows OS (3.x, 95, or NT)
- 8MB of RAM (16MB preferred)
- 8MB free space on your hard drive (15MB preferred)
- 2x CD-ROM drive (4x recommended)

Macintosh System Requirements

- Apple Macintosh or Power Macintosh (or clone) running System 7.0.1 or later
- Apple Open Transport or Mac TCP and Thread Manager
- 8MB or RAM (16MB preferred)
- 8MB of free space on hard drive (16MB preferred)
- 2x CD-ROM drive (4x preferred)

For All Systems

A modem (14.4bps or faster is recommended for optimum performance).

Installing Internet Explorer

Internet Explorer Version 3.01 for Windows 95

You must be using Microsoft Windows 95 to run Microsoft Internet Explorer 3.01. Locate the IE-Win95 folder in the MS-IE directory on the CD.

Double-click on the IE301M95.EXE file. Follow the instructions that appear on your screen to complete the installation.

Internet Explorer Version 2.1 for Windows 3.1

You must be using Microsoft Windows 3.1 to run Microsoft Internet Explorer 2.1. Locate the IE_WIN31 folder in the MS_IE directory on the CD.

Double-click on the DLMINI21.EXE file. Follow the instructions that appear on your screen to complete the installation.

Internet Explorer Version 2.0 for the Macintosh

Double-click the Internet Explorer installer icon, located in the MS Internet Explorer Folder, to install. Follow the prompts that appear on your screen to complete the installation.

Note: Eudora Light is an Internet Mail client application that is included in Microsoft Internet Explorer 2.0 for the Macintosh. Documentation for Eudora Light is not included. To download the Eudora Light Manual separately, visit the Microsoft Internet Explorer Web site at: http://www.microsoft.com/ie/iedl.htm#mac.

Installing Earthlink Internet Connection Software (for Macs and PCs)

To install Earthlink as your Internet service provider, follow these steps:

Installing Earthlink for the Macintosh

To install Earthlink on your Macintosh, follow these steps:

1 From the Earthlink folder, double-click "Total Access Installer."

2 Follow the onscreen instructions.

Installing Earthlink for Windows

To install Earthlink for Windows, follow these steps:

1 From the Earthlink folder, open either the Win31 (for Windows 3.1x) or the Win95 (for Windows 95) depending on your system.

2 Run the Setup.exe File and follow the onscreen instructions.

Appendix *B*

TIPS FOR USING LYCOS TO SEARCH THE WEB

To search the Lycos catalog, just enter one or more words (better known as a "search query") in the text entry box on the Lycos home page or search results page. Next, press the Enter key (or click the Go Get It button). Lycos will display the results. If you need to customize or refine your search, however, Lycos provides an easy way for you to "fine-tune" your search.

The Customize Your Search form is a tool that Lycos provides to make searching its index easy for you to do. It's especially helpful if you need to do any of the following:

- Make your search wider or more narrow

- Have the search match ALL words in a query rather than ANY single word (which is the default setting)

- Search for special variations of a given term (for example, to search for several possible spellings of a word AND some other word)

Most of the time you won't need to use this search form at all if you only want to perform "wide" searches of the Web. However, Lycos gives you other Search options, which you can change if you want to search for different types of information, such as pictures, sounds, and sites that have been categorized by subject.

You can also "refine" your search by making it narrower or wider. You can have the search match ALL words in your query rather than the default ANY word. You can also search for a number of terms which are DIFFERENT from the number you entered (for example, to search for several possible spellings of a word AND some other word).

The search form gives you two ways to control your search: *Search Options* and *Display Options*. You'll notice that both Search Options and Display Options are pull-down menus. Simply click the down arrow in each of these pull-down menus and look at the selections that are available.

USING SEARCH OPTIONS TO SET TERMS TO MATCH (BOOLEAN)

You might wonder why you can't do Boolean searches on Lycos. You might also want to know what exactly a Boolean search is. Boolean searches are those queries that let you search the Web for very specific combinations of words. For example, you might want to see all instances of peanut and butter together, but only where they appear without jelly.

Although you can't perform true Boolean searches on Lycos, you can come very close by using the

Search Options features. Just keep these simple guidelines in mind:

- AND searches are possible by selecting the match all terms (AND) option and then entering whatever words you want in the search box. In the above example, you'd simply enter peanut butter.

- NOT searches are a bit trickier. You may currently prepend (that is, begin) a term with a hyphen to make it a negative indicator, like this: -jelly. This will only reduce the score for sites containing the word jelly, not remove them entirely. The good news is that the first set of results you get will most likely give you what you want: peanut butter without jelly.

By default, Lycos will find all documents matching any word you type in your query (except for certain words like "a" and "the" which are generally not meaningful in a search). If you type "jeep cherokee" as your query, Lycos will find all documents containing either "jeep" OR "cherokee." This is the match any term (OR) Search Option, and is what you get when you type a query into the form on the home page, or if you select the match any term (OR) option on the Customize Your Search form.

Sometimes you might want to find only documents which match ALL the words in your query. This is the match all terms (AND) option. Try it on the form and then see what Lycos returns for "jeep cherokee" when you use the "OR" option and when you use the "AND" option.

SYMBOLS YOU CAN'T USE IN YOUR SEARCHES

You can't use + in search terms. A common instance of this is the term C++, which gets stripped down to c. Unfortunately, this leaves a single letter which, being shorter than three characters, is ignored. This

behavior can be annoying, but Lycos is in the process of choosing the best solution to solve it (and related problems) without affecting the speed and performance of conducting searches. For now we suggest you search for related terms: Instead of C++, for instance, you might try programming languages. Hopefully, Lycos will fix this soon.

You also cannot search for numbers. The current version of Lycos strips out all numbers at the beginning of words. This causes problems if you search for 3DO, 4AD Records, or any other letter-number combination.

The problem is that numbers are a whole different breed of cat from letters. Lycos is trying to teach its retrieval engine to determine for itself which sequences of letters are words and which are not; once they do, you'll be able to make these searches.

SYMBOLS YOU CAN USE IN YOUR SEARCHES

At the present time, you can use the following symbols in your search queries:

- (-) As we mentioned earlier, you can use the - symbol to help narrow down your search. For example, to search for bank, but without river turning up in the search, you would type bank -river in your search query. This is similar to the NOT Boolean search term.

- (.) Use a period at the end of the keyword to limit it with no expansions. Bank. will bring up only results with the keyword "bank" and ignore expansions like "bankers" and "banking."

- ($) Put this symbol after the keyword to make the search engine expand it. The search term "gard$" will bring up results like "garden" and "gardenias." This feature is great if you don't know how to spell a word, or if you aren't sure what you're looking for.

LIMITING YOUR SEARCH TO A SPECIFIED NUMBER OF TERMS

You might also be wondering why you need "match 2 terms," "match 3 terms," and so on. These options give you more flexibility in your search. Suppose you wanted to find references to Sarajevo and Yugoslavia. But you're not sure whether Sarajevo is spelled "Sarajevo" or "Sarayevo." So you enter your query "Sarajevo Sarayevo Yugoslavia." To get the best results, you can use the Search Options.

You can't use match all terms (AND) because that would give you only documents which contain both spellings of "Sarajevo" AND Yugoslavia, and there probably aren't any of those. You could use match any terms (OR), because that would return all documents that contain any of these three terms, but you would also get lots of documents you don't want in the list.

Here's what you do: Enter "Sarajevo Sarayevo Yugoslavia" as your query, and choose match 2 terms. This selection will match at least two terms in each document. Since it's quite unlikely Sarajevo will be spelled two different ways in the same document, the results returned will have references to BOTH one of the two spellings of Sarajevo AND Yugoslavia.

USING THE SEARCH OPTIONS TO SET THE SELECTIVITY OF THE SEARCH

You can change the Search Options to adjust the selectivity of the Lycos search engine. When set to "loose match," you will get more documents, but they will tend to be less relevant to the query you've made. Often, particularly when you are beginning a search and wish to cast the widest possible net, this is exactly what you want.

If you want the Lycos search engine to be more selective, change the Search Option from loose match to "strong match." Lycos will return only documents which have a very high relevance to your query. If you are on a slow dial-up connection, setting the selectivity to "strong match" can save you time by reducing the number of irrelevant hits downloaded to you.

You should try out the effect of changing various selectivity settings on the form. Try some searches with various selectivity settings to get a feel for how it affects your results.

SETTING THE DISPLAY OF THE RESULTS PAGE SIZE

Lycos always gives you all the results or "hits" matching your query, even if there are hundreds or thousands of documents. If the number of hits is large, however, Lycos does not display them all at once, so you don't need to wait a long time for the whole page to come to you. By default, Lycos displays 10 hits on each results page. Once you've looked at those 10, you click on the "Next 10 hits" link at the bottom of the page to get the next 10 hits, and so on until all the hits are displayed.

To change the default from 10 hits displayed on each page, you can set the number in the Display Options pull-down menu. Simply choose another value from 10-40 results per page.

SETTING THE AMOUNT OF RESULTS DETAIL YOU WANT DISPLAYED

You can also control the amount of information you want Lycos to display about each result. There are three levels of detail you can choose from:

- Standard (the default)
- Detailed (all information displayed)
- Summary (the minimum amount of information is displayed)

INTERPRETING THE RESULTS OF A SEARCH

The percentage numbers are simply Lycos's way of showing you how close it thinks each site will match what you're looking for, based on the words you asked Lycos to search for.

When the Lycos search engine compares each page to your query, it gives higher scores to pages that contain the words as you typed them in. It also looks for pages that mention these words early on, rather than far down in some sub-section of the site. The page with the combination most like the words you typed in is ranked at the top and assigned the number 1.000. Other sites are ranked below and assigned numbers based on how much or how little they resemble your search terms.

This means that if you asked for Hungarian goulash, then a site titled The Hungarian Goulash Recipe Page will end up above sites that mention Carpathian goulash, salad, and Hungarian bread or some less precise combination.

The percentages are in no way a rating of how good Lycos thinks any page is. They're simply a tool to help you narrow down your choices.

CREDITS

CHAPTER 1

Why America Online Sucks Web site Copyright 1995-1996 James Egelhof. Portions Copyright America Online, Inc. Used with permission.

GL Web's Rainbow Query is a production of Atlantis InterNetworks. Used with permission.

Gay Resources Web site designed and maintained by Christine Kossman. Copyright 1996. Used with permission.

CHAPTER 2

DivaNet Search Page Copyright 1996 Wynn Wagner III. Used with permission.

CHAPTER 3

Gay and Lesbian Star Trek Web site Authored by T. D. Perkins. Used with permission.

Tinsletown Queer Web site Copyright 1997 Nicholas Snow. All worldwide rights reserved. Used with permission.

Pansy Division Web site Copyright 1995, 1996 Pansy Division and Woodworks Digital Design. Used with permission.

Cemetry Gates Web site layout and design by Scott Krajewski. Morrissey picture by Reprise Records. Used with permission.

Derivative Duo Web site designed by Kim McKoy, May 1996. Used with permission.

Parterre Box Web site Copyright 1996 James Jorden. Used with permission.

Hello, Dolly Web site courtesy of Kenny Hom.

Theatre Central! Web site Copyright 1992-1996 Andrew Q. Kraft. All rights reserved. Used with permission.

A-R-K Web site Copyright StoryWorks. Used with permission.

Angel Web Web site Copyright StoryWorks. Used with permission.

ArtAIDS Web site courtesy of Gordon Joly.

CHAPTER 4

Draginatrix Web site Copyright 1996 Mediapolis, Inc. The Draginatrix and the Data Lounge are trademarks owned by Mediapolis, Inc. All rights reserved. Used with permission.

RuPaul's House of Love Web site Copyright 1996 RuPaul's House of Love and World of Wonder. Used with permission.

KeanuNet Web site Copyright 1996 Nautilus Books, Inc. Used with permission.

Bette Midler Unofficial Web site created by Jason Matthew Stewart. Used with permission.

Time in New England Web site designed for Time in New England BMFC. Used with permission.

Steve and Mark's Madonna Page courtesy of Steve and Mark's Madonna Page.

Elizabeth Taylor Image Gallery Web site courtesy of the Silver Screen Siren Web site.

CHAPTER 6

Gay Games Web site reprinted courtesy of Sjoukje Postma.

ACT-UP Paris Web site Copyright 1996. Reprinted courtesy of Yves Menager.

Gay Men's Health Crisis Web site reprinted with permission. Design by Proclus, Inc., in memory of Benjamin Mason.

BOY2BOY Network Web site Copyright 1995. Courtesy of Colorado AIDS Project.

POZ Web site Copyright 1996 POZ Publishing LLC. Production and Engineering by Mediapolis, Inc. Used with permission.

CDC National AIDS Clearinghouse Web site used with permission. CDC NAC is a government-funded organization; all materials within the Web site and documents found on the site are public domain and can be downloaded or reproduced.

CHAPTER 7

Loving More Magazine Copyright 1996 Loving More Magazine. Used with permission.

Without Restraint BDSM Home Page Copyright 1996, SM/Leather/Fetish Community Outreach Project. Reprinted with permission.

Deviants Dictionary Web site edited, designed, and maintained by Des de Moor. Copyright 1996 Des de Moor. Used with permission.

Transexual International Web site Copyright 1996 Transexual Menace International. Used with permission.

Life Sucks Web site reprinted with permission.

Gen-X Bears Web site Copyright 1996, Gen-X Bears International. All rights reserved. Used with permission.

Resources for Bears Web site Copyright 1996 by Resources for Bears, all rights reserved. Used with permission.

CHAPTER 11

Servicemembers Legal Defense Network Web site Copyright 1995-1996 Servicemembers Legal Defense Network. All rights reserved. Donated, designed, and created by ApolloMedia Corp. Used with permission.

Interfaith Working Group Web site composition, mission statement, and Interfaith Working Group Logo Copyright 1996 Interfaith Working Group. Used with permission.

CHAPTER 12

Canadian Gay, Lesbian & Bisexual Resource Directory Web site courtesy of the Canadian Gay, Lesbian & Bisexual Resource Directory.

Borland Online Web site Copyright 1997 Borland International, Inc. Used with permission.

CHAPTER 13

Rancho Mirage Travel Web site Copyright 1996 Rancho Mirage Travel, Inc. Designed by Mass Media Transit, Inc. Used with permission.

Pride InfoNet Navigator Web site Copyright 1996 by Pride Travel Information Network, Inc. Reproduction prohibited without permission. Used with permission.

All Continents Web site courtesy of All Continents Travel.

Welcome to Lizard Country Web site Copyright 1996 Lizard Head Expeditions, Inc. Used with permission.

Quistory Web site Copyright 1996 Quistory Publishers, Ltd. Used with permission.

Rainbow World Directory Web site Courtesy of Rainbow Marketing, Inc. Copyright 1997 Rainbow Marketing, Inc. All rights reserved.

Pink Web Web site Copyright 1997 kpmedia group. Used with permission.

CHAPTER 14

Wynn Wagner's Web site Copyright 1996 Wynn Wagner III. Used with permission.

North Carolina Gay & Lesbian Attorneys Web site Copyright 1996, North Carolina Gay & Lesbian Attorneys, Inc. Used with permission.

Fannon & Stomberg Web site used with permission.

GayLawNet Web site compiled and maintained by David Allan. Copyright 1995-1997 David B. Allan. Used with permission.

Viatical Settlements Web site Copyright 1996 Wynn Wagner III. Used with permission.

h.e.r.m.p. Web site Copyright 1996 ApolloMedia Corp. All rights reserved. Designed and created by ApolloMedia. Used with permission.

INDEX OF SITE NAMES